Successfully You!

Successfully You!

Reversing Your Misfortune

LEIGH VALENTINE

DESTINY IMAGE® PUBLISHERS, INC.

P.O. Box 310, Shippensburg, PA 17257-0310

"Speaking to the Purposes of God for this Generation and for the Generations to Come."

This book and all other Destiny Image, Revival Press, Mercy Place, Fresh Bread, Destiny Image Fiction, and Treasure House books are available at Christian bookstores and distributors worldwide.

For a U.S. bookstore nearest you, call 1-800-722-6774.

For more information on foreign distributors, call 717-532-3040.

Reach us on the Internet at www.destinyimage.com.

ISBN 10: 0-7684-2613-8

ISBN 13: 978-0-07684-2613-7

For Worldwide Distribution, Printed in the U.S.A.

1 2 3 4 5 6 7 8 9 10 / 12 11 10 09 08

DEDICATION

IN loving memory and dedication to the best friend a girl could ever have—my mother Mary Middleton. She always believed in me and motivated, encouraged, and stood by me through the hard times. I love and thank God for her special zeal for life and all the love she generously showed her friends, family, and especially how much love she showed her only grandson. Everyday I wish I could pick up the phone and call her—I have *so* much I want to tell her.

ACKNOWLEDGMENTS

To my wonderful and gracious parents, Doctor Robert and Mary Middleton, thank you so much for all your love and support. Although we had many challenges, I can look back now and see God's hand of mercy was on all of us. To my grandparents, Leon and Ella Middleton, who showed me small-town goodness, integrity, and love, took me to summer Bible school, and gave me my first Bible.

To my maternal grandparents, Papap (John) and Rowena Shuman. Papap taught me a lot about business, was a true entrepreneur ahead of his time, and had the good sense to go to Florida every winter! Although my grandmother died right after I was born, I was given a beautiful piece of china she hand painted and gilded. She also left a legacy of love and generosity.

To my son, Joshua, who is a miracle in every single way. He is bright, loving, and generous with his time, hardworking, and musically talented. I love you with all my heart. I will always fight for you to fulfill the call of God on your life. You have been a tremendous support to me in writing this book, particularly in giving me encouragement and computer time.

A special thanks to my mom's favorite sister, Nancy Ann Shuman Hock. Aunt Nancy you have been such an encouragement and blessing to me all these years. I love you dearly and thank you for teaching me the importance of having a closet full of shoes! Special thanks to all of my cousins: Sue Dailey, Teddy Hock, Johnny Hock and Julie Williams. Thanks for all the childhood memories and those yet to come. To my brother, Rob Middleton—we weathered many storms together. You're always in my thoughts.

A special thank-you to my executive assistant Debbie Brown for keeping chaos in order—for toiling with me on this endeavor. It really helped that she is a walking encyclopedia!

To Don Milam, Dean Drawbaugh, and the Destiny Image Publishing team for believing in my message and in my pursuit of giving God my very best.

To my sister, research assistant, and editor, Shae Cooke, for her endless hours of researching my material and hunting down the smallest of details, assuring the validity of all my endless stories. I so appreciate your brilliance, creativity, and patience. God has joined us forever.

To those in my life who have made an impression from childhood to the present. Those whom God called into my corner to champion, uplift, uphold, and pray for me, and cheer God on in the process! These are my friends and colleagues, some I hardly know, and some whom I haven't met, yet they have inspired me in various ways and may not even be aware of it. Although I cannot name them all, I love you fiercely!

To my college roommates Leslie Fairbairn, Joan Joslin, Debbie Elliott, and Karen Rich, and at Stephens College, I met my dear friends Joel and Mindy Chernoff, and my best friends at Incarnate Word Academy, Lanni Marrs, Nancy (Kenkel) Knutson, and Bobby Klemmer. I love you all!

I would also like to gratefully acknowledge the pastor who attended to me and prayed for me roadside, as well as Mrs. Frances Allen, Byron Clark, Darlene Bishop, Norvel Hayes, Myles Munroe, Tim Storey, Lance Wallnau, Oral and Evelyn Roberts, and my nanny, Gwen.

It goes without saying I give *all* the glory for restoration and success to my Lord Jesus Christ who because of the pouring out of His precious blood at Calvary and the power of His resurrection, saved me, and is continually saving me.

ENDORSEMENTS

Leigh Valentine has once again written material that is good for the soul. Her book *Successfully You* is not only motivational, but gives you step by step instructions on how not to sit in your setback, but how to spring forward into your comeback.

—Tim Storey
Storey Dreams

Do you really believe the promise that is given to us in Romans 8:28 that "all things will work together for your good?" In *Successfully You*, Leigh Valentine paints a beautiful picture of God's grace taking us from a chaotic mess to a divinely orchestrated destiny. Leigh shares that it does not matter where you have been or how badly you have failed, God is able to artfully turn your circumstances around. As you read this book, your faith will rise and you will be catapulted into your God-given purpose!

—Darlene Bishop
The Solid Rock Church, Ohio

Leigh Valentine has been a tremendous blessing to our ministry. Her love for souls and passionate desire to see lives changed for God's Glory will transform your life, family, business and church.

—Drs. Kenneth and June Robinson
Restoring Life International Church
Baltimore, Maryland

Leigh Valentine is an amazing phenomenal woman. This book inspires and encourages you to fulfill your dreams and passions. She is intimately acquainted with turning challenges into triumphs. Her love for God, love for life, and her love for others are demonstrated throughout her entire life. This is a must-read book for all.

—Council Woman and Pastor of Family Victory Fellowship,
Sylvia Jordan
Southfield, Michigan

I thought I would read the first three chapters, but I could not stop reading this book. It is unique, exhilarating, and encouraging—one young woman's story about overcoming difficulty and reinventing herself to support her son. I believe this book will help many who struggle with difficulties.

—Dr. Michael Chitwood
CPA, Financial Adviser, and Entrepreneur

CONTENTS

Misfortune pursues the sinner, but prosperity is the reward of the righteous... (Proverbs 13:21 NIV).

Jesus of Nazareth, without money and arms, conquered more millions than Alexander, Caesar, Mahomet, and Napoleon; without science and learning, He shed more light on things human and divine than all philosophers and schools combined; without the eloquence of schools, He spoke words of life such as never were spoken before or since, and produced effects which lie beyond the reach of any orator or poet; without writing a single line, He has set more pens in motion, and furnished themes for more sermons, orations, discussions, learned volumes, works of art and sweet songs of praise, than the whole army of great men of ancient and modern times. Born in a manger, and crucified as a malefactor, He now controls the destinies of the civilized world, and rules a spiritual empire which embraces one-third of the inhabitants of the globe.

There never was in this world a life so unpretending, modest, and lowly in its outward form and condition, and yet producing such extraordinary effects upon all ages, nations, and classes of men. The annals of history produce no other example of such complete and astonishing success in spite of the absence of those material, social, literary, and artistic powers and influences which are indispensable to success for a mere man.

Philip Schaff (1819-1893)

INTRODUCTION

I F there's one thing I hope you glean from this book, it's that failure is
never final. We blow it. We fail. We mess things up. Even when we feel
like a failure, Jesus is there to place a hand on our shoulder and say, "Get up!
Don't quit! I'm with you. Stand tall! You're forgiven. I love you, and I'll
never let you go, no matter what!" The only way we can fail is to stay down
and not permit God's hand upon our lives. You were created to be unique—
successfully you, and I pray and trust that you take that truth to heart!

In writing this book, I've experienced even more of His transforming
power because there's power in our testimony. The miracle of what He's
done for me cannot be denied or taken away—it's everything to me. When
we acknowledge His power and credit the power of His blood in our lives,
our faith becomes a testimony to others. Faith without action is dead
though, and action without faith is too. We need faith and action working
together to make our story real and powerful. (See James 2:14-26.)

What's your story? How has God transformed your misfortunes? Can
you recall when God has been there for you, whether in good times or in
bad? Did you ever feel an inexplicable power at work in a difficult circumstance? Have you ever felt a sudden peace overcome you that you couldn't
explain? Put yourself in remembrance of these things. Trust that God has at
least nudged you at some point in your life. Sometimes we forget the places
where God has helped us. Sometimes we haven't credited Him with those

things. Trust that when you do—when you discover Him in your life, those discoveries will become defining moments that will help you move forward in your calling. There's a reason you are alive! Ask God, "Why am I here? What's my purpose? Why did I take that U-turn? What do You have for me? Defining moments will make you bold and courageous; will give you the zeal you need today to move forward in your calling, purpose, and in the appropriation of the blessings you've missed and the ones yet to come.

You don't have to memorize a million Scriptures to tell your story. Sometimes the Lord will give you a life-verse that almost says it all! If you don't have one, perhaps you need to encounter the Lord afresh or for the first time. It's vital—crucial to have a story because the enemy, satan, cannot stand against the powerful testimony of a believer. Go back and count your blessings if you have to. You'll be surprised when you discover what the Lord has already done in your life.

When you consider the divine power of revelation in the biblical stories of the woman at the well, the woman with the costly oil, the lame man at the Gate Beautiful, and the blind man Bartimaeus, they confirm the power of God to transform lives. They all met Jesus. They all encountered the power of love.

I encourage you as you read to look for those divine defining moments in your life. Because Jesus loves you, there will be more than one defining moment in your life. If you miss one, He loves you enough to provide another and another and yet another and another so that eventually by His grace and His breath breathing life into you, you will enter the great adventure of His purpose and destiny for you.

The choice to leave your comfort zone is the beginning of a wonderful journey, but it won't always be easy. At times it might be downright risky, but it will also be the most exhilarating and awesome ride of your life. No possession, notoriety, accolade, or accomplishment on this earth can hold a candle to the time of your life God wants you to have!

In this apathetic world of ours, trust that wonders have not ceased, that possibilities have not paled, and that hope is a very real foundation in your life. Joy is the outcome of a life centered on God. When you can anticipate God's help and deliverance and actually experience it for yourself, whether recovery from addiction, the restoration of broken relationships, the healing of emotional wounds, the realization of peace in the midst of personal wars, or the recovery of finances, you'll want to shout out your story—while experiencing unspeakable joy.

TRANSFORMATION

Hannah wept bitterly because she was barren until she heard the word of the Lord through the prophet, Eli who told her to go in peace because God would grant her request. Then, the Bible says, her whole countenance changed. She went her way (see 1 Sam. 1:17-18). She didn't even have a child and wasn't even pregnant yet, but her whole being was transformed such that there was joy in her heart when she sang, "My heart rejoices in the Lord; my horn [strength] is exalted in the Lord. I smile at my enemies, because I rejoice in Your salvation" (1 Samuel 2:1).

The shepherds, who were known as some of the poorest, loneliest people on earth turned from fear to praise and glorified God because of the Good News of the birth of a Savior. Even as they walked back to their hard, cold, lonely lives in the beautiful yet dangerous hills and fields, they had hope!

You too can turn your hardship into a story of salvation and praise that will continue to influence others as you trust God and experience His joy. Your story can become a roll of praise that echoes and covers the earth and draws in generations even yet unborn—because human impossibilities are God's possibilities.

I hope my testimony teaching does that for you.

Part I

NOBODY KNOWS
BUT JESUS

WRECK FOR JESUS

The car slammed into the Corvette and a body flew out of its T-top, through the air, and across the three-lane highway into a ditch. The Corvette rolled airborne and landed atop the thrown body, its back tire pinning the woman to the ground. I pulled off to the side of the road and quickly ordered my wife and children to stay put because I didn't want them to see the horrific scene. I raced to the woman's side, while at the same time signaling a passing trucker to call 911 on his CB radio. Heavy traffic roared past as I knelt close to her face. Her eyes didn't open and I didn't see her mouth move but to my amazement, I heard a heart-wrenching little cry rise from the very depths of her being. "Jesus, help me! Jesus, help me!" —*Witness and first person on the accident scene.*[1]

JESUS wasn't on my mind as I left my pageant director's house in Kansas City to drive home to St. Louis several hours earlier that awful Sunday morning. Unconsciously, I'd left God behind six months prior in the aftermath of winning the Miss Missouri crown.

For weeks I trained with Robert as he coached me for the upcoming Miss U.S.A. pageant in Miami, and because of it, I was in the best shape of my life physically: toned and tanned, rehearsed and poised. To anyone watching, I was a "model" of success as I loaded my suitcases filled with expensive gowns and clothing into the trunk of my new Corvette that was the color of champagne.

Outwardly, I was. I certainly looked the polished part standing there beside my expensive car that glistened like gold in the early morning Missouri sun. Everything screamed starlet including my long hair and designer sunglasses, and the outfit set off with expensive high heels and Gucci handbag. I had worked hard to get to that point—my outward transformation wasn't without pain and sacrifice. As a competitive swimmer and runner, I swam mega pool lengths every day, and jogged six miles every other day, doggedly training to get in shape for the pageant. Moreover, I had to breach comfort zones and deal with many insecurities and inner fears.

This pursuit of the crown was more than winning a title—it would feed my inner heart crying for approval and praise, like a hug and hearing my dad say, "A job well done; I'm proud of you," or the accolades of my peers. In my quest to feel worthy, I sought approval in the eyes of others, not realizing that that type of approval is not always important. Knowing that people liked me meant a lot, and there was nothing like words, or a certain look, or even a crown to prove it. To be told that I was beautiful and talented, or smart and able, in some way strengthened me; but I didn't really believe those things about myself, so the sporadic ego boosts wouldn't last very long. Leaning on and depending on others kept me bound to a rollercoaster ride of emotions.

Often lonely as a child, I craved attention. As a teen, I felt that I let my family down so often that I wanted to show them that I really *could* accomplish something worthwhile. Winning the crown in Missouri temporarily

fueled many of those needs, but that fateful day I was coming off the high, and really needed the boost that this new title would give me. Just as fast food acts as a temporary salve for hunger but provides little nutritional benefit, the spoils of worldly success that I'd binged on felt great for a while but provided little in the way of long-lasting emotional or spiritual fuel.

The stress was so great at times that my hair fell out almost in handfuls as I also struggled with an eating disorder, inner personal torment, family heartache, hard decisions, and the consequences of compromises. In truth, it was a miracle I even looked the part of a beauty queen. The make-up and possessions were a façade hiding the truth of the battle waging within.

OUT OF THE THRONE ZONE

Opening the T-top of my beloved Corvette, I settled in for the 230-mile drive, dropped a tape into the player, and turned the music up full blast perhaps to drown out my uneven thoughts of potential failure. The warm April breeze mussed my hair as I accelerated from the onramp and onto the interstate heading for home and closer to the Miss U.S.A. title. I shivered inside with uneasiness.

Did I even really trust worldly success for the long-term benefits I needed? Fear and insecurity inspired my dreams and what the world offered fueled and guided them. *Fame, wealth, acceptance, pride, self-esteem...oh this life is so great, fun, and exciting,* I thought as I drove along.

It all felt so good, even though I had to compromise a few values along the way which produced some guilt. Sometimes my pursuit of stardom felt so right, and at other times it felt so wrong. *Why can't I feel deep joy? Why isn't it lasting? Why do I feel confused and sometimes so undone?* My ultimate goal was to become an actor and I had already received offers to audition for soap operas in New York City; but deep inside, I had a nagging suspicion that I was on the wrong road.

Oh yes, anticipation was there, excitement was there and I determined not to take my eyes off of what *I thought* I wanted. However, behind my pageant smile was that feeling of emptiness and meaninglessness—a life void of God. I'd veered *off* His path and dreams for my life and this wrought a measure of torment.

I sought my identity through the approval of others and by the outward manifestations of what the world thought of me. Consequently, when things went wrong, I couldn't see past what it meant to me and often these things became huge obstacles. My passions flowed from areas of past pain and my passion for purpose was no exception.

Certain things vie for our affections and sometimes they are legitimate and need attention; however, oftentimes the need, in truth, is merely a pleasure. Then we feel as though we must fulfill the need to be happy, which keeps us busy chasing a false "want" instead of pursuing a legitimate need. I needed Jesus Christ as my affection and sole source of happiness. Instead, I placed my affection in the need for the world's approval and the need to belong. While busy chasing what I considered necessary, I had no time to focus on God.

MATTERS OF THE HEART

We have only to turn on our television sets or open a magazine to see how the jet set live, and many of us do. Today's society loves to nose into famous people's lives to see what designer labels they're sporting, who their latest flings are, who's divorcing who, what their homes look like, and so on. With their lavish lifestyles, we see them spend extravagant amounts on new cars, posh dinners, and exotic getaways.

With the onslaught of reality television shows and the leeway given to tabloid magazines, there's not much that the general public has to guess about. Fifty years ago, television studios and magazines only showed us the glam and seldom the pain—but now lives are deliberately exposed because of the fascination to print dirt. Perhaps you're someone who has had this happen to you.

What should cause us to wonder, however, is the fact that many of these well-known people eventually fall—in spite of their fortunes and fame. They are arrested for drugs or drunk driving, they commit adultery, they attempt or commit suicide, they are obsessed with plastic surgery or being thin, they get caught in lewd acts, they contract AIDS, they're found dead in hotel rooms, they become misers, eccentric, over the top, cheaters, and have mental and emotional breakdowns, rehabilitation centers are full with such people.

Success, fame, and fortune don't exempt people from falling prey to the enemy's wiles and the pull of this world into making the wrong choices. Although no one is immune from the pull of darkness and its consequences, public figures' problems and sins are thrown into the spotlight for all to see.

Wrong choices are made when in the pursuit of what we think will make us happy. But unless God the Creator is the One fulfilling and meeting our needs for happiness first, we're just grasping at the wind. Joy Himself is the foundation and very cornerstone of happiness, because happiness without Him is fleeting, no matter how much fame or wealth we accrue.

Motivation and Heart Check

So too, God wants to inspire our dreams, to fuel them with His power, to guide them with His love and faithfulness. He wants us to trust Him as the source of our success, and if we do, we will enjoy the spoils of divine success even more!

I didn't handle the pressures of the world well without the wisdom and inspiration of God. He lifted me up with favor, and I let Him down. If God suddenly raised you up with sudden fortune or fame, how would you handle the change and the pressure? Trust that the enemy will be your paparazzi, following your every move and looking for an opening to destroy you. God wants to give you every blessing He has for you; and the enemy wants to quickly steal it all away. He'll find inroads through your mind and through the idols of your heart. If anything other than God fills those places, satan will use that for his gain and your destruction.

More importantly, if your heart is not God-filled, you cannot glorify God and eventually any surrogate will be your downfall. He tells us to above all else, guard our hearts, for it affects everything we do.[2] Over 800 times the Bible speaks about the heart—why the emphasis? Why did God think it that important to include it so often in His Word? And why do we pay so little attention to the heart? Hello? My friends, the Bible isn't known as, "The Book of Life," for nothing!

The heart filters all pain, sorrow, dreams, visions, hopes, goals, love, anger, hate, and so on. It *affects* everything too, such as our sleep, (that's been a big one for me) our health, happiness, relationships, potential for success, emotions, and our peace of mind. If your heart is heavy, you know how hard it is to accomplish anything, right? When you are out of God's will your heart will naturally feel heavy. You should feel a grieving in your Spirit that something is out of whack. But, if the condition of your heart is healthy, you'll be emotionally and spiritually healthy, and trust that this affects your physical health as well.

Years ago in Beaumont, Texas, I was ministering at a church with Brenda (not her real name), a friend of mine from Rhema Bible Training

Center in Broken Arrow, Oklahoma. Our hearts were so heavy for the move of God. In particular, there was a beautiful young woman we wanted more than anything to be healed of terminal cancer. She was in her 20s, and the devil was doing his best to kill her. We prayed and prayed for her for several afternoons until we almost lost our voices. Finally when it seemed like we were getting nowhere and just about ready to give up out of shear exhaustion, the Holy Spirit clearly showed us why our hearts were so heavy. The young woman was full of bitterness and unforgiveness—we eventually learned that she had been hurt by one of the pastors and she had let this experience fester and grow. She admitted that she had hate in her heart. The great thing is that it all surfaced, and she cried out for the Lord to forgive her and have mercy on her. She had a *true* heart-change that brought about her healing.

Let your heart convict you. God wants to show you a better way to live. Sometimes your healing will come speedily as you totally release those who have hurt you. Many times as you get rid of bitterness, healing can flow. Not forgiving someone doesn't hurt the other person as much as it hurts and kills you. The heart is a hiding place too. Hidden sin dwells there like lust, gluttony, unforgiveness, jealousy, and covetousness, and eventually these things flow from the heart and seep into our lives adversely affecting all that we do. This is why we must keep our heart in check: daily seek God the Father and ask Him to reveal the things that don't line up with His Word and will for our lives. Ask Him, "What is displeasing to You? Show me Jesus."

Seek Him through prayer and through His Word. What does God's Word speak to you about what is in your heart? What does God say? "Search me [thoroughly], O God, and know my heart! Try me and know my thoughts! And see if there is any wicked or hurtful way in me, and lead me in the way everlasting" (Ps. 139:23-24 AMP). Cry out for God so you can personally have a heart change.

The Holy Spirit counsels us, urges us to give attention to His words, tells us to "incline" our ears to His sayings, to not let them depart from our eyes, and to keep them in the midst of our heart because His words are *life* to those who find them and *health* to our flesh (see Prov. 4:20-22). What is hindering you from coming to Jesus? What is in your heart? Ask Jesus *today* to guide you.

THE FINALE?

By the time of that fateful day, I had let God's sayings depart from my eyes and heart. Although I didn't realize it at the time, God could see past my designer sunglasses and into the God-shaped void in my heart that wasn't filled with Him, like I had promised when I first surrendered my heart to Him a year or so prior. Little by little, the rewards of the world edged Him out of my heart and was replaced with a pursuit of status, promises of an acting career, fame and fortune. Although I captured a worldly throne, I had ventured way out of the throne zone of God.

Along the route home, I pulled into a truck stop diner for a quick bite. Noticing a long line to pay for my piece of pecan pie, I lost my patience and stormed out with my pie. I didn't even put on my seat belt before tromping on the gas pedal and peeling away from the diner.

My anger dissolved, as did my hunger as I finished the last bite of the sweet treat. I relaxed for the rest of the journey, anticipation and eagerness for what lay ahead returning and mounting with every passing mile marker. The sun felt warmer now that it was higher in the sky and was streaming through the open sunroof—it felt good being on the open road. Feeling better now that I'd released some of my pent-up angst, I actually looked forward to getting home and into my own bed, and in seeing my mom and dad, even though they now lived apart. Winning the Miss U.S.A. crown might redeem their faith in me—I'd messed up so much in the past. Having an alcoholic father made me feel as if I could never achieve enough to make up for the reality of his lack of attention. I was always looking for a bigger achievement, a larger goal, always trying to achieve, achieve, achieve, never at rest.

How wonderful it would be to see a look of pride in my father's eyes again. They glistened when he and my little brother saw me crowned Miss Missouri. It was incredible even having him there because throughout my life his binge drinking didn't make him very reliable. As a child I sometimes confused his undependability with a lack of love, though he often assured me that I would always be his little girl. At times he'd brag that I was his favorite daughter and then laugh because I was his "only" daughter! Even in spite of my failings, Dad always boasted that whenever I walked into a room people would know I was there because I would light it up. If I could win this Miss U.S.A. pageant and become a successful actress afterward, that would really take it over the top, or so I thought. Perhaps it might even bring my family back together again.

> *I was always looking for a bigger achievement, a larger goal, always trying to achieve, achieve, achieve, never at rest.*

Suddenly I couldn't wait to see my mom, who really was my best friend and interested in all my endeavors. Everything would be just fine; it just had to be. After all, at 21 I had more than most young women could ever hope for, and with the Miss USA Pageant only a month or so away, a happy life shone ahead of me as brightly as the noonday sun glinting off the hood of my car.

LIFE-THREATENING COLLISION

But every hope came to a screeching halt as a car appeared out of nowhere, swerved, and clipped me, and then homed in on me like a jet-fast missile seeking its target.

"No...stop...STOP," I screamed, "STOP!" There was no way to avoid the collision—no place to turn and no time to escape. I just closed my eyes in terror as the car crashed into me sending my car flying and flipping on impact.

Up through the T-top roof and into the clouds I went soaring...into the sky and across the highway, landing with a sickening thud atop what felt like a rock of crushed glass. Then everything went black.

RESURRECTING
THE IMPOSSIBLE

I was surprised she found strength to cry out as she did. I tried and tried to lift the car, but it wouldn't budge and all I could do was comfort her as best as I could and pray. "Help her Lord!" There were burns, blood on her arm and back, there had to be broken bones. I turned away for a second to talk to the trucker and when I turned back around, couldn't believe what I saw. The Corvette had lifted mysteriously off her and now was lying next to her. There was no way she could have pulled herself out from underneath it, no way could she have lifted it off, no way I could have done it. In shock I realized, God must have sent angels to lift that ton of weight. God had to have intervened. I'd heard about angels intervening in people's lives but now witnessed it firsthand.

Just before the ambulance crew arrived to take the young woman to the nearest hospital 30 miles away, she opened her eyes for a moment and appeared to be in shock, delirious, and in excruciating pain. "Is my face OK?" she asked in a small whisper.

Here she was almost near death, and now she was asking me if her face was OK. I told her, "Young lady, don't worry about your face—it's just fine. It's a miracle that you're even alive!" —*Ongoing account from accident witness*

⋘—◆—⋙

THERE I lay in a broken, bloodied heap trapped by a mess of twisted fiberglass and steel. One moment a beauty queen with everything to live for, and the next a lifeless rag doll with nothing to live for.

But this wasn't the end of my story, because the angels didn't lift that ton of steel for nothing.

Cruelly tossed out of an earthly throne zone pursuit, I was about to enter into a divine zone of miraculous U-turns. But to pull through, I'd have to draw upon every seed of promise and every shred of hope that God could deposit in my life.

Some dreams don't die as abruptly as mine did but rather ebb slowly like the embers in a dying fire. Others tumble, leaving much debris. Some dreams fizzle before the fire even gets going, leaving only a residue of unfulfilled expectations and ashes of hopes. Joe DiMaggio said of the suicide of his former wife, Marilyn Monroe, "*She had everything to live with but nothing to live for.*"

Do you have a dream that tugs at your heart? Maybe you have everything you need to live on this earth but nothing "to live for." Do you sometimes have an unsettling feeling as if something is missing but you can't figure out what that something is? Have you envisioned your future and anticipated success only to be disappointed as adversity, calamity, or disaster hits?

When something tragic happens, our lives instantly change forever; and so too with daily disappointments, because like cankerworms they have the potential to eat away at our dreams, and before we know it we think that there is no hope left.

> *Perhaps there's some horrible secret in your past or one that you're struggling with now.*

How do you find courage to tackle life when your heart has broken over your circumstances and you believe all of your dreams, hopes, and ambitions have died, in stark contrast to what you've imagined for your life? What do you do if you're the one who keeps flubbing up? Is recovery possible? How do you handle the blows? How do you get turned around?

We all want favor, want someone to choose us, want to prosper, want approval, but many of us feel as though we're not probable candidates for greatness. You may feel as if you've driven yourself into dead ends, that there are more subtractions than additions, more division than multiplication in your life—rejection. Stumbling stones are there and you don't know how to remove them, or you've resolved just to let them be and stay where you are.

Perhaps there's some horrible secret in your past or one that you're struggling with now: an eating disorder, an affair, addiction, lust, embezzlement, a divorce, an abortion, sexual abuse, a crime. I've lived with the shame of some bulimia, drugs, and alcohol, and for years I hid the shame of childhood sexual abuse and an alcoholic father. I understand your pain and physical and emotional heartache. I truly can relate to you—I have been there in more ways than these written words can describe.

You may be thinking, *What about this illness I am living with every single day? My life is out of control. How can I be healed? How can I solve this mess?* Life is full of crises that can defeat us if we're passive about them or if we fear them. No matter the crisis though, be it a terrifying medical diagnosis, unexpected financial ruin, a painful broken relationship—you can emerge victorious. There is resurrection power for a new life. I have personally experienced it. I have been raised from emotional and physical death several times!

JOEY'S MIRACLE

God cares about us so much—everything about our lives—and He'll often do the seemingly impossible, even in those daily things that affect us. Take Joey, for instance, my son's kitten and favorite cat. Joey had fleas and I'd asked my girlfriend, Robin who was visiting overnight, to help me read the back of a flea and tick medicine box to see whether the product was meant for a dog or a cat. "Cat," she said, and so we applied the liquid preparation to the back of Joey's neck.

For some reason, I awoke at 5:00 A.M., and couldn't get back to sleep. This was unusual for me to be so wide-awake, because I'm not a morning person! Suddenly I had a craving for a hot cup of my favorite coffee so I ventured downstairs to the kitchen to grind some beans. As I passed through the library, I saw Joey lying down and thought it odd. He was usually at my heels following me into the kitchen for his breakfast. As I waited for the coffee to brew, I went to head back upstairs and passed by Joey again, and still he lay there, barely moving. Something was wrong, and I swooped him into my arms.

"Robin, Robin," I cried out while running into her room, "Help, the cat is sick—he's siezuring or something!"

She sat up groggily, wiping sleep from her eyes. "Hurry, Robin, the cat—he's sick."

"It's probably just a hairball," she ventured.

Suddenly—blood poured out of his mouth—and I had the terrifying thought that I'd perhaps misread the directions on the box of flea and tick application. Did we overdose the kitty?

Robin thought it was a hairball, but I was sure the cat was dying. We went back and forth that way for a while until Robin finally said, "Call the vet."

First, I called my good friend, Byron, and asked him to come over right away. "Come quick Byron, we need you. Joey is dying," I cried.

We found the Dr. Lanny's home number in the telephone book. Miraculously, he answered the call: "Check the trash can for the box—read the label—it's probably an overdose."

Then he instructed us to put Joey in the sink to rinse him off. At that point, Byron arrived, not believing anything was wrong with Joey until he saw the blood pouring out of the poor creature. As Joey convulsed, he helped me hold him. With every seizure, the cat's eyes would roll into the back of his head. He helped me wrap Joey into a towel, and then he drove us at 90 miles an hour to the vet's office. All the way, we prayed—pled with God to save this little kitten's life.

Robin stayed at home to get Josh up and ready for school, and read the back of the box again. "Leigh, I read it wrong!" she said when I called. "I cannot believe it—I read it *wrong*!" She was so upset. "This medicine is for a large 60-150 pound dog, not a small eight pound cat! Please forgive me, I'm so sorry!"

I can't tell you how this grieved me—this small, dear animal had brought such joy to Josh's life. Would he blame us for killing his cat?

A nurse met us at the animal hospital and immediately hooked Joey up to an IV. I didn't know what else to do but break out into tongues—my prayer language—and intercede for Joey. "Please, Lord, have mercy...don't let this cat die! Please Jesus; cancel the effects of this medicine!"

By the time Dr. Lanny arrived, Joey's condition had deteriorated. Two of my girlfriends arrived and tried to calm me—but I was beside myself. "What had we done?" They tried to pull me out of the surgical room, but I wouldn't leave until I knew Joey was OK. About two hours later, the doctor said, "I know you love this kitty, and you want to save him because he's your son's favorite cat, but I don't think he'll make it." He talked about kidney failure, and possibly brain damage because the seizures wouldn't stop. There was nothing left to do but wait. And pray!

"Come on Leigh," said my girlfriend, "Let's go and pray, and then get you home." We drove around the countryside praying—even groaning in travail for this wee cat. "I've killed my son's cat—I can't believe it," I cried to her. I couldn't get over what I'd done.

"Listen," she said. "God loves Joshua, and He cares about every detail of his life. God will take care of this—let's just believe God!"

That night, after Josh returned from school, I just prayed he wouldn't notice Joey missing. Saturday, he finally asked, "Where's my cat Joey?"

I didn't know how to tell him, so called on Byron to help. Byron explained what had happened. "Joey might not make it, but we're going to trust God. Don't blame your mom though, if he doesn't pull through. All we can do now is wait until Monday." Byron didn't give Josh the gory details, but just encouraged him to believe God for a miracle.

That night, I was so tormented feeling that I'd poisoned the cat that I couldn't sleep and headed downstairs to sleep on the sofa in the library. At 4:00 A.M., I was awakened. A still, small voice said, "I have healed Joey. I

have healed his liver, his kidneys, and his brain—he'll be back to normal. Pick him up after church."

If this is truth, I thought, *I'll be so relieved,* and I instantly fell back to sleep.

After church that morning, I wondered if what I heard was truth. It was Sunday—the vet always took Sundays off. Nevertheless, I had to find out so I called the animal hospital. Dr. Lanny picked up the phone—I couldn't believe it.

"How'd you know I was here?" he asked. "Did you see my car in the driveway? I was just about to call you." Then he told me about how he'd gone into the office expecting to find Joey dead—to bury him really, but to his amazement found the cat sitting up and purring like crazy. He said that Joey ate two bowls of food.

"In 30 years of practice, I have never seen anything like this!"

Of course, I hopped in my car and dashed straight to the hospital to get Joey before Josh got home from church. I praised God all the way there. Joey was a hundred percent normal, just as the Lord had said he would be. The doctor walked out with me to my car. Pointing up to the sky, he said that it had to have been a higher power at work and that although he wasn't a believing man; it had to be a total miracle.

I tied a pink bow around the kitten's neck for when Josh got home. "Joey! Joey!" Josh screamed, running to his favorite cat now purring at the window. What an incredible miracle this truly was. But wait! It gets better. Even though Dr. Lanny is now retired, Joey's story still lives as a testimony of just how much God cares for His creation. One day I asked the new vet if he'd ever heard of Joey, and indeed, he'd heard about it so much that he went into Joey's files himself to check things out.

You know, we all mess up or miss the mark at times but God always has our best interest at heart. He knows what hurts us and He wants to help us in every way, whether at home, in our ministry, or in our business.

I have made horrifically bad decisions, but in spite of myself, God has given me a measure of success and much joy. All of us mess up, but many go on to lead successful, happy lives. How do they do that? Most people suffer misfortune or wheels of misfortunes that cause life setbacks, disappointment, or lost hope for life's ambitions, goals, and dreams—that may be why you picked up this book.

Listen, we're coming through some pretty dark days right now, and the way the economic forecasters are calling it at the time of this writing in 2008, there may be darker days ahead for our nation, which affect each of us. The United States is on the verge of recession; the dollar is spiraling, the economy hurtling.

According to the news at home and abroad, we're living under threat of more terrorist attacks. Natural disasters have claimed the lives of hundreds of thousands. How many sons and daughters have we lost in the war in Iraq? Cancer is rampant, depression is epidemic, pedophilia is rising, moral values are plummeting, crime is escalating, finances are dwindling, the national debt is climbing, our troops are fighting controversial wars, taxes are skyrocketing, thousands of unborn babies are dying, suicide is on the rise, people are losing their life savings, there are threats of nuclear attacks, kidnappings, and hijackings—oh my Lord, have mercy on us. What's the secret to getting through life unscathed? How do we move on, press in, rise to greatness and our full potential in light of every drawback, setback, and fear?

WE NEED DIVINE SUPERNATURAL POWER

I believe it will take supernatural strength and help to get through the days ahead. When you've bottomed out and there's no place to go, when you've depleted every resource for help, when you're so tired of fighting, of making mistakes, of suffering consequences of unwise decisions—how can you turn your life around?

What if all your troubles are beyond your control? What if you're at the mercy of something such as a debilitating illness, famine, natural disaster, even a tragic accident? What if an economic downturn throws you into bankruptcy and you lose your business, your home, or perhaps your spouse leaves you? What's the secret to getting through even now in your present circumstance?

There is a supernatural answer to rising above all obstacles that manifest in our lives and to experiencing inner peace that satisfies the longings of the heart for a meaningful reason to press into our respective callings.

> *What if all your troubles are beyond your control?*

CONNECT WITH GOD

Connecting with God is the answer. Sounds simple doesn't it? It's truth. David, a "man after God's own heart," a true God chaser, knew what it meant in his own life to be connected to God. He was in grave and imminent danger of being taken and destroyed that no human means were left for his escape.[3] In his hour of deepest need and in one of his greatest setbacks, David knew what God was capable of doing in his life, and he cried out as we see in the Psalm 54:

> *Save me, O God, by Your name; judge and vindicate me by Your mighty strength and power. Hear my pleading and my prayer, O God; give ear to the words of my mouth. For strangers and insolent men are rising up against me, and violent men and ruthless ones seek and demand my life; they do not set God before them. Selah [pause, and calmly think of that]! Behold, God is my helper and ally; the Lord is my upholder and is with them who uphold my life. He will pay back evil to my enemies; in Your faithfulness [Lord] put an end to them. With a freewill offering I will sacrifice to You; I will give thanks and praise Your name, O Lord, for it is good. For He has delivered me out of every trouble, and my eye has looked [in triumph] on my enemies* (Psalm 54:1-7 AMP).

With conviction, David knew that God could save him, vindicate him, hear him, help him, uphold him, cut off his enemies, repay his enemies for their evil, and deliver him out of all trouble. This knowledge can only come about by knowing God well enough to know what He can do. Sometimes we are so wounded that our spirit reaches out to Him for us. Thankfully, my spirit knew to cry out to Him as I lay on the ground unconscious right after the car accident.

It's sad that we have to hit rock bottom, or be deplete of strength or fiber of pride, or wait until every plan backfires, or become physically or emotionally helpless before we accept and appreciate divine help. All too often we seek to connect with Him when we have no choice but to become vulnerable enough to entrust our lives in the hands and care of God, just as I had to do that fateful day when it was all my spirit could do to cry out to Him.

After connecting with God, that is coming into a relationship with Him, former news anchor and broadcast professional Doris McMillon[4] said that her hunger for the material things "has faded over the years, and I have discovered that my relationship with God is what endures and gives me hope and strength for whatever challenge I face."[5]

The Bible takes the reader on an incredible adventure showing how far God will really go to supernaturally show Himself to those who are committed to a relationship and to fully serving Him. The Bible is full of one miracle after another.

Regardless of our limitations as human beings, our potential for greatness, overcoming darkness, and restoring what we've lost is unlimited when we have the power of the Almighty behind us as He claims victory and backs His words with awesome miracles of provision and recovery.

"For I know the thoughts and plans that I have for you," says the Lord, "thoughts and plans for welfare and peace and not for evil, to give you hope in your final outcome" (Jeremiah 29:11 AMP).

We all want hope! I know I want to be happy, successful, accomplished, and to use the utmost of my potential without wasting any part of it. I desire emotional health, strength, and real power to do what's right. Inherent in our DNA is the desire for good, deep joy, and to connect with someone greater—much greater than ourselves who can teach us how to be great in love, how to live without fear, and how to press in to our destiny.

To Resurrect the Impossible

Millions of people are curious about how to handle their present and see into their future. Why? For the most part, their curiosity is rooted in fear; uncertainty grips them so they reach out to find hope, inspiration, and insight.

Some people venture into the New Age realm of thinking, rely on karma, or have sought the wisdom of Eastern mysticism. There are those who consult gurus or inner guides to help analyze a situation or to try and secure their future. Many seek counsel with psychics or seers to see what lies ahead, or even worship angels with the hope of acquiring supernatural insight or intervention. Others read mountains of self-help books in hope of finding the secret to moving ahead successfully, either personally or professionally. Even some believers in God and Jesus seek help from those types of resources.

I don't believe that I'm part of some large force that moves the universe or that I'm in some way God, and am in control of everything that happens within my realm. The concept that our thoughts and feelings align with vibrations in the universe to attract the things we want frankly scares me. Proponents of this thinking liken it to the universe as a shopping basket, claiming all we have to do is place an order for the things we want with our thoughts. I can't rise above my failings, shortcomings, or fears by altering my consciousness; and so far, the power of my own thinking hasn't created powerful outcomes. I don't even want my own life to serve my own best interests. I don't want to be my own hero, either. I realize that I need someone to save me from myself, and so far I haven't found that someone in the world. I am hopeless at saving myself. What good is seeing into my future if my hopes depend on me or on the sorry state of the world? How will simply seeing into the future *empower* me to change anything?

I've found that real power comes from following Jesus Christ. Jesus was God made flesh on this earth. (See John 1:14.) He came in the flesh. He took on bodily form so God could touch us. When God reaches out and embraces us, He touches us through Jesus Christ.

RESURRECTION POWER TRANSFORMS

His resurrection transformed the lives of the disciples. They hid when He was crucified, but when they saw the risen Lord (and some had to see *and* touch Him), they knew that all Jesus had said and done proved that He was indeed God in flesh, the Savior. I don't know about you, but if I knew Jesus when He walked the earth doing all the awesome things He did to heal and deliver people, I don't think it would have taken the resurrection to prove it to me that He was indeed God. I would have said, "Well buy me an 'O' for 'Oh this *has to be* God!'" He made claims *and* backed His words with awesome miracles and deeds: changed water into wine; cast out demons; healed lepers, diseases, the paralytic; raised the dead; restored sight to the blind; restored and cured deafness; fed the multitudes; walked on water; calmed a storm with a command; He Himself rose from the dead, and appeared to His disciples after resurrection!

Just as Christ backed His words and did all those things 2,000 years ago, God and all of Heaven backs up every inspired Word in the Bible *today* with the same and even greater miracles available for your life—a promise of divine power flowing in, for, and through you, and of His protection.

And these attesting signs will accompany those who believe: in My name they will drive out demons; they will speak in new languages; They will pick up serpents; and [even] if they drink anything deadly, it will not hurt them; they will lay their hands on the sick, and they will get well (Mark 16:17-18 AMP).

He can supernaturally heal you or your circumstances.

When you believe, the same power that raised Jesus from the dead is the power that lives in you through the Holy Spirit. This is your rich inheritance as a co-heir with the risen Jesus.[6] In His life you are re-born, and hope becomes your treasure:

By having the eyes of your heart flooded with light, so that you can know and understand the hope to which He has called you, and how rich is His glorious inheritance in the saints (His set-apart ones) (Ephesians 1:18 AMP).

He was, is, and always will be the real thing. Life with God is the real thing! It's a supernatural life—one that will thrill and engage you. Satan has tried to counterfeit what was always meant for God's children to experience and enjoy here on earth. You don't need a clairvoyant to see into your future; God can speak to you personally through the Bible or His voice; He can send an angel to you with a message; He can speak to you through a modern-day biblical prophet or seer, through your circumstances, or through a friend or peer. He can supernaturally heal you or your circumstances too through a praying believer. As a believer, *you* can pray for your sick loved ones and see them recover!

Christ said that we would do what He could do and even more so[7] when the Holy Spirit came, the One who would teach us all truth. I encourage you to examine God's way for your life if you haven't already. If you have and still find it hard to overcome and press forward, take a closer look at the resurrection power available to you to live a supernatural, abundant overcoming life.

The resurrection is vital! Without the resurrection our faith is useless (see 1 Cor. 15:14). This resurrection is proof of who Jesus is and that He did accomplish what He set out to do, which was to provide the *only* means of redemption for humanity. Of all the religious leaders of time, only Jesus has physically risen from the dead, walked on water, claimed to be God, and raised others from the dead. He has conquered death. Why trust anyone subject to physical death when we have a Messiah who is greater than death itself?[8] When you're facing death, you'll be asking that question of yourself.

Counterfeits will rise to tell you that their way is the right way, but you can't figure out if something's counterfeit unless you study the real thing! Any banker knows that the only way to identify a counterfeit dollar bill is to know what a genuine dollar bill looks like.

RESURRECT THE HOPE OF YOUR CALLING

If your dreams have died because of calamity, disaster, failure, or tragedy, or even because of your own sin or perceived failures, I want you to know that Jesus can resurrect the hope of your calling in this life! There's no need to stay tied up in knots over a problem or to be stopped by some mountain of sin, sickness, disability, poverty, or lack that's in your path. You don't need to feel ashamed, dirty, or not worthy. As a born-again believer, you have the resurrected Christ in you—the very glory of God—and He has anointed you to release and manifest that glory into your life. When you came to accept Jesus into your life and heart, these things became possible.

He can resurrect your deepest innermost desires. He can resurrect your health, finances, relationships, and save, protect, and restore all that you've lost. You *can* live a life of success. The resurrection is more than just an event that happened once in history a few thousand years ago. It's the source of power you can experience in your life *every* day.

HIS PAIN FOR YOUR GAIN/HIS GAIN

The same power that resurrected Jesus from death to life is available to you. "And whoever continues to live and believes in (has faith in, cleaves to, and relies on) Me shall never [actually] die at all" (John 11:26). He died for your gain. "Do you believe this?" (John 11:26). To everything dead in your life that you hold dear, He can resurrect and give life. We are dead to sin and alive to God in Christ. (See Romans 6:11.)

When you know Him intimately, you'll experience the power of His resurrection first-hand. If you tap into it, you'll see amazing transformation in your life. And when you die, you'll live, so there's no reason to fear death anymore. That's the God's-gain part. It's not His will that you should perish but that you have everlasting life—He wants to spend eternity with you. (See John 3:15-16.)

When you expect the glory and resurrection power in your life, expect to know the solutions to your problems, and the power will explode through you like dynamite to blow up every obstacle, every mountain. Ask and receive, ask and receive—whatever you ask for from the promises of His Word, expect to receive it in liberal doses because that's what He promises. Moses asked to see the glory and he saw so much of it that his face shone when he descended the mountain. Jesus, coming back to earth after

the resurrection, shone with the revelation of the glory of God by the power of the Spirit of God.

> *For it is the God who commanded **light to shine out of darkness,** who has shone in our hearts to give the light of the knowledge of the glory of God in the face of Jesus Christ* (2 Corinthians 4:6).

That same Spirit lives in every believer and follower of Christ and shines through us. Just as God created the sun to light the day and said, "Let there be light," (see Gen. 1:14) He's saying, "Let there be light in you—Christ in you, the hope of glory." Let there be light in your life. Light makes darkness flee. The light is the glory of the Lord in you. He is the lamp unto your feet—the lamp that will light the path for you, that will topple and move mountains.

Each time He works powerfully on your behalf; your confidence grows.

Jesus said "If you only have faith as a mustard seed...." If you have even a little knowledge of who Christ Jesus is, and who Christ Jesus is in you, you'll be confident enough in the wonderworking miracle power of God in your life. People who have experienced the power of Jesus in their lives have that confidence.

Each time He works powerfully on your behalf, your confidence grows because you're increasing in knowledge and understanding of the power of the Spirit of the living loving God dwelling in you. Each time He works, you'll gain the wisdom to apply that knowledge to your life daily. Notice that godly wisdom and understanding are things we have to find, thus we have to seek—we have to take action. Blessed is the person who finds and gets wisdom and understanding!

> *Happy (blessed, fortunate, enviable) is the man who finds skillful and godly Wisdom, and the man who gets understanding [drawing it forth from God's Word and life's experiences], for the gaining of it is better than the gaining of silver, and the profit of it better than fine gold. Skillful and godly Wisdom is more precious than rubies; and nothing you can wish for is to be compared to her. Length of days is in her right hand, and in her left hand are riches and honor. Her ways are highways of pleasantness, and all her paths are peace. She is a tree of life to those who lay hold on her; and happy (blessed, fortunate, to be envied) is everyone who holds her fast* (Proverbs 3:13-18 AMP).

At certain times in my childhood and early teens, God left seed deposits of hope that helped me believe for the impossible. Every seed He planted in me and in my life increased my faith level for those times when I would need Him most. Certainly I would need to cling to Him as I lay broken along the highway, but had it not been for the knowledge of the wonderworks He'd already done and for His drawing power in my life as a child, I couldn't have believed for the resurrection of my hopes and dreams.

FOR THE LOVE
OF A FATHER

"Bob, where have you been? You missed the entire father-daughter dinner...how could you leave her here *waiting* for you like that...!"

I strained to hear more. "Be honest Bob. You never wanted Leigh Ann to even be born...she is your daughter...you have to stop drinking and be here for her...."

You never wanted Leigh Ann to even be born... Did I really hear that? It was more than I could bear so I tossed back the bedcovers, scrambled out of bed, and sped down the hall, blinded by tears. "Where have you been...is that true daddy?" I screamed while pummeling him with my fists with all of my strength. "You...you didn't even want me to be *born*? I hate you...I hate you!" I cried.

THE EARLY YEARS

I was born in Des Moines, Iowa, where my dad was finishing his medical residency at the hospital. My mom was a music teacher and also sold Stanley Home Products. The year my mother was pregnant with me, her picture and an article about her Stanley Home Product parties and business appeared in *Life* magazine showcasing her achievements and congratulating her as a highly successful woman in a primarily man's business world. It's fun to look at that picture of her even today, knowing that she was pregnant with me in the picture.

I was literally born into a sales world. A true entrepreneur before her time, my hard-working and kind mother of Pennsylvania Dutch German descent was the greatest person in my eyes. Pretty inside and out, fashion conscious and multi-talented too, Mary Middleton had a million-dollar personality such that everyone who knew her loved her. She could win anyone over with her genuine interest and caring spirit.

My doctor father wanted to practice specialized medicine in the state of Illinois; however, when Stanley Home Products offered my mother a great manager's position in St. Louis, about four years later, we moved there. But the decision to follow my mother's dream was not without a battle between my parents, and this would prove an underlying menace to my parent's relationship. Nevertheless, Mom was very successful in her new position and became quite the motivational speaker, soon leading the nation in sales for the company. My father as well had settled quite nicely into his thriving medical practice in Florissant, a city in St. Louis County. With two lucrative incomes, we lived very well.

A year after we moved to St. Louis, when I was six, to my delight my brother Robbie was born—even though I had wanted a sister! I dearly loved him. He was strong and all boy. He loved to play all sorts of sports and tried to imitate Dad—walking and talking like him, putting on sunglasses, reading the newspaper, and crossing his legs like Dad.

My best friend was Jeannie. Inseparable, we rode our bikes together and played from sunup to sundown with boundless energy. She was my closest friend and often stayed at my house because Mom would leave us on our

own to play or she'd be away on a trip somewhere, so I learned how to cook and entertain my friends.

I adored spending time with Jeannie's family though, as there was so much love there. Her mom was always so attentive and caring with kind words for me; and my mom and she played Bridge together. Her dad was an attorney who was home every night to spend time with Jeannie. He was affectionate toward her and gave her lots of hugs—which I craved of my own father.

Jeannie and I studied hard, made honor roll in school, and often enjoyed free tickets to St. Louis Cardinals' baseball games. "The Cards" were my favorite team. I'll never forget watching the World Series; it leaves me breathless even now when I think about it.

CRY FOR ATTENTION

My family had an enviable, wonderful, comfortable life, however, sometimes these things masked dysfunction. To neighbors and others our family looked picture perfect. I had many pretty dresses to wear, we lived in a nice house in the suburbs, my parents were successful, and we had a membership at the country club. Nevertheless, to me everything felt very wrong, and it wrenched my heart in mega proportions. My insides hurt so badly all of the time, mostly because my parents never seemed to be home.

From the time I was born, I was in the daily care of nannies or sitters and after my brother was born, both of us were. Nannies arrived and left faster than you could say, "Pleased to meet you," because my father was fickle when it came to someone caring for me or keeping the house clean, and with neatness and organization on both counts. You can imagine how insecure this left me after over 30 good-byes, especially so because I seldom had the chance to say good-bye. Oftentimes I'd just awaken to somebody new in my life. Some were let go for having boyfriends over on the sly, others because of my tantrums, who knows! It was all so hard on my brother and me because we missed our parents so much.

GWEN, A GIFT FROM GOD

There was no one nanny more precious to me than my beloved Gwen who had been with me since birth. For six years, she treated me as her own child, and when we moved from Des Moines, she moved with us to St. Louis to help take care of me during the transition. This precious African American saint hugged me often and loved to pray and sing. She'd hold me in her lap in our rocking chair and rock back and forth back and forth and sing to me. "Swing low...," she'd croon in her deep and raspy gospel voice, "...sweet char-i-ot..."

Whenever I'd cry for my daddy, she'd say, "You got Jesus...you got Jesus, child!"

One of her favorite tunes was *Nobody Knows the Trouble I've Seen*[9], and she often sang it as she went about her housekeeping duties.

Nobody knows the trouble I've seen.
Nobody knows but Jesus.
Nobody knows the trouble I've seen.
Glory Hallelujah!

Sometimes I'm up,
Sometimes I'm down
Oh, yes, Lord.
Sometimes I'm almost to the ground
Oh, yes, Lord.

I never shall
Forget that day
Oh, yes, Lord,
When Jesus washed my sins away,
Oh, yes, Lord.

No one could possibly know how troubled my heart was to awaken one day and learn that Gwen had to return to her biological family back in Des Moines. *I* was her real family! She'd been my constant companion and now she was leaving me too. That meant my peace and happiness went with her, and I felt alone and abandoned.

For days, weeks, even months afterward, I grieved the only way I knew how, through whining, screaming, and even tantrums because it was all too much for my young heart to process. How else could a lonely 6-year-old react to having an umbilical cord ripped away from the one who seemed to care for her most?

Even to this day I think of this awesome woman who showed me the love of God through her actions. Sometimes I still feel the void in my heart. I begged Dad to go and see her, and finally, about four years later, when he had to make a business trip, we dropped in to see her in Des Moines, Iowa. Gwen just about fell off her porch chair when she saw us driving slowly down the street searching for her house. "Doc, doc...Leigh Ann...oh Leigh Ann...I've missed you so much!" She gave me a million hugs and said, "I've prayed...I've kept praying, 'Jesus, let me see them one more time—I just want to see my family one more time.'"

Her hugs felt *so* good. Now I see this divine appointment of her in my life as one of the seeds the Lord planted early on to set the stage for things to come. God had seeded her into my life so I could experience His love through her. Again, evidence of the drawing power of God in my life.

I'm certain that her love and the love of Jesus working through her ful-filled a desperate need I had and prepared my heart for receiving Him as my personal Lord and Savior later on. Her actions and the love of God that shone through her planted a seed for later harvest.

ENTER THE ENEMY

My incessant and excessive screaming and tantrums really started, I believe, when she left. Gwen wasn't there for comfort—no one rocked me or held me as she did; nobody filled the void left by my parent's busyness as she did. Nobody exemplified the love of Christ as she did. No one could take her place, and one by one the nannies filed out the door.

However, one nanny marched in one day whose attention I *didn't* want. I felt like a battered soldier in a cruel dictator's army. She was pitiless and a perfectionist—the perfectionist part, no doubt, was what prompted my father to hire her. Perfection with a "p" for pressing clothes—she ironed everything, including underwear, sheets, towels, and socks; and Lord help me if I wrinkled or messed up a crease in anything she ironed for me. Did I mention starch? Even the clothes stood at attention in her presence and they didn't dare soften.

She ironed everything, including underwear, sheets, towels, and socks.

My old clothes looked brand new and she determined that I'd keep them that way, even when going outside to play with Jeannie. Jeannie's mother would sometimes say, "You look so nice, are you *sure* you're sup-posed to be outside in your good clothes, Leigh Ann?"

The old battleaxe nanny had a wooden spaghetti spoon that she'd chase me around with and then use on me as her weapon of choice when I didn't sit up straight enough or if I talked at the dinner table, even if I got a speck of dirt on something. That's the "p" for pitiless part. She'd curse in Italian, and hiss and scream at me for the slightest infraction, which left me a mess. I wasn't an angel per se, just a little girl—a little spoiled, a lot insecure, and perfection wasn't my strongpoint. Cold, mean, and a real sourpuss, this woman didn't have one ounce of the usual warm-hearted, fun-loving, forgiving nature of a typical Italian mama, which is what I desperately needed!

I'm so glad that I'd known the love of Gwen because had God not placed her in my path beforehand, there's no telling how detrimental the effects of this nanny's cruel ways would have been on my young life and in later years. In light of this person's cruelty, I could hold fast to the love I'd once known and believe for it again.

HAPPIER TIMES

My pretty bedroom became my retreat for tears, and the window where I'd press my little nose up to watch for and will my parents to come home to help me, was my hope. Peering off into the distance toward the highway, I'd scream at the top of my lungs, "Mommy, Daddy, please come home, I need you *now*!" Then I'd watch for their car to come down the road right away to save me, then wonder why they didn't. Of course I didn't know they couldn't hear my cries. But I'm convinced God heard me and sent Daddy home early one day in what could only have been a miracle because he usually worked late into the night.

Daddy arrived right when the nanny was chasing me through our backyard yard screaming while wielding that awful wooden spoon. He was so shocked, and I can only imagine what was going through his head as he realized that Miss Perfect wasn't so perfect after all. I was so grateful that he finally believed me and saw the truth of how she treated me.

Exit the battleaxe. Can you say, "P" for "Praise God!"

There were some happy, normal times with my parents though, like when my mother would take time off work to take Jeannie, my girlfriends, and me to Camp Fire Girl's camp.

Daddy's parents lived in Greenfield, Illinois, and were of English and Irish descent and very Baptist. Many of my ancestors were preachers, musicians, and political figures. In fact, we are direct descendents of Arthur Middleton who signed the Declaration of Independence.

I loved the drive up to Greenfield, where we would eat Grandma Middleton's famous pot roast and homemade pimento cheese sandwiches. She would ask grandpa to walk Jeannie and me to Vacation Bible School some summers, and I loved running free and learning about Jesus who loved children. We would all sing old hymns like "Onward Christian Soldier,"[10] and "At the Cross."[11]

Grandpa Middleton owned a pharmacy and drug store and was sweet, kind, and soft-spoken. People in town called him "the man who walked like a streak of lightning" because he always walked so quickly to and from the store. He was fun and good to me, and I remember him showing me how to put nickels on the train tracks to flatten them.

Even more fun than my days at various camps were the summers I spent in Pennsylvania with Uncle Clair and Aunt Nancy and my four cousins, Sue and Teddy, and the twins Johnny and Julie. This time with family was a welcome change from spending holidays in towns with racetracks and gambling places. Because of my father's penchant for betting on horses, I got quite good at figuring the odds—not the best environment or foundation for raising a child.

Aunt Nancy, my mother's sister, was the most amazing stay-at-home mom and a great cook, and Uncle Clair had a thriving construction business building highways all around Bloomsburg, Pennsylvania. They lived in a big house on the hill and had a small retreat on Lake Carey near Tunkhannock, Pennsylvania. My brother and I loved being with them because they were wonderful in giving us attention and love, and showing us patience and generosity. For instance, Aunt Nancy spent hours in the cold lake water teaching me to water-ski, and she also taught me how to garden, cook, and buy shoes! She also drove her jeep like Mario Andretti through those Pennsylvania hills to pick apples at harvest time. We ate a lot of Pennsylvania Dutch food like shoofly pie, and huge sub sandwiches called *hoagies*—the most delicious sandwiches. Being with her was so much fun. Had it not been for those happy summers away, I don't think I'd have had any semblance of normalcy. Those times often kept my hope for happiness alive.

Daddy, a Beloved Doctor

I loved my father, and his patients loved him too. He'd often not charge people who couldn't afford medical care, and he never turned anyone away. From delivering babies for everyday people to providing medical care to famous sports figures, wrestlers, and some shady Mafia members, "Doc's" clientele ran the gamut of people like Cashes Clay (Mohammed Ali), George Foreman, Stan (the Man) Musial, as well as a few questionable figures like "Big Rick." I can't tell you how often Dad was called out in the middle of the night to put this gangster's hands back together after a "confrontation."

One day I asked him, "Daddy, do you believe there is a God?"

"Honey, I *know* there is a God!"

"How do you know?"

"If you ever have the chance to see a baby born, or if you ever deliver a baby, you'll know that only God could have created such wonder."

Dad's sense of awe when it came to the preciousness and miracle of human life, his big heart, gentle sense of humor, and kind ways attracted people. I don't know, however, that he *loved* his work as a general practitioner and surgeon per se because his heart always was to become a specialized surgeon in his home state of Illinois. Bitterness and anger toward my mom sometimes surfaced at home about this, exacerbated by his binge drinking; however, I know he made the best of things because he did love his patients and oh, they sure loved him.

SHOCKING REVELATION

As great as my daddy was at making people feel good, gambling and alcohol were serious sicknesses in his life. When on a bender, sometimes he wouldn't come home at all and he went through money like water on his frequent trips to Las Vegas. My mother lived in torment because of these addictions as well as suspected affairs, although she never talked about it and never, ever complained to me. I mean never ever said a discouraging word! She always covered his sin—this dark side—and tried to act as though all was well. Perhaps she sensed that the sacrifice he made for her career drove him to it, and simply tolerated it because of guilt.

For whatever reason, I'd sense her inner hurt and even as a little girl affirmed my love to her throughout the tough times. On days when she needed that affirmation the most she'd invite me to cuddle up with her on the sofa, and then she'd hold me close all night long as we watched old Doris day and Vivien Leigh movies on television while eating Jiffy-Pop popcorn.

In fact, I was named after Vivien Leigh from "Gone with the Wind" fame. How well I remember crying at all of the sad parts with Mom.

My father's problem with alcohol and gambling worsened though and as it did, he became less and less reliable and seldom showed up for school things or my swim team matches. On one such day, I looked forward, for quite some time, to Dad taking me to a father/daughter banquet. I was giddy with excitement in my new pink and black velvet dress and waited for Daddy to come home, but he never showed. My mom explained that he'd probably stayed late with a patient though he never called. Finally at 1:00 A.M. he staggered through the door reeking of alcohol.

Long since tucked in bed I lay there listening to my upset mother as she confronted him in the family room. This was the first time I'd ever heard her actually talk to him like that. "Bob, where have you been? You missed the entire father-daughter dinner...how could you leave her here *waiting* for you like that...!"

I strained to hear more. "Be honest Bob. You never wanted Leigh Ann to even be born...she is your daughter...you have to stop drinking and be here for her...."

This is when I heard those awful words.

You never wanted Leigh Ann to even be born. It unnerved my father when he found out that I'd heard him say that. Deeply repentant but reeking of alcohol, he tried to pick me up to quiet and calm me. "Honey—that is not true what your mother said. I do want you, I do love you!"

He held me but his hugs didn't linger. They never lingered, and I always wondered why. I'd get the pats usually, that was all, and I remember craving more of him. I wanted bear hugs as Uncle Clair gave me. My father's affirmation helped for the moment, but those negative words hurt for a long time.

Abba Daddy God

When our parents seem to fail us, we can always rely on God the Father. Jesus called God His Father, but in a special, more endearing way, "Abba." This is an Aramaic word that translates like *Daddy*. Jesus introduced us to a Father in Heaven, not as a harsh ruler or someone unapproachable, but as Daddy God, someone we can turn to and who will give us more of Himself the more we crave Him. Our heavenly Father is our *Abba*, our Daddy, the most perfect Father we can have. He cares about, loves us, and watches over us—a loving Father who never lets us down.

Our Daddy loves us so much that not only did He love us from Heaven but came down to us from Heaven as Immanuel, God with Us, Jesus Christ. In Jesus, God became Immanuel, God with Us and He really and *truly* is with us!

The Bible says that nothing can come between us and the love of Christ, the love of God made visible in Jesus our Lord (see Romans 8). Even negative words from our earthly parents cannot come between us and the love that the Father, Daddy God has for us.

Words that Hurt, Words that Heal

Negative words on a young life—any life for that matter—are powerful and they can wreak much damage because they can embitter us. As adults, we might hear or overhear words such as, "We never should have hired him," or "I wish I never married you!" Hearing such negative words is like getting punched in the gut because these words can destroy, hinder, and hurt us in many ways.

The old childhood saying that "sticks and stones may break my bones but words will never hurt me," isn't true. Negative words can cause some of the deepest and worst-wounding experiences we have in life. Bones may heal but hearts that words have broken take much longer at any stage of life.

Just as negative words affect us, positive words have greater influence to build up, heal, bless, and encourage. God created His ordered world with words, but we can create chaos in our worlds with unhealthy, embittered, trashy, belying, underhanded, critical, hurtful words.

> *Just as negative words affect us, positive words have greater influence.*

"Death and life are in the power of the tongue..." (Prov. 18:21). Overhearing that my dad wished I were never born hurt me so deeply. Because I hadn't resolved in my heart that what I'd overheard wasn't true, when my mother started to travel more often, I felt even more rejected and alienated. My mother was an incredible mom, but her timing for travel was not the best in light of my need for security and more attention. She attended more and more out-of-town meetings and rallies and won more glittery diamond awards for her outstanding sales performance—which meant more strangers caring for me, additional strain on my parents' relationship, and I felt less and less safe even in my parent's love. I also felt less secure at home. Never would this become more apparent than the day the thief came to steal that last shred of security from me.

Chapter 4

SOMEBODY *PLEASE* LISTEN

Couldn't anyone see I need help? I need a savior, someone to rescue me from my torment and the fear of being violated again, or worse yet, murdered by this horrible man....The fear night after night that he would kill my brother, mother, and father. Where is this Jesus my grandmother and Gwen used to tell me about? He isn't in our church, for sure. Nobody will listen...

WHEN I was nine, my mother left me in the care of a teenage girl who lived across the street from us. Not wanting to miss hanging out with her friends, she took me along to her girlfriend's house just down our street.

The girls, busy curling their hair, left me to myself and it was a while before they discovered that I had disappeared.

I had just come out of the bathroom when someone (it turned out to be the girl's 19-year-old brother) with a nylon stocking over his head and wielding a huge silver knife grabbed me and put his hand over my mouth. At first, I thought it was a game or someone playing a trick on me but when I heard the basement door lock behind us, I really got scared. He dragged me downstairs, flung me on the sofa, and violated me. To keep me from crying out, he kept his hand on my mouth and as my pain escalated, I stopped struggling, and helpless against his strength, withdrew into a dark, still place inside of me as a way to endure and wait for the horror to end. After what seemed like an eternity the sitter called for me, and finding the basement door locked, she began pounding on it. "Leigh where are you? Are you playing hide-and-seek?"

"Go into the washroom now, blow your nose, and put a smile on your face," my terrorist commanded in a whisper. "If you tell your parents...if you tell *anyone* at all, I'll kill you *and* your family with this very knife!" he said as he flashed the knife in front of my face to make his point.

Terrified, I ran up the stairs and out of that evil pit and away from the demonized youth's murderous glare.

*...kill you and your family...kill you and your family...*I couldn't shake free of those threats. It would be a long time before I could escape his horrible glare and words. The filth and horror of what happened wouldn't go away even though later at home I tried to soak it away in the tub. *Scrub...maybe if I scrub harder I can get it all off.*

I took bath after bath but nothing worked. The filth wouldn't rise above the bubbles.

HEAR ME, PLEASE...

Perhaps if my mother had done something about it, some of that dirt would have gone away. When I told her something bad had happened to

me, she acted so strangely and somewhat unconcerned, in my mind's eye. Perhaps that was her way of dealing with something so terrible, but it didn't help me deal with it. She didn't even ask me for details or call the police. I don't know what went on in her heart that day for her not to just cuddle and comfort me; I needed it so much.

Inside my heart screamed because the violation and fear was far beyond my innocence to comprehend or lend words to. The only hope I had was my dad. Surely he would do something...make it all better...*something* to help me get rid of the dirt, shame, and abject terror.

Daddy got home and my mother immediately intercepted him and took him out of earshot of me. I heard them discuss something and it gave me hope. *Good—Dad will storm into the house, scoop me into his arms, and make me feel safe and clean again before racing out to beat up that evil man who'd hurt me.*

Nothing happened.

He didn't do a thing.

He didn't champion, protect, nurture, or stand up for his little girl. My parents simply sent me to bed as though it were an ordinary night. *Thump, thump, thump* I'd hear my wee heart pound like a jack hammer in fear for countless sleepless nights afterward as I lay curled up under the covers terrified, wide-eyed, alone, and lost in a space between childhood and adulthood. If I did succumb to sleep, I'd awaken in fear from nightmares with my pajamas soaked in sweat. Even the sound of my beating heart scared me. With no outlet, I wondered what would happen if I told Jeannie's parents about what happened, but I thought that if I did they wouldn't ever allow me back to their place again or let her come over to play. As darkness fell on my last possibility, I felt very alone.

One summer at Aunt Nancy's home, I almost opened up and told my cousin Sue, who was slightly older than me, was beautiful, tall, and the intellectual type! A reader, she loved to learn things and I thought surely she'd be able to figure something out, to understand—maybe she'd read of things like that happening. One day we were gabbing and sharing secrets and I figured that because she was older she would know things about boys that I wouldn't know. I didn't even know how to explain what happened! Averting her eyes, I focused on her wall of horse knick-knacks, but just as I was about to blurt it out, fear gripped me. *What if Aunt Nancy never invites me back for my summer vacation? What if Uncle Clair thinks badly of me? This is the only good thing I have to look forward to every year—I can't risk it.* We didn't have a large extended family and to lose them would devastate my brother and me.

Not to fault my parents or anyone else, in those days people didn't talk about "certain things" and mostly just swept them under the proverbial shag rug hoping something would just make it all disappear. In my child's mind, I thought I'd explained everything adequately but maybe not enough, now that I think of it in hindsight. Alternatively, perhaps my mom felt too uncomfortable dealing with it. And my father was intelligent enough to know the police and court systems of the day, and it's possible he didn't want to see his little girl dragged through it all. Thus, it's possible that they *did* try to sweep it all away with a pat and kiss goodnight.

It didn't work.

Dad called me a "rail" because I'd become so skinny. Although he was a doctor, my rapid weight loss didn't sound an alarm that perhaps something wasn't "quite right."

When I ran away from home, they still didn't get it and besides, where could I escape the nightmare if I didn't have an outlet even to help me express the abuse I suffered.

Baths, baths, more baths. They became an obsession as I tried to cleanse myself of that day. *Why didn't mom and dad fight for me? Why did they do nothing?*

One day it became clear—I suddenly knew why they didn't even try to make everything OK. *They don't love me.* Indeed, to my just turned 10-year-old fifth-grade mind, it *appeared* they didn't believe me and probably didn't even want me around, I reasoned. Also, my parents said I had to go to school and I didn't want to go because the bus stop was right in front of this guy's house. So one day I took a razor from Dad's bathroom and carved several lines down each side of my face. Blood trickled from the wounds. *Now I was as ugly outside as I felt on the inside. Now they'd see that ugliness and ask "Why?" Now they'd see how painfully my cuteness was violently wrenched away from me. Now I won't have to wait at the bus stop near that guy's house...I don't want to go to school ever again.*

"What have you done to your beautiful face? Why have you done this?" my mother gasped and screamed on discovering me in the bathroom. "Why—why?" she cried again as she first shook me and then clasped me close.

I didn't have answers but not for lack of trying. Earlier I'd tried to find them in my small white Bible I received during catechism class. I tried to read it and find help, but things were just too difficult in there to understand, and in frustration I hurled it across my bedroom.

"I love you Leigh Ann, I love you. You are my precious daughter. It's going to be OK. We'll get through this!" she encouraged.

But I didn't believe her and felt so confused and worse now that I had upset my mother. More guilt, more shame, more to keep inside of my heart.

For weeks I couldn't go to school but when it was time to return, my mother rehearsed with me what I would tell everyone about what happened to my face: "Tassie, my cat scratched me." I'd have to lie because my precious cat never scratched!

It was all just too much for my little heart to wrap around.

Couldn't anyone see I needed help? I need a savior, someone to rescue me from my torment and the fear of being violated again, or worse yet murdered by this horrible man, this crazy pervert who lives a few doors down from me...the fear night after night that he would kill my parents, my brother. Where is this Jesus my grandmother used to tell me about? He isn't in our church, for sure. People didn't really talk to Jesus at our church; they just dressed up nice, smiled a lot, and pretended to listen to what the pastor had to say. *Is there a God? If yes, how can I find Him? My dad sort of believed in God. Grandma said Jesus would listen. I need someone to listen!*

These things weighed on my heart later that day as I sat on my perfectly-made bed in my pretty color-coordinated bedroom. My eyes wandered to the little white Bible, open on the floor where I'd tossed it earlier. When I picked it up a verse beamed at me:

The grass withereth, the flower fadeth: but the word of our God shall stand for ever (Isaiah 40:8 KJV).

Although I didn't quite understand what the words meant, I memorized and tucked them into my heart for no special reason. At night in bed, I'd recite the verse and a measure of comfort, peace, and hope would come.

PARENTS AREN'T PERFECT

Now I want to stop right here to tell you something. Even though I perceived things as a child about my parents that shaped the ways in which I

might see things now as an adult and more importantly as a believer, I know that my parents loved me very much. A strong-willed child, it doubtlessly wasn't easy raising me, especially as a first-born. As you'll see later on, we indeed did develop a stronger relationship particularly once God healed all of our hearts and we all came to know the wonderful power of the love of Christ.

The only perfect parent is God

I'm certain Mom and Dad wished they could have done some things differently or made better choices; and likewise, I could have done things differently. Nevertheless, I also know that they always wanted the best for me and brought me up the best way they knew how in the midst of *their* circumstances and challenges. The only perfect parent is God, and if we don't have Him as our model in our own lives, it's that much harder to be a parent.

Today I've learned to seek the good that I experienced and avoid dwelling on what they did wrong. While parents typically feel loads of guilt and focus more on the things that weren't great while raising their children—things they could have done better—there's nothing they can do except learn lessons, forgive themselves, seek forgiveness, and pray for their children. Similarly, children too must learn from their experiences, forgive their parents and themselves, and keep their parents covered in prayer.

Parenting isn't for cowards, in that we have to be fearless and watchful over our children and guard them—I mean really guard them.

When I moved my son Josh into his own room as a little guy, I'd leave my bedroom door open so I could hear him, and I never slept so deeply that I wasn't aware of every breath he took. Things haven't changed! I still instinctively know when he has difficulty sleeping, if something hurts, if he's feeling insecure in some way, or if something's bothering him. Parents' hearts break for their children when they share their hurts or when they have to learn harsh life lessons too young.

WHY BAD THINGS HAPPEN

One of the hardest questions people pose to Christians is, "If God loves His people, why do bad things happen to them?"

That's a huge question, one which even theologians have struggled with because God is so infinite and we are finite beings unable fully to understand the eternal, omniscient, omnipresent, omnipotent infinite ways of God. First know, however, that God's love is real.

The Book of Job gives us insight. Satan attributed Job's righteousness to all of the blessings he had. The accuser told God that the only reason Job was so upright was because of all the stuff he enjoyed—his massive land holdings, material possessions, large and healthy family, and so on; that if Job didn't have those things it wouldn't be long before he'd lose trust in God. God disagreed, but agreed to satan's request to test Job to prove his loyalty to Him regardless of Job's position or stature in life. God gave the devil permission to do anything he wanted to Job except to kill him. Now I don't know about you, but I don't know if I would have had the patience of Job considering all the enemy did to him. From boils to plagues to losing his family and all of his possessions, his suffering was awful.

Job's reaction? *"Though He slay me, yet will I hope in Him"* (Job 13:15 NIV). He was saying, "I depend solely on God and I trust in Him alone. Even if I die, I know that I'll come forth as gold."

...Naked (without possessions) came I [into this world] from my mother's womb, and naked (without possessions) shall I depart...blessed (praised and magnified in worship) be the name of the Lord! (Job 1:21 AMP)

Is it strange that God would give satan permission to do all this? God did it for His own glory, for the honor of Job, to explain providence, and to encourage us even today. Job didn't understand *why* God allowed the things He did, but he knew that God was *good, just, loving, kind, merciful,* and so he continued to trust in Him.

God's greatest goal is that we should become like Jesus, His Son. This is His great purpose for our lives.

And we know that all things work together for good to those who love God, to those who are the called according to His purpose. For whom He foreknew, He also predestined to be conformed to the image of His Son, that He might be the firstborn among many brethren (Romans 8:28-29).

When we understand the truth in this Scripture deep in our inner beings, we will better grasp why we have trials and difficulties, and can trust that what happens is working for our good. The good that comes about is God growing us into the image of His Son through every trial, mistake, hardship, or bad thing that happens to us. What the devil meant for bad, God means for good and will make right.

God can deliver us from all the bad stuff. We live in a fallen world and would that be conducive to His purpose—that we grow and develop into that mature stature of Christ Jesus? Sometimes it's hard for us to wrap our minds around *all things working for our good* because cause and effect says that good brings good and bad brings bad. How can bad things bring health, peace, plenty, triumph, hope, joy, happiness, success?

Edward Payson,[12] great pastor in the 1800s, preached the following in one of his sermons entitled, "God's Ways Above Men's":[13]

> If God's ways and thoughts are thus high above ours, ought we not implicitly to believe all his declarations: to believe that all he says and does is perfectly right? Is it not reasonable for children thus to believe their parents? For a sick man to trust in a skilful physician? For a passenger unacquainted with navigation, to trust to the master of the vessel? For a blind man to follow his guide? If so, then it is certainly much more reasonable for such ignorant, short-sighted, fallible creatures, as we are, to submit and trust implicitly to an infinitely wise, good, and infallible Being; and when any of his words or works appear wrong, to ascribe it to our own ignorance, blindness, or prejudice, rather than to suppose that there is any thing wrong in him. Is it not more likely that we should be wrong or mistaken, than that God should be? If so, we ought to praise him, when his conduct appears wise and right, and to impute it to ourselves when it does not, and to believe and to submit to him implicitly in all things.

Payson's faith and belief had to have rubbed off on his own daughter, Elizabeth Prentiss, who published a best-selling book, *Stepping Heavenward*,[14] that revealed her yearning to know God, even though she suffered through the death of her two children and had major health issues.

This inner hope is God in us—Christ *in* us. In the end, everything will be OK not because we deserve things to be OK but because of God committing His only Son to die and because the Son agreed to die for us in our place. Paul said that "when we were still powerless, Christ died for the ungodly. Very rarely will anyone die for a righteous man, though for a good man someone might possibly dare to die. But God demonstrates His own love for us in this: While we were still sinners, Christ died for us" (Rom.5:6-8 NIV). Jesus said it Himself that He didn't come for those who were well but those who were sick (see Luke 5:31). I'm sick, you're sick, and He died for us because of the Father's love. His Word says, in fact, that He draws us with loving-kindness (see Jer. 31:3).

WE'RE FORGIVEN

How do you react in suffering, or when you see an innocent suffer? Does it make you wonder? Job's reaction should be our reaction too when something happens that we don't understand. Rather than doubt God's goodness, we should trust Him. The Bible says that we should. "Trust in the Lord with all your heart and *lean not on your own understanding; in all your ways acknowledge Him, and He shall direct your paths*" (Prov. 3:5-6 NKJV).

God is holy (see Isa. 6:3; Rev. 4:8) and we are sinful (see Rom. 3:23; 6:23). He says:

As it is written, none is righteous, just and truthful and upright and conscientious, no, not one. No one understands [no one intelligently discerns or comprehends]; no one seeks out God. All have turned aside; together they have gone wrong and have become unprofitable and worthless; no one does right, not even one! Their throat is a yawning grave; they use their tongues to deceive (to mislead and to deal treacherously). The venom of asps is beneath their lips. Their mouth is full of cursing and bitterness. Their feet are swift to shed blood. Destruction [as it dashes them to pieces] and misery mark their ways. And they have no experience of the way of peace [they know nothing about peace, for a peaceful way they do not even recognize]. There is no [reverential] fear of God before their eyes (Romans 3:10-18 AMP).

Every millisecond we are alive is only by God's great grace. None of us deserve His grace. In fact, even the most terrible suffering on earth is nothing compared to what we, as humanity deserve—an eternity in hell. Someone once said that this world is the only hell believers will ever experience but this world is the only Heaven unbelievers will ever experience!

But God also proves His own love for us that "while we were still sinners, Christ died for us" (Rom. 5:8). *God still loves us* even though we have an evil, sinful nature. Yes, hallelujah, God loves us enough that He died to take the penalty for our sin and wickedness (see Rom. 6:23)—all of it was heaped upon His shoulders. All we have to do to be forgiven and live eternally in Heaven with Him is believe in Christ Jesus: "For God so loved the world..." (John 3:16). Even greater news, God doesn't revisit our sin once there's been a thorough work of repentance.

To illustrate, a Bible translator worked with the elders of an Inuit tribe and in trying to translate the Scriptures into the Inuktitut language, he couldn't come up with the word for "forgiven." The elders finally came up with a word: "issumagijoujingnainirmik" which means, "not able to think about it again." God never again thinks about our sin once He's forgiven us. As far as the east is from the west, God says that He will remember it no more (see Heb. 10:17).

THE REDEEMED

It was never God's plan that we be terrorized or sick or even that we die, but He knew that we would fail so He sent Jesus, His very own Son, to

suffer and die for us that we might be redeemed from the curse. As we give our hearts to God, He will heal, restore, deliver, and save us from the works of darkness. God says, "I know My plan for you, for good and not for evil..." (see Jer. 29:11). He says He will give us hope in our outcome, so why doubt Him?

God never said that it was only out of the pit that we could find Him, or only at the end of the road. We can find Him all along the way, at any juncture or at any pit depth. Even when we're riding high, we can meet Him. Wherever we are, the journey with Him can begin. The way actually begins the moment we shed pride and confess to God that we can do nothing to save ourselves. That's when He saves us—when we call out, "Help me, Lord. I can't do it without you!"

That's when transformation happens and you become a new person, a new creation in Christ Jesus. He wipes your slate clean and then, if you allow Him to, He'll raise you up in His knowledge, grace, power, and love! When you truly come to God, you'll be able to love everyone—even those you haven't liked—because God will put love in your heart. This is the way to know you love God—that you love others.

Some time after my mother became a Christian, she took Aunt Nancy, her only sister, who was visiting, to church with her one day. Mom, wanting to be certain that Aunt Nancy *heard* the message, made certain to sit up front, much to my aunt's consternation. At the end of the sermon the pastor said, "Someone here needs the Lord. You need to come forward and receive the Lord into your life."

My aunt, while studying the carpet perhaps not to meet his gaze, suddenly saw a vision of Jesus in the pattern of the carpet. The image of Jesus seemed to get bigger and bigger. As crazy as it sounds, this compelled her to go forward when the pastor called again, "Is there anyone here who would like to give their life to the Lord today?"

Normally, Mom, being her older sister, would have nudged her up there. However, that day, she held back, knowing that this was a decision only her sister could make. Aunt Nancy, much to her joy and relief said, "Mary, will you walk forward with me," and she gave her heart to Jesus.

A few days later, when her husband picked her up at the St. Louis Airport, he said with a sarcastic edge to his voice, "So Nancy, I guess you're *born again* now?"

She replied, "Yes, as a matter of fact I am!"

"How do you know?"

"I know," she said confidently, "because I love people I couldn't love before."

After God got through with her in the area of forgiveness, He set to work in her life and she's actually enjoyed many blessings, including her family and health. She has such a generous and giving heart—the Lord has certainly used her.

SURRENDER ALL

Are you willing to let go of the past so God can begin His great work in you?

Surrender! Give Him everything. Put it all into His hands so that He can lead you into His perfect plan. He's your Savior, and then He's your Lord! As Lord of your life, you give Him the reins to lead you in the direction He would have you go. You belong to God and Jesus alone—no one else holds claim to your life. God will heal past wounds, and He may have

to take you briefly into your past to clear the debris so you can move forward. This is necessary because sometimes our past binds us so that we can't fully live in our present. Are you willing to let go of the past so God can begin His great work in you?

EMOTIONAL HEALING

I had to surrender my wrong thinking that arose because of the abuse and my lonely childhood. Every time you let go of something, you'll move forward. However, if you hold on to something that debilitates your thinking or stunts your spiritual growth, you may not be able to fully accomplish all that God has for you.

God doesn't focus on your past except to heal you and to show you how you can learn from mistakes so that you don't repeat an unhealthy pattern. This may require the breaking down of strongholds by prayer or prayer and fasting. After we let go, snap go the chains that bind and we can move forward with no more looking back negatively. Paul said,

> *"...but one thing I do, forgetting those things which are behind and reaching forward to those things which are ahead. I press toward the goal for the prize of the upward call of God in Christ Jesus"* (Philippians 3:13-14).

It's easy to fall back on the bad things and then throw a pity party for yourself as guest of honor. We may even justify an outright sin because of something that happened to us in the past; but we have to let go. We can't be victorious or successful unless we get rid of the baggage. That baggage also includes any unforgiveness that remains in our lives. Yes, this can be hard especially when people have so defiled or hurt us that it seems an impossible task. Remember that in forgiving someone we're not justifying what they did to us, but instead we are forgiving them and lifting them up to the Father to deal with. God won't supernaturally heal our emotional pain or wounds of the past inflicted by someone unless we deliver that person into His hands.

Allow God to right every wrong ever done to you. It's OK to say, "God, help me forgive," because He'll show you how. When you truly forgive someone, God will move by the power of the Holy Spirit to heal your wounds and erase the pain. You may not forget the wounds, but you'll be able to look back and see God's handiwork and faithfulness to deliver you from their ill effects. God can heal your mind and emotions.

> ## *It's OK to say, "God, help me forgive."*

First, He works deeply on the heart so you can move ahead in those areas and into His plan for your life. God can set you free from the fallout of living in a dysfunctional family by showing you the errors in your parents' ways. This, for the most part, takes getting out of the boat and trusting God—as Peter did when he walked on water toward Jesus (see Matt. 14:29). Jesus extends His hand to you to hold onto as the Holy Spirit moves in to clean house and remove the obstacles that set you back. Remember, it takes action on your part and willingness, and submission to let Him bring you up and out of it.

THE DRAWING POWER OF GOD

I have chosen you...I have chosen you... the joy welled up in me and the words kept ringing in my heart like church bells on a quiet Sunday morning. "Hope...hope."

———◇———

VULNERABILITY and fear festered like cancer in me for a while. For a time, I was still afraid of waiting for the bus at the stop near that guy's house. Because there was no one to cry out to, my spirit cried out in pain. From the depths of my being, I called "Help!" but I didn't know to whom I cried.

But God always takes care of His children. He sees and listens to the cries of the innocent. I know this to be true because He showed up one gorgeous day when I was about 12 years old.

I was playing in the living room, while my mother napped on the sofa, and had walked over to the window to watch for my friend, Jeannie. Just as I wondered when in the world she'd get there, I felt the presence of

Someone right next to me, as close as my skin—almost under it! I couldn't see anyone, but a presence enveloped me in a warm cocoon of powerful, glorious love wrapped in an inexplicable sense of security! Oh my goodness. It was awesome being in the presence of this warm, loving Being. As I basked in that delightful Presence, a voice said to me, "I love you and I have a plan for your life and I will take care of you...I have chosen *you*!"

*I have chosen you...I have chosen you...*the joy welled up in me and the words kept ringing in my heart like church bells on a quiet Sunday morning. "Hope...hope."

For the first time in I don't know how long, I smiled for real as the heavy oppression, the darkness, the weightiness of despair lifted not only from me, but also from our house. This wasn't imagined. I felt so happy and free and wanted to scream for pure joy. Even the yard seemed different—the blue spruce trees more beautiful than ever. My mother awoke startled as I ran excitedly through the house yelling at the top of my lungs, "Mom...I heard a voice *speak* to me and it said 'I have a plan for your life'; it's like I'm chosen or something!"

My mother said that my voice kept getting excitedly higher and higher in pitch. "Maybe I'm going to feed hungry children like I see the Feed the Hungry people do on television! Mom...mom...are you listening to me?"

Papap Shuman sometimes admonished Mom, "Mary, *listen* to your daughter." I reminded her of that. "Mom, what did Papap used to tell you? This is important Mom...very important!"

"OK honey," she said pointedly, "I *am* listening...you don't have to be so loud! Calm down, settle down. I can hear you."

Finally, I got her attention and to keep it I yelled even louder. "Mom...I'm chosen! I'm going to do something great. I heard this voice and I felt this—"

"Honey, your voice is so loud you could be a preacher."

You have no idea how prophetic those words were coming from my mother's mouth—almost as though God had planted those words for her to say at just the right time. It had to be, because in our Presbyterian circles women just didn't preach; and no one preached like those evangelists on television did. Our pastors were monotone and lifeless compared to them. "Boring," I used to say.

Was it God who spoke to me? It made me wonder but not for long. Somehow, I knew that I'd connected with the One who could lift my insecurities, my fears, my shame, my loneliness, the rejection, the pain, my yearning for approval. To think He cared enough to have a plan, to speak to *me*. This was my grandmother's Jesus, it had to be! Suddenly, I wanted to pour my soul out to Him. I'd heard the voice of my grandmother's Jesus—the One I could talk to, the One who would listen.

Ah...now that verse that I'd picked up off the floor and memorized earlier made sense. The Word of God—what He spoke to me—would never fade away, and I was glad of it. Now I had His audible word as well as His written Word to hold fast to, and I would need to in the coming darker days when they were all I could cling to, to save my life. Even though I'd venture away, His drawing power was constant and it ran as a thread through my childhood and teen years.

School Days

When I turned 14, I heard that the man who had molested me was serving time in prison for murder. Yes, murder! I was fortunate to have escaped him but it was hard to escape the horror of that day. The following years, for the most part, were a blur as the agony, despair, and feelings of worthlessness overtook me.

My early teen years were turbulent, and I hung out with a terrible crowd. Dad decided to take me out of the public school system and place me in a strict, private all girl's Catholic prep school in Normandy, Missouri, with the hope that I'd make new friends and get a better education. At first, I hated that he took me away from my friends. However, I grew to appreciate what my dad did for me, and those years at Incarnate Word Academy became some of the best times of my life. I started to see the world from a different vantage point. The nuns stressed providing a good education and pushed us to read and be creative, and to think about humanity, charity, people around the world, and global issues. Most of all, I felt safe in that environment and thrived.

I gained more confidence and actually did extremely well. Surrounded by great friends, Lani, Bobbie, and Nancy, with whom I'm still close, I excelled socially and academically.

Perhaps this school was in God's plan for me in that it gave me a desire to know more about Him. Yes, it was traditionally Catholic and didn't preach the salvation message per se, but many biblical moral basics were there and it really turned me around. Had I not attended, I don't believe I would have done well in college. Without realizing it, my father's decision made a huge difference in my life. Certainly it fueled my hunger to know more about God, who He was, and what He meant in my life.

One summer I traveled with a group from school to study at the Universidad de Santiago de Compostela in Spain. After more than a few sips of my "cognac con leche," I got up the nerve to talk to Sister Angelina. I blurted out, "Sister Angelina, why did you become a nun and give your whole life to this work, because I see how committed you are. Tell me, why are you doing this. Why?"

"When I was younger I was engaged to be married and a young man left me and broke my heart. So I decided to become a nun and work in the convent for the rest of my life," she said.

"Do you know God? Did He tell you to do this? Does God talk to you? Is He real?"

"Not really," she said, "I just felt this was the right thing to do."

Over the following months, I quizzed her and the other nuns more. Their answers bothered me in a way because it seemed most went into the convent because of hurts and wounds. Not being Catholic, I didn't understand how someone could dedicate her whole life to God—give up even romantic love, for God. "Do you know Jesus? Do you know God? Why do you pray to all of these saints?" I so wanted the truth and determined to find it.

Does God talk to you? Is He real?

Catholicism's traditions perplexed me too. As the only non-Catholic girl in the school, I went through all of the rituals and motions of Catholic tradition in chapel, mostly to fit in better. Strangely, even though we read a lot of Shakespeare and other literary greats, in class, we were seldom encouraged to read the Bible. That was reserved for the priests. I was hungry for God, nevertheless. At least I was in His "house" and that much closer to answers.

After graduation, I applied to Ivy League schools and one accepted me but I opted to attend the University of Tampa in Florida where I registered with the name "Lisa," as part of a standing tradition with my mother. When she attended college, she used the name "Jan," although her name was "Mary." My dad always called her "Jan" after that, and so it was that I would change my name too, more for a lark! I thought Lisa sounded more glamorous, Hollywood, British English, and *proper* than Leigh did, especially for the affluent U of T.

However, the unofficial name change didn't help me focus on schoolwork or change me in any way because I was still a damaged person looking for love and acceptance. Later the Lord emphasized that I should change my name back and actually said, "I named you Leigh for a reason!"

Names are still as important to God as they were in the Bible times. They held an important place in biblical revelation because often a person's name was the revelation of his or her character. Often when a person's state or character changed, so did his or her name. Consider Abram to Abraham, Sarai to Sarah, Jacob to Israel, and Saul to Paul, for examples. While God hasn't yet revealed to me the significance of my name, and what it means to Him, I trust that the reason He named me Leigh Ann is a good one!

One day much later while attending a Charles Capps meeting in Richmond, Virginia, I heard a voice say clearly, "You'll be with child, and you'll have a son. Name him *Joshua*. He will be a light to the nations and many will come to know me through him." There was no doubt in my mind that this was God's voice, and I wrote everything down that He told me.

TEN MONTHS LATER, JOSHUA WAS BORN.

Even though I was going through a very difficult stage in my marriage, God moved forth to bring His seed into the world. My son's name carries with it the DNA of his divine purpose—and I'll never call him by any name other than the one the Lord gave me for him.

If you want to change your name, I urge you to pray about it first. It could be God has a special name for you, or, the name you have could be the one He destined for you. What Father doesn't want a good name for

His child? Ask Him, "Lord, what's my name? What do you want my name to be?"

ENTER GOD'S REST

His great love and mercy are amazing. God goes to great lengths to show us how tenderly He loves us. Though things might scare us, He wants us to surrender our fears to Him. He is our strength and our enabler.

We don't have to figure out how He will fix a problem, or take care of a situation—we can rest in the truth that as we keep our hearts and faces focused on Him, He will complete His will for us.

He gives strength to the weary and increases the power of the weak. Even youths grow tired and weary, and young men stumble and fall; but those who hope in the Lord will renew their strength. They will soar on wings like eagles; they will run and not grow weary, they will walk and not be faint (Isaiah 40:29-31 NIV).

He frees us from sin and guilt and wants us to receive the freedom of His sacrifice. When He knocks, we can answer because He has ripped wide open the separating veil so that we can have complete freedom in communication with Him.

God revealing Himself to me as a child gave me rest from my weary young soul, and I can still rest in those words years later. As I look back on my life today, I can see the footprints of His protection so often. He never left me forsaken, even if I stumbled as I went on my own way thinking that I knew better than He did.

It's vital to remember His promises to you and every word He speaks to you. Remember with a grateful and thankful heart the times He encourages you and heals you, all of those times His love lifted you up and held you—when you do, you'll be renewed by His love and all the more trusting and confident in Him. These remembrances will calm your fearful thumping heart! His are heavenly words birthed in Heaven, and if you hold fast to His sayings and treasure them in your heart, they will influence your actions for the rest of your life.

God has a *plan* for my life, just as He has a plan for yours. No one can or will do the purpose He created for you alone to fill. When God places dreams, promises, or desires into your heart, things that you're praying for or believing in, things you cry out for or hope for, you don't have to struggle or force these things to happen. You don't have to become anxious or worried wondering if it will happen because the Creator of the Universe has planted it in your heart! If you cherish it enough, the Bible says that you *will* enter into His rest.[15] No maybe. You will. The rest of God is a place of complete trust, where you know that you know that you know for certain that God will see you through, just as He's promised. Failures and lack of success won't have a hold on you.

DO YOU *SEE* THIS WOMAN?

"Finally I felt free of the shackles that had bound me for so long with feelings of unworthiness, insecurity, and insignificance."

———◆———

THE transition from the strict Catholic school to the more liberal University of Tampa environment wasn't something I was ready for. This "in" crowd was comprised of many rich kids looking for a good time.

Feeling somewhat out of place, once more I found myself looking for acceptance. Of course, the partiers welcomed me warmly, and soon I was partying with the hardiest of them—Tampa Spartan's John Matuszak and Freddie Solomon, in particular. At 6′9″ and 280 pounds, John, or "Tooz" as we called him, eventually went on to play in the NFL after his studies, and later went to Hollywood to in hopes of beginning an acting career. I think my father had some misgivings about the university when he met my mammoth happy-go-lucky friend! Tooz partied hard and gained a reputation for disturbances on and off campus, but he had a big teddy bear heart, too.

The Houston Oilers drafted him in 1973, and then he did a stint with the Kansas City Chiefs before joining the Oakland Raiders for five seasons and helping win two Super Bowls. He gained quite a bit of weight in 1973 and won the World's Strongest Man competition but had the title withdrawn after news of his drug use was exposed. After football he went to Hollywood and he appeared in quite a few movies with the likes of Nick Nolte in "Caveman"; Ringo Starr, Dennis Quaid, and Shelly Long in "Ice Pirates"; and Steven Spielberg's "The Goonies" in 1985. He was also seen on television. Worn down by years of drug use and steroids, John's heart gave out during a television production in Hollywood in June 1989.

One night after a concert, my friend Howie invited us to a party he was holding at his parents' condominium at the Roney Plaza apartments in Miami Beach. Members of the music groups Chicago and the Bee Gees were going to be there, so I was excited to go.

The party had already started when my boyfriend, Michael, and I arrived, and drugs were flowing freely. About an hour into the party, one of my classmates passed out and someone called an ambulance. In a near comatose state, they rushed her to the hospital.

People were partying hard at this stage and someone offered me some drugs. Stupidly I accepted, not even connecting the possibility of bad drugs being the reason that girl was wheeled out unconscious.

Everything felt fine until a few hours later when sudden paranoia gripped me and I started to "see" things. Feeling myself weaken physically, I could no longer walk but couldn't tell anyone because I feared they'd call the ambulance as they did for that other girl.

Somehow, I managed to crawl to a closet to hide so that people wouldn't find me. Curling up into a tight ball to make myself very small, I hid as far back into the dark space as I could. Some would call them "hallucinations," but what I experienced over the next few hours was straight from the pit of hell—from satan himself. Tarantula-type spiders crawled over me like big, ugly, furry, demons. In my spirit, I knew these harbingers of death were fighting to pull my spirit into a black tunnel, into the very pit of hell. I would die, and never live to fulfill what I was supposed to do.

Thick darkness closed in, strangling me. Was this the spirit of death? I'm sure it was. Hell was real and I was headed there. I felt the pull of my spirit away from light and "saw" these demons try to pull my spirit out of my body.

The Holy Spirit though was drawing me back because suddenly, I had a vision flashback of my praying Baptist grandmother, and knew to call out to God.

"God, I am going under for the last time...please don't let me die. I want to live...help me God...I don't want to die...!"

Death knocked but I refused to answer. Instead, clinging to the seeds God had planted in my life years before—my precious grandmother who'd given me that little white Bible—the Voice that knew my name was with me.

I must have passed out because the next thing I remember is crawling out of the closet around noon the next day, the partiers long-since gone. In 12 hours, nobody had missed me—even my date had not searched me out.

It was a wonder I didn't feel sick, hung-over, or still fearful. In fact, I felt wonderful! Hope filled me to the very top of my being and I couldn't remember a time I wanted to live as much. As I gazed out over the sparkling waters of the ocean from the terrace, a feeling washed over me of light, hope, and a true possibility for happiness. Looking heavenward toward the billowing clouds in the sky, I saw beauty in them for the first time in my life. Finally I felt free of the shackles that had bound me for so long with feelings of unworthiness, insecurity, and insignificance. *I knew that I knew that I knew* that Someone divine had pulled me out of my grave. Now I just needed to find out why.

Jesus Sees the Best

Jesus excelled in seeing the best shining through the worst. The Bible records that in a divorcee, He saw a loveable and kind saint (the woman at the well); in a ruthless and relentless oppressor, He saw a powerful and convincing evangelist (apostle Paul); and in a gutless friend, the one who denied Him three times, He saw a martyr who would boldly die for his faith (Peter).

As Jesus sat at the dinner table with guests at a religious man's house, a woman whom they remembered by her mistakes, failings, and sins stumbled in and made her way to the feet of Jesus. She pushed past all the religious and judgmental spirits to find Jesus. Weeping over His feet, she broke an expensive vial of perfume over them and then wiped His feet dry with her hair. Those gathered had to have noticed her, she was totally out of place in this elite, "do-gooder" crowd. Yet Jesus said, *"Do you see this woman?"* (Luke 7:44). What did He mean? Of course they all saw her. Who could miss her? While the others probably questioned her doggedness and reputation and even what she was doing there among them, Jesus said, "I tell you, her many sins have been forgiven—for she loved much" (Luke 7:47 NIV).

She saw God when others didn't, but even more touching was that God saw her when others didn't. She poured out all that she had at the feet of Jesus, weeping in the knowledge of her enormous debt in the face of His innocence. Jesus saw her, *really saw her*, as the Father saw her and He said, "Your sins are forgiven" (Luke 7:48). Wow! The world saw a dirty woman with a past. God saw a beautiful woman with a great future. She had a pure heart in His sight.

Jesus heard her heart; for she didn't want to die, but she knew that she was dead in her sin, and that only Jesus could take that ugliness away and set her on her feet again. When she fell at the Savior's feet, she fell as a broken, dirty, and sinful woman before the throne of a loving Father, who heard her, understood her, and lifted her up from the heap of her mistakes. There's an old hymn by G.M. Taylor that starts out, "Oh to be nothing, nothing! Only to lie at His feet, a broken and emptied vessel for the Master's use...."

There is great healing in love.

She lay at His feet as nothing, a broken and emptied vessel for His use, emptied so that He could fill her, so that His life through her would flow. She wanted only to be led by His hand, an instrument of praise ready and willing to live a life of fullness in Him.

> *And we have known and believed the love that God has for us. God is love, and he who abides in love abides in God, and God in him* (1 John 4:16).

When we come before the Lord in prayer and empty ourselves of heartaches, hurts, grief, agony, and injustice, when we pour our pain out to Him, He refills our spirit—our inner self with Himself: "In Him we live and move and have our being" (Acts 17:28). God is Love—He fills you with love (see 1 John 4:16). There is great healing in love. It is a mighty trade off—your pain for healing and purpose. Your sin for His sanctification. Darkness for light. Ashes for joy.

When you give Him your pain, He'll touch you with His love. This impartation of love into the very fabric of your being will refresh you very much.

> *Bless (affectionately, gratefully praise) the Lord, O my soul; and all that is [deepest] within me, bless His holy name! Bless (affectionately,*

gratefully praise) the Lord, O my soul, and forget not [one of] all His benefits—Who forgives [every one of] all your iniquities, Who heals [each one of] all your diseases, Who redeems your life from the pit and corruption, Who beautifies, dignifies, and crowns you with loving-kindness and tender mercy; Who satisfies your mouth [your necessity and desire at your personal age and situation] with good so that your youth, renewed, is like the eagle's [strong, overcoming, soaring]! (Psalm 103:1-5 AMP)

"FOR MY BENEFIT..."

At only 39 years old, King Hezekiah was deathly sick. A prophet, Isaiah, told Hezekiah that God said he would die. Hezekiah called out to God, pleaded with Him for more time—and changed God's mind. God healed Hezekiah of his terrible boils and even confirmed his healing with a miraculous sign in the skies. Hezekiah was so thankful that he penned a poem whereby he compared himself to a piece of thread cut off from a loom and like a lion with broken bones.[16]

Have you ever felt that way? When you think there isn't a thread of hope left? When you feel beaten and broken like a Mack Truck hit you? Trust a near-death experience to get us focusing on the meaning of life and a lead into humbleness.

You can be the most successful person in your community, but what good does it do if you're facing imminent death? It doesn't matter if you're sitting in first class on the plane or in the cattle car in economy class, if the plane is going down, all are looking death in the eye.

Could it be that death brings life to us—makes us more alive? Certainly it gets us thinking about life! Sometimes we *think* we're dying but we're not.

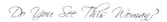

It just *seems* that our problems are insurmountable.

You kept me from the pit of destruction.

There's a story about a woman who went horseback riding. Everything was going fine until the horse got out of control, bucked, and threw her to the ground head first. Unfortunately, her foot caught in the stirrup and as the horse bucked, her head kept hitting the ground over and over again. The horse showed no signs of stopping or even slowing down. Just when she thought all hope was lost and before she lost consciousness, the manager of Wal-Mart came to her aid and unplugged it!

Sometimes our plights aren't nearly as severe as they seem—but Hezekiah's plight was genuinely grave. He wrote of his mournfulness about his infirmity (some scholars believe he had bubonic plague) but closed the poem with a beautiful tribute to God, praising Him for answering and then committing to walk with Him in all of His ways for the rest of his life.[17] Hezekiah learned a valuable lesson: "Surely it was for *my benefit* that I suffered such anguish. In Your love You kept me from the pit of destruction; You have put all my sins behind Your back" (Isa. 38:17 NIV).

The good news is that God is quick to forgive. He's quick to save. He's quick to move us forward. He's quick to heal. He's quick to transform. God preserved the story of Hezekiah in several books of Scripture so we would be encouraged and find hope.

NEVER TOO LATE

It's never too late to come to the throne of God—to the very feet of Jesus to say, "I want to live." It doesn't matter what the world sees of you or in you,

He sees you and knows your heart better than they do, and better than you do. The act of coming before Him with all of your ugly, sinful garbage, with your pain and suffering, with your poverty of spirit and soul brings Him to that place of saying, "Do you see her as I see her? She's absolutely beautiful in My eyes," and at the end of the day, that's all that counts.

Poet Annie Johnson Flint knew pain. Orphaned as a child, and later suffering all sorts of ailments including cancer and rheumatoid arthritis, she heroically and triumphantly endured her long life of pain. She'd spent so much time in her sickbed that she needed tons of pillows just to cushion the agony of her raw bedsores. However, she demonstrated to the world through her writings that we could glorify God in the midst of trials and the worst pain. She truly lived the realities of the following poem:

He giveth more grace as our burdens grow greater,
He sendeth more strength as our labors increase;
To added afflictions He addeth His mercy,
To multiplied trials He multiplies peace.

When we have exhausted our store of endurance,
When our strength has failed ere the day is half done,
When we reach the end of our hoarded resources
Our Father's full giving is only begun.

His love has no limits, His grace has no measure,
His power no boundary known unto men;
For out of His infinite riches in Jesus
He giveth, and giveth, and giveth again.[18]

Part II

THOSE DEFINING
MOMENTS

SEARING TRUTH, SCARRING LOVE

"God told me you were dying. He said if I didn't pray and intercede, you wouldn't live...."

THESE were the words of my college professor, Mrs. Allen, when she took me aside after class a week after God's divine intervention at that party in the high-rise condo. When she'd walked into our classroom that morning, the first thing she said to all of us was, "This is the day the Lord has made, we will be glad and rejoice in it!"[19] This was the norm for our "eccentric" teacher. The students thought she was nuts because she would walk around campus talking under her breath in an incomprehensible "language."[20]

Understand that this was a secular campus in the 1970s, so everyone looked at each other as though to say, "Man...far out...I want what she's on...." We loved her in spite of her eccentricities, for she was sweet, endearing, and a great teacher.

Just as my boyfriend, Michael, and I were about to leave class, she cornered me. "Lisa, I need to speak with you. What happened to you last Saturday evening? The Holy Spirit woke me up and I knew you were dying. I prayed for you all night...."

I was speechless.

"I felt as though you were in a serious situation and near death, so I interceded as God told me to. I just want you to know, Lisa, that the Bible says that God looks to and fro throughout the whole earth, searching for someone whom He can use."[21]

Whoosh! Was I the one? Did He in fact find me in that dark and sinister closet because He'd chosen me? Her words reminded me of that day as a child when God told me that He had chosen me. The Voice who knew my name. He knew me. He knew me by name. I started to believe as I realized that Mrs. Allen had heard God's heart for me, and prayed for my life.

"Come on over to my house on Sunday for lunch and I'll explain more," she said, inviting Michael at the same time. Michael accepted but I felt a little apprehensive about going. However, when Sunday came, I almost couldn't wait to get there.

The love of God was evident the moment we stepped in the house—and even in the home-cooked meal she'd prepared for us. What a meal it was! She served southern-fried chicken and gravy, mashed potatoes, and green beans. When she brought out mouthwatering homemade biscuits and wonderful southern grits, I was in Heaven.

After we had filled up with food and warmed to her even more, she invited us to the patio to sit for a spell. As naturally as one would open a newspaper, she opened the Bible and read to us about the life of Mary and Joseph and about how Jesus was born of a virgin to live and die not only for us, but also for all of humanity. She shared her testimony and then shared that this same God could do for us even more if we would allow Him. The air was electric with conviction and for the first time in 19 years of living on this planet, I heard the Word of God read by someone who really knew Him.

I had sat in a church all my life that now seemed as dry and dusty as desert air in contrast to the words that leapt off the page from a woman after God's own heart, alive and fiery hot for Jesus! What a difference the Word of God has when coming from the mouth and heart of one who knows Him personally. As I returned to my dorm room I knew that I wanted to know the God of Mrs. Allen, the very one who had healed this precious woman's body of cancer. If He could heal her, could He heal the cancer of my heart?

GLORY IN THE DORM ROOM

I dropped to my knees and called upon His name, "Jesus, Jesus!" I wanted Him...all of Him! "Oh Jesus, I need You in my life the way Mrs. Allen has You." The words of her testimony resonated in my spirit:

I was near death with cancer...the surgeons opened me up to operate only to find that Jesus, the Great Physician had healed me—totally! The doctors marveled and closed me back up.

Boldly now I prayed and with great faith, because if God could heal Mrs. Allen that deeply, He could heal me, save me. "Jesus," I prayed with all of my heart, "please come into my heart and be my Lord and Savior. Forgive me for all my sins. I believe You died for me and on the third day that You rose from the grave. Take my life and make something good out of it. Take my fears, take these hurts, wounds, and all of this rejection. I hate these things—and I give all of them to You."

Jesus filled my college dorm room and I believed I was born again. Hallelujah!

I knew that I knew that I was saved from my old life and was now free from the power of death. Oh! Praise the name of Jesus! Thank You Jesus!

Then I called upon the name of the Lord: "O Lord, I implore You, deliver my soul!" For You have delivered my soul from death, My eyes from tears, And my feet from falling (Psalm 116:4,8).

I shall not die, but live, and declare the works of the Lord (Psalm 118:17).

I did not have to fear death; for we never die. I'm sorry, Shirley MacLaine, but there is *no* reincarnation, for it is "appointed to men to die once, but after this the judgment" (Heb. 9:27) and if you truly know to be absent from the body is to be present with the Lord (see 2 Cor. 5:6).

> *For the first time in my life, loneliness fled, darkness ran, evil cowered, and hope reigned.*

God etched and seared these truths into my soul and scarred me with His love, and for the first time in my life, I was scarred in a good way—a delightful way—a beautiful way. I felt scarred and beautiful. Scar me with Your love Lord! Use me, God!

For the first time in my life, loneliness fled, darkness ran, evil cowered, and hope reigned higher than any wound I'd suffered at the hands of dysfunction, of crazed people, and most of all, of myself.

God's eye searched to and fro the earth for the one whom He could use *to bring me* unto Himself. I owe my life to Mrs. Allen's faithfulness to God.[22] Now He would use me in the same way.

THE INTERCESSORY HEART

There are dark places you've walked through where the devil could have killed you. For some reason God spared your life and kept you alive. Understand that often it's because the Lord has laid you upon someone's heart to pray for you. Remember this when God lays someone on your heart. Pray on the night watch, and don't let up until you feel a release in your heart to stop.

Intercession is the ultimate in prayer effectiveness because intercessory prayer is bold confidence that ensures deliverance, secures healing, averts judgment, encourages repentance, blesses, brings restoration, and can even cause the Father to change His mind about something![23] These prayers are requests we make on behalf of others, when the needs of another find a place in our prayer time before God's throne. Everyone needs prayer! You've never met anyone in your life who hasn't needed it or whom you can't or should not pray for—and that includes your enemies, those whom you're in conflict with, those who seem out to get you, and those who plain annoy you.

Years ago when things started to go downhill in our marriage, I'd heard that Oral and Evelyn Roberts were in town and staying at a nearby hotel. I contacted them and asked if they would pray for Bob and me, and they immediately carved out time for us. I'll never forget how Oral and Evelyn got on their hands and knees on the hotel room floor to pray with us. They prayed with fervor, sweetness, passion, compassion, and expectation for well over an hour. Especially Evelyn, she just wept in prayer and was so sensitive to my pain. It was such a powerful time. Suddenly, Oral asked, "Would you mind praying for us? We really covet prayers."

This shook me up for a moment. Here was this great man of God asking *me* for prayer; it was humbling to pray for them. We all need prayer—

especially so our leaders. For the next hour, we all began to pray. It really touched me that we were able to pray with them alone for such an extended period.

Oral and Evelyn Roberts have impacted the world with their healing crusades, and I've personally met hundreds who were healed in their meetings. I'm convinced that the reason they could establish one of the largest Christian universities in the world, the reason they could raise up thousands of students who know how to hear the voice of the Holy Spirit, is because they knew how to pray, and they prayed. I was blessed to tell them that even my only brother, Rob, graduated from there.

They were such mighty intercessors and warriors in the spirit. They exuded compassion and passion for God and people in such a deep way that forever scarred my heart for the good. It's one thing to see these people on television everyday, but to see them walk the talk, and even more so in person, convinced me that these were mighty saints of God.

Compassion must flow through our hearts in the Person of the Holy Spirit. He makes intercession through us to the Father, guiding us as to what specifically to pray for as it concerns the one for whom we are praying. Intercession is calling down Heaven to bring the accomplishment of the Father's will on earth as it is in Heaven.

An intercessor has a heart after God's own heart, has a heart for people, compassion for the lost, the misled, the hurting, the sick, the wondering and the wandering. An intercessor lives a life of repentance and is radically set apart for God, confident that He hears prayers and will answer them. It takes unconditional love to intercede for others and the belief that God can do a great work in everyone because He does not will that any should perish.

Often the intercessor prays the Word of God and has good knowledge of the Word and his or her blood-bought right and authority and power against the devil. This is why intercession is so effective in spiritual warfare because it defeats satan's strongholds over people: binding the powers of darkness and unleashing the forces of Heaven to attack and wage war on satan, thus taking more territory for and people into the Kingdom of God. Intercessory prayer is powerful, and although some have a special gift of intercession, as Mrs. Allen had, it's something we all can do as we spiritually grow and mature. With it also comes awesome blessings of the Lord and best of all, His glorious presence because such prayer is good and right and it's pleasing and acceptable to God!

First of all, then, I admonish and urge that petitions, prayers, intercessions, and thanksgivings be offered on behalf of all men, for kings and all who are in positions of authority or high responsibility, that [outwardly] we may pass a quiet and undisturbed life [and inwardly] a peaceable one in all godliness and reverence and seriousness in every way. For such [praying] is good and right, and [it is] pleasing and acceptable to God our Savior, who wishes all men to be saved and [increasingly] to perceive and recognize and discern and know precisely and correctly the [divine] Truth (1 Timothy 2:1-4 AMP).

Whether someone cries out to Jesus on our behalf or we call to Him ourselves, we have to trust that He hears us. The most important thing to remember is that it's OK to cry to Jesus. King David cried out, "To You I will cry, O Lord my Rock..." (Ps. 28:1). Tell God, "I will cry to You Lord...." (See Psalm 28:1-2.)

Immutable God is our Rock, the immoveable foundation of all of our hopes and our refuge in times of trouble. God wants us fixed in our determination to flee from past hurts and sorrows, and run to Him as our stronghold whenever we're in danger or suffering. Whether it's the onslaughts of the strongholds of our own minds, or that of the wiles of the enemy, cry to Him. God stands fast and firm.

CRY FROM STRENGTH, DESPERATION, AND PERSISTENCE DON'T GIVE UP

A cry is the natural expression of sorrow—and it's OK to cry out in our pain or for deliverance. However, if we cry from the depths of our being to anyone else but Jesus, it's like crying into thin air.

As His children, trust that if you are crying out to no one in particular, perhaps because the pain is too deep and you can't even think straight; trust that the depths of your pain connects your spirit to the Spirit of the Living God who is the Holy Spirit, and that He will intercede for you to the Father. Your pain can be released in prayer to even help others.

Look at the Syrophoenician woman, in Mark 7:24-37, who had a very sick daughter and was desperate to find this Man whom she heard could heal her child (see Mark 7:24-37). Jesus had disappeared into Gentile country for some rest and quiet from those who sought Him out. Word had traveled quickly and people knew that Jesus was the One who had answers to their problems.

...the pain is too deep and you can't even think straight...

The first thing we notice about this woman is her tenacity. She boldly sought Him out, even though she was a Greek (a Gentile) and not supposed to be associating with Jewish people, let alone Jesus. She didn't give up and threw herself at His feet and cried out, begging Him to heal her daughter because she knew and completely believed that Jesus was the only One who could provide healing. She was in a desperate state.

At first, Jesus seemed indifferent to her plea, explaining that He was the Savior of the Jews; in other words, it wasn't the right time for the Gentile. Nevertheless, she didn't go away. It wasn't a pathetic plea, but an *impassioned* outpouring of *determination* and *belief* that *only* He could heal her daughter. She was persistent and refused to give up. Jesus honored her attitude. Her heart cried for a miracle for her little girl, and Jesus performed a miracle for this little one to honor her mother's faith.

She returned home, found the child lying on the bed, and the demon gone. Hallelujah! Stop and think for a moment. What do you need God to do for you? Cry out to Jesus; cry out to Jesus with passion and determination, then watch the miracles come to you! Don't give up!

Then they cry to the Lord in their trouble, and He delivers them out of their distresses. He sends forth His word and heals them and rescues them from the pit and destruction. Oh, that men would praise [and confess to] the Lord for His goodness and loving-kindness and His wonderful works to the children of men! (Psalm 107:19-21 AMP)

No matter what you're going through, whether it's come about because of bad choices, or not, Psalm 107 proclaims the same answer: Call out to the Lord in your trouble and thank Him for His goodness and wonderful works.

Sometimes we suffer because of humanity's rejection of God, or because of generational sin, or simply because we live in a fallen world that's filled with sin. Other times, as my later life would attest, we suffer because we deliberately ignore God and choose our own way, but even so, even when we've despised His counsel, if we call to Him in our trouble, He will bring us out of darkness and out of the shadow of death, snapping our chains.

I have had regrets over the years. But despite wrong decisions, God transformed my life anyhow, and I praise Him for that. He can restore and transform your life, too! Don't give up the fight and always be thankful.

Cry Out for Your Life's Purpose

God promises, too, that when you cry out for purpose and meaning, He will quench your thirst. Answers *will* come! The purpose for your living will be revealed. Even when things are barren, when all of your spiritual and earthly resources are dried up, He'll answer and replenish, restore, and refresh you. He'll lift you up as He lifted me up countless times from childhood to adult life—again and again, as often as you call out to Him. Take time to read Psalm 107 in its entirety, which reveals the enormity of this truth.

Here are more promises just for you:

I will cry to God Most High, Who performs on my behalf and rewards me [Who brings to pass His purposes for me and surely completes them]! (Psalm 57:2 AMP)

When the righteous cry for help, the Lord hears, and delivers them out of all their distress and troubles (Psalm 34:17 AMP).

The Book of Psalms contains countless accounts of people crying out to God. We can come to God with our heart cries because of who He is: He is tender, merciful, loving, kind, steadfast in His love, remembers not your sin, and He is good. He's ready to forgive and is abounding in mercy and loving-kindness to all who call upon Him. God is merciful and gracious, slow to anger, abounding in truth. The Father is faithful from generation to generation, mighty Lord God of Hosts; God is faithful.[24]

The Lord of Hosts has power no enemy can withstand. He's your refuge and fortress upon whom you can lean and rely on in complete trust and confidence. He delivers you from your enemies, from the "snare of the fowler," His truth and faithfulness are a shield and a buckler. He doesn't chide, nor is He contending, He doesn't hold a grudge, and His anger doesn't last forever. He loves and pities His children. He knows our frame, remembers, and imprints us on His heart.[25]

REMEMBER HIS WORKS

When you read through the Psalms, notice how the psalmists end their heartfelt cries with a shout of praise. They remember His works and thank Him for them![26] Call up His works and remember the days of your healing and deliverance. This builds your faith in Him and in His willingness and faithfulness to save you. It creates expectation in your heart for what His Word surely says He'll do. Scour the Psalms and the Bible for situations where He intervened, and thank Him. Thank Him for the healings you've heard of elsewhere. Look what happens when you recall His works with awe and worship Him: "*The Angel of the Lord encamps around those who fear Him [who revere and worship Him with awe] and each of them He delivers*" (Ps. 34:7 AMP).

Return to your First Love often in remembrance and He will demonstrate the fire of His love to you in unimaginable ways.

When God calls out to me, and when I call out to Him, we are connected in a supernatural way that causes me to seek Him and cry out to Him even more—heart cries that He faithfully answers.

AN ANOINTING
FOR THE BETTER

"Leigh Ann, I want you to go back in there and I want you to let Me flow through you. I will use this...."

M Y father had always wanted me to attend Stephens College, a private women's school in Columbia, Missouri. Finally I agreed when I learned that the college specialized in fashion, so I moved from Florida back to my home state of Missouri to earn a Bachelor of Arts degree in fashion merchandising and business administration.

One day a girl from class who had won the title of Miss Missouri the previous year told me about the upcoming 1977 pageant. "Try out for it," she encouraged. "You have a good chance of making it."

Eight-hundred girls tried out in Columbia, Missouri, and I became one of the 80 finalists chosen to go to the Four Seasons Resort at the Lake of the Ozarks in Missouri. So, I set out on this new adventure, even though it seemed the worst possible time to do so. My savings had all but dwindled because of my father's declining finances. How would I afford the clothes and everything I would need for the pageant?

Someone lent me a swimsuit but I didn't have anything to wear for the evening gown competition. In desperation one day, I bought a stunning peach evening gown from an expensive boutique in St. Louis, even though I wasn't quite sure that I had enough money in my bank account to cover the check that I wrote. I bought it anyway because I was so scared I would be laughed off the stage if I showed up in something right off the rack.[27]

I also felt as though I were going it alone. My parents were in the midst of divorcing and my mother and I weren't on the best of terms because she was dating a man I didn't approve of, so asking her help for the pageant, or even to accompany me was out of the question.

Dad, bless his heart, was unreliable and seldom showed up at things when he promised he would, so while all the contestants seemed to have their chaperones or supporters with them, I arrived all by myself with no one to champion or assist me—or so I thought, before God showed up.

Yes, I had God on my side but I was yet spiritually young and didn't have a solid and firm biblical foundation from which to draw. As well, I didn't totally trust my earthly father who I could see, so how could I easily learn to trust my Heavenly Father—whom I couldn't even see. There was a real battle of my mind, therefore, in learning how to trust; mistrust was one of the strongholds in my life. More importantly, and the reason why I didn't completely trust Him, was that I didn't know much about the workings of the supernatural power of the Holy Spirit in my life and my potential *in* Christ Jesus.

HE HAD A PLAN

Consequently, when I walked into the hotel by myself on the first day of the pageant, every girl looked more beautiful and more talented than I could ever be. They had designer clothes, talent, and poise, and looked me

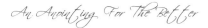

up and down snottily as though to say, "And you think you even have a chance?" Freaking out I thought, *what am I doing here*, and ran for my car. However, just as I turned the key in the ignition of my car, the presence of the Holy Spirit invaded that space and a voice in my heart said to me, "Leigh Ann, I want you to go back in there and I want you to let Me flow through you. I will use this. You're not in this for yourself. There are 80 girls in there who need to hear that Jesus Christ is alive, and if you go back in there and tell them about Me, I will anoint you."

Now, I had no idea what the anointing was but it sounded good, and if God was with it and in it, then I was all for it! I walked back into the hotel and put a smile on my face with new-gained confidence. (You'll notice that when I feel the Lord's presence, I smile and smile and smile...I can't help it, it's awesome.)

God had a plan but the devil had a plan too, and for the next three days, the enemy's plan became quite apparent. I went through torture. Many of the contestants were downright nasty! Some of the girls hated that I was a believer, and one found my Bible and threw it at me, "Why are you reading the Bible here," she snapped at me. Another was so jealous that she hurled her cosmetic case at me. Whoa! My heart was like, *I'm here to win and witness, and satan, you're not stopping me! In all these things, I am more than a conqueror through Him who loves me.*[28] Sometimes we have to be as forceful as Jesus was with the enemy, with the righteous anger of God flowing through us and directed at the enemy. The enemy is bent on destroying our health, finances, successes, and spiritual acuity by trying to steal God's Word from our heart. To dismantle the destroyer of destiny, we have to speak the Word of God at him and then trust all of Heaven to back us up.

It's important to cling to the promises of God. Oh how I clung that weekend to Him. I knew I was where God wanted me; it was my position and I wouldn't let the enemy steal it. I had told the enemy: "Devil, get off my promotion!" God had big plans for me to win that pageant, and I resolved to fight valiantly for them.

MIRACLE CROWN

One part of the pageant required that the contestants gather in small groups to discuss issues that were important to them. I had no idea what to say but God put big words in my mouth about communism as it related to the world issues of the day. The judges gave me an "A," for this supernatural intelligence that only God could have downloaded in me at that stage of my life. God's presence was so strong and with every step, He made me feel elegant, worthy, smart, and beautiful—and I just couldn't wipe that smile from my face.

Deciding to sing was a venture of courage

On the night of the finals that would include the talent competition, I was so scared because I didn't really have any talent except for a smidgeon of musical training, and I knew that this part could break me. The only thing I could remotely do (and I mean remotely is sing, so I found temporary refuge in a bathroom stall and prayed the only prayer I knew by heart, the Lord's Prayer. I whispered, "Our Father, which art in heaven, hallowed be Thy name, *Thy will be done....*"

God dropped faith into my heart and He said, "I will allow you to win, but use it for My glory."

Deciding to sing was a venture of courage because I could not carry a tune. My mother studied concert piano with Leonard Bernstein and graduated from the Eastman School of Music. She could play seven instruments flawlessly, was a songwriter, choir director, and a music teacher, so *of course* her daughter would be musical too, right? Wrong. I took vocal lessons, piano, and clarinet, but to no avail—no ear for music, though I loved music and still do. All my teachers eventually said, "Keep your money Ma'am— take her home!"

But as God is my witness, I sang like an angel that evening. As I belted out the last drawn-out note of "What I Did for Love," I saw my dad and then 15-year-old brother in the audience. Dad, in true form, missed the other events, but this night, miracles of miracles, there he was. Tears streamed down his face as I ended the score with a flourish because he knew that I couldn't sing a note on key and my brother said something like "This has to be God!" I sang with the power of Almighty God flowing through me for a beautiful performance—it was definitely a miracle, and the judges gave me a perfect score. Later, reporters interviewed my dad and he testified about how amazing it was that I sang in tune, but to me the greatest miracle of all was my dad being there to see and hear it.

Then the time came for the judges' decision.

We were down to the four finalists and I was one of them.

Third runner up...

Second...

First...

And God had His winner...Miss Missouri for 1977, Leigh Ann Middleton!

I know what it feels like to receive a crown and a sash that says, "You made it," but it's nothing—nothing compared to the crowns of life we'll receive in Heaven for endurance. However, we don't receive these crowns so that we can walk down the golden streets of Heaven and show them off. No, we receive them and should desire them for one reason and purpose only: to cast them at the feet of the Master to tell Him how much we appreciate everything He has done for us. How glad and joyful we are that we can give Him all the glory for whatever work we might have done.

"Oh thank You Jesus," I prayed from the relatively quiet sanctuary of the women's room shortly afterward—feeling an unction to slip away from the celebrations to tell Jesus how awed I was by His faithfulness and love. It was my way of casting my crown at His feet. Wow—this was just a foretaste of what God had in store for me. What a great feeling for once to have the secure knowledge of someone loving me just the way I was and seeing the "beautiful" in me when I couldn't.

I didn't have to perform for God—He performed through me. It reminds me of what Mother Teresa said. She likened herself to a little pencil in God's hand and that however imperfect she was, God writes beautifully.[29] "He does the writing;" she said, "the pencil has only to be allowed to be used."

He trusted me with so much, and for once in my life, I didn't run away as usual in my discomfort. It was hard to believe I'd won...but I had, and supernaturally, too; of that I was certain. In line with God's will for my life, I felt full and sated by His tremendous love and supernatural blessings.

FROM VICTIM TO MISSION MENTALITY

When you firmly resolve to let go of your wheel of misfortune, time becomes your friend because your times now are in God's hands. You're on a different wheel now—the wheel of purpose and blessings, healing and deliverance, salvation and grace: the Potter's wheel. Salvation is not salvage. God doesn't recycle you. No survivor or victim mentality is needed! It's about God transforming you. This is a time when you will not determine your destiny, but you will discover it through the turning of events as God and you work together for the good and His glory.

It's not about, "I survived financial ruin," but about, "God saved me from financial ruin." It's not, "I survived cancer," but, "God healed me from cancer." It's not about, "I averted the accident," but about how "God protected me." Then as He molds you, it's not, "Oh, I don't know how I'm going to get through it," but, "I can't wait to see how God gets me through this." You adopt a mission mentality.

He seeds you with clear purpose, planting the plans of His heart within your spirit. He molds and fashions you sometimes slowly, sometimes quickly, into the vessel He needs you to be—shaping your heart to live and abide in Jesus and to be like Jesus. During this process God may show you that your desires aren't His, as He did for the children of Israel who wanted a king and received Saul as their king. It took God over 50 years to teach and convince them that His desire and choice was far better, because most of the kings who reigned led them the wrong way.

"I can't wait to see how God gets me through this."

This process takes a lifetime but God is a patient Potter, and now you are on His destiny wheel of favor where He molds your life through His divine providence. Therefore, there is no such thing as good luck or fortune, because it's all about the blessings and favor of God—from divine appointments with people, be they on airplanes, on QVC—wherever you go, or to meet your exact needs. As you resolve to stay on the Potter's wheel and obediently and willingly allow Him to turn and turn the wheel to shape you into a unique vessel of purpose, He will fill you with Heaven's treasures that will flow in and through you for His glory.

He says,

My grace (My favor and loving-kindness and mercy) is enough for you [sufficient against any danger and enables you to bear the trouble manfully]; for My strength and power are made perfect (fulfilled and completed) and show themselves most effective in [your] weakness (2 Corinthians 12:9 AMP).

So that you can say,

Therefore, I will all the more gladly glory in my weaknesses and infirmities, that the strength and power of Christ (the Messiah) may rest (yes, may pitch a tent over and dwell) upon me! (2 Corinthians 12:9 AMP)

INCREASING FAVOR

Even when we fail to understand our circumstances, it's vital we cooperate with God believing He knows what's ahead and what's happening. Though there may be times when it seems as though God is disinterested, trust that He's working out His purpose. In fact, we should all be of the conviction that God *is* working things out. A great example of God setting the stage to work out His plans was with the young Jewish woman, Esther.[30] For

12 months, Esther was prepared and groomed herself for the upcoming selection process, whereby King Xerxes would choose His queen—who would reign as the Queen of Persia. The king provided everything she and all of the contestants needed to look beautiful: maids-in-waiting, perfume, jewelry, skincare products, massages, facials, manicures, fancy clothes, elocution lessons, you name it, they had it all. As soon as this young woman walked before him, the king said with certainty, "That's the one! I want her!"

...She had a deep inner assurance that drove her with passion...

"Now the king was attracted to Esther more than to any of the other women..." (Esther 2:17 NIV) and the king had no idea she was Jewish, but this was all in God's perfect plan to save His people. God had set a perfect stage and now His plans would really unfold because of Esther's willingness and confidence and conviction that God would work all the details out. With the first part of God's plan accomplished—with the setting of the stage of the mission to save His people, things would start to happen and become apparent.

God will never abort His plans for your life, even if He seems galaxies away from your circumstances—don't doubt that He is working out His plans and purposes. God is more than able to accomplish what He sets out to do, so don't equate His silence with noninvolvement.

Esther anchored herself in the belief that God was working it all out, and she had a deep inner assurance that drove her with passion to do everything in the best way she knew how—with a mission mindset.

You will encounter blips along the way and some of them may appear life-threatening, but bring them to Him with a mission mindset that no matter what, you want to be a part of God's overall plan, and you will be rewarded.

Charlie Duke, former NASA astronaut turned successful entrepreneur, was one of only 12 men to walk the moon. He said that when he came to know Christ sometime after his space adventure, he didn't see angels or hear music and there were no blinding lights, but he knew what he knew, that it was real and the following day he awoke with an "insatiable desire to read the Bible." As a man used to adventure, of his walk with God he said, "It cost the government $400 million for me to walk three days on the moon—and it's over. But to walk with Jesus is free and it lasts forever."[31]

Walk with Jesus and you will move beyond, way beyond what you could ever accomplish by your own strength in your lifetime. Drive your stake into the ground and walk with God!

TRIVIAL PURSUITS

"In search of my dreams I sought what I thought I needed to fulfill them, but that's a slow, dangerous, and uncertain road."

THE next few months after winning the Miss Missouri pageant were a blur with numerous obligations such as traveling to Jamaica, L.A., New York City, and Las Vegas; interviews with news and entertainment media; parades; speaking engagements; television appearance offers in New York; modeling and photography sessions; not to mention invitations to restaurants and clubs; offers of expensive gifts, and the attention of many men.

Nothing could prepare me for the onslaught of lures and dangling glittery carrots. Suddenly my eyes were on the kingdoms of the world, and I lost sight of my First Love, Jesus. No church, no prayer, no Bible reading, no time for God. He no longer had first place in my life as He once had. He wasn't even on second stage because I'd subconsciously invited other "gods" in. Gradually, I dropped classes at Stephens College so that I could fulfill my commitments traveling around the country as Miss Missouri. Suddenly, I was taken out of jeans and put into gowns—I wasn't the same Leigh Ann Middleton I was before I received the title.

Because I couldn't fill my life with the promises of God, how could I align it according to His divine plumb line, according to His will? So, although full of success, I started to feel empty. It's like filling up on empty calories that do the body no earthly good. Because I needed to be filling my heart with the things of God to push out the unchecked issues that plagued it, my needs turned into idols of the heart. These idols became strongholds that caused me to compromise my values and made even minor obstacles seem like a giants.

Moreover, the further I strayed from the loving care of the Lord and His Kingdom ways, the more tarnished, dull, and void my heart felt, and the further away I was from His perfect plan for my life. So six months into my reign as Miss Missouri, and only a month away from the U.S.A. pageant, I wasn't in the greatest of places. I'd picked up too many of the enemy's temptations along the world's highway to fuel my single-minded pursuit of the Miss U.S.A. crown, and soon they became a mountain that all but obscured the vision He'd given me.

STAY ALERT

No one should ever forget we have an enemy who is on his job moment-by-moment. That's not to say that we're to blame the devil for everything, mind you, as in a Flip Wilson "The devil made me buy this dress," fashion, because we're also in a battle with our own minds. However, the devil is always at work setting traps, placing temptations ahead of us, planning ways to steal from us or destroy us, or the people whom we love. Sometimes he works all of his diabolical schemes at the same time.

He's not your friend. Satan is a liar and the truth is not in him. He will do all he can to keep you *away* from God, *away* from your greatness in Christ Jesus, *away* from all of the good and spectacular things the Lord has for you. Jealous, he knows God loves *you* and unlike the devil, you, as a loved

child of the King of kings, as God's beloved daughter or son, will spend eternity with the One who cast the evil one out of Heaven.

THE THIEF

The thief comes only in order to steal and kill and destroy. I came that they may have and enjoy life, and have it in abundance (to the full, till it overflows) (John 10:10 AMP).

Satan's a trickster! Of course, he'll give you all the things you *feel* you need, but they are things that will keep you away from God. If it's fame, you'll have it. If it's drugs, he'll make it easy for you to get them. If it's money, he can make you rich. If it's humankind's approval, he'll give you their favor. However, before you're sucked into the contract and sign on the devil's dotted line, be sure you read the fine print!

Have you ever seen a prescription drug commercial on television? Pick one, any one. The first 59½ seconds regale us about the benefits:

...your pain will go away, you'll have a new lease on life, you'll be able to ride a bike, do things you couldn't do before, your depression will lift, you'll conceive, you'll have stamina, you won't sweat anymore, your freckles will fade, your cellulite will vanish, you'll get a good night's rest, no more liver spots, incontinence will not be a problem anymore, and so on and so on and so on....

The last second mentions the multitude of side effects, as the announcer *very* quickly states that, "Side effects may include heart attack, still birth, stroke, paralysis, warts, uneasiness, palpitations, feelings of suicide, liver failure, decreased sexual drive," and so on and so on and so on!

Trust that the devil *won't* tell you that the fame, money, drugs, sex outside of marriage, and the favor of the world may keep you from God and send you to the fiery pit of hell that God never meant for you. The devil is a drug pusher and relentless, and says things such as, "You'll be able to handle sudden fortune *and* serve God, so go for it."

Listen, there's nothing wrong with wealth if God gives it to you, but if it's a gift from satan, flee from it because it'll give you warts and misery. It won't be easy. Jesus says that through Him you may have life, have it to the full, and trust that *no sorrow is added to what He gives you*—you don't even have to read the label if it comes from God.[32]

NO SORROW WITH SUCCESS

When the world makes money, sorrow comes with it as part of the curse of the Law. If a person of the world falls in love, the love is full of sorrow because there's fear with that type of love—fear of loss. However, as believers, we are inside of the blessings of God, such that prosperity from God has no sorrow associated with it and love has no sorrow.

Now hope does not disappoint, because the love of God has been poured out in our hearts by the Holy Spirit who was given to us (Romans 5:5).

We are free from the curse of depression and sadness, worry and anxiety, because the blessings of God come with peace and joy, confidence and trust—in short, they fulfill us.

When you look to God for His blessings, you can trust they will deliver what you really need. All too often we perceive what we need and try to find it in the world, but I urge you, don't let your needs miscue your priorities

which will result in compromises—something I know all too much about. This is why I felt a gnawing and annoying ache of something missing and gone wrong, as though I'd stepped *away* instead of *toward* the provision that God knew I needed to fulfill His plans. In search of my dreams I sought what I thought I needed to fulfill them, but that's a slow, dangerous, and uncertain road. When we search for *God's* dreams for us, He gives us even supernatural things to help us accomplish them.

Always remember God's intervention in your life, otherwise, the enemy will try to make you forget so that you believe your accomplishments were done by your own strength or merits.

This is perhaps why the thrill about what lay ahead, as I drove home that day, was somewhat empty and why I had so much anxiety. God wasn't in my plans; matters of my heart and the world had edged Him out of my memories and hope for my future. Therefore, as I looked ahead, I was looking at doing it all by my strength—and the future loomed like Mount Everest, making me anxious and worried.

GRACE TO CHOOSE

The truth is, once we experience God, it wrecks us for anything else in this life because nothing even remotely holds a candle to His presence and power—not fame, fortune, others' approval, massive success—nothing—but I didn't know that. He gives us the grace, however, to choose the path we want to take but we cannot choose the consequences of our chosen path. We can't have it both ways. Either we're dedicated to living His way and being blessed by Him, or we live like the world, overcome by sin and death. We choose the Kingdom of light or the kingdom of darkness. Blessings or curses. There are no grey areas.

To the Israelites, God got right to the point and said, "I have set before you life and death, blessing and cursing."[33] I'd already tasted of the blessings of God in my life, but I was about to find out what can happen when one steps outside of the circle of blessing. I'd opened misfortune's door to allow the destroyer of my destiny to run rampant.

FINDING THE WORD AGAIN

Because of the jealousy of my college roommate after I won Miss Missouri, I decided to move into another dorm room with someone else—a nice Jewish girl from Chicago! I think at this stage, God was sending me a message because when I walked into her room, I saw her Bible on a table and discovered she was a Jewish believer. Mindy and I became instant friends, as sisters, and our time together helped me re-focus. (Mindy later married Joel Chernoff from the music group, *Lamb*, and today they have three children. We're still great friends.)

CONSIDER THE CONSEQUENCES

So many people forget the principal that consequences follow actions, and that's why many of our difficulties arise. I'm not certain who coined the phrase, but I like it: "Every effect has a cause and every cause produces an effect."

Consequences follow actions, and that's why many of our difficulties arise.

Nothing that we do in life is without consequences. The devil often entices or tricks us into thinking that the situation we are in is an isolated

event, and he gets us to believe that what we do, or are about to do or say, will have little or no effect on others. He is exceedingly skillful at getting us to become preoccupied with the temptation he puts before us. We focus our whole attention on it and become oblivious to everything else, including the consequences of our actions. The enemy may even send false friends cautioning you not to "do this or that," because, for example, "it wouldn't be good for your career." However, always consider the consequences of whatever anyone tells you as it relates to God's plan for your life—always opt for God's will—not others'.

Influential Contact

For constant, true success, remain in contact with God! Don't stray—don't lose communication with Him. That's the most important principle of success. King Solomon, one of the most successful people who ever lived, forgot this principle. In all of his wisdom and riches, he stopped acknowledging God and this change in motivation became his eventual downfall.

Here's the formula for continual success in your life—the foundation for success. Memorize it!

Lean on, trust in, and be confident in the Lord with all your heart and mind and do not rely on your own insight or understanding. In all your ways know, recognize, and acknowledge Him, and He will direct and make straight and plain your paths (Proverbs 3:5-6 AMP).

Constant contact! Acknowledging God in every endeavor.

Solomon was born with a silver spoon in his mouth and succeeded the throne of his father. He amassed a lot of wealth over his lifetime and pursued his dreams and love of building, art, and nature. His achievements were incredible and known the world over, and he was known to be very wise about human frailty and the world around him. Important people from all over the known world consulted him—he had it all, wisdom, fame, fortune, an incredible reputation. But guess what? He found no satisfaction in all of it. In essence he said, "I looked at all of my accomplishments, everything I've worked for, and it was all vanity—self-gain and a striving after the wind and a feeding on it."[34] In other words, it was all empty without God. Futile because he did it *his* way. Materialism defined his success and he realized how empty that was.

If you have an opportunity and you go for it, keep this foundational principle foremost in your mind. Recite it to yourself and ask, "Am I seeking God's counsel? Have I glorified Him in all of this? Am I compromising anything? Anyone? My faith? Is this principle the core and very motive why I seek this opportunity? Am I giving things back to God? Am I sowing to God? Be diligent and fervent about this foundational principle and you'll experience more consistency in your life.

IF YOU GET LOST...

Is your heart hardened today? Maybe you're so busy you don't even realize you are lost. God may tug at your heart but the yank of the world may seem to pull you toward what seems more promising in the natural.

For My thoughts are not your thoughts, neither are your ways My ways, says the Lord (Isaiah 55:8 AMP).

Stray too far from His thoughts and His ways, and you may get lost. When you're lost, you're far away from the one searching for you. Yikes!

Getting lost is not good! Separation from God especially causes a great void. We all wander at some point in our lives, and sometimes we're on the receiving end of loss. Have you ever lost something? It's not a good feeling. You may have lost your health, or a loved one, a husband to a younger woman or a child to drugs. Perhaps you've lost a fortune or your good name. Perhaps you were the one who took something away or went away and created loss in the life of another.

What man of you, having a hundred sheep, if he loses one of them, does not leave the ninety-nine in the wilderness, and go after the one which is lost until he finds it? And when he has found it, he lays it on his shoulders, rejoicing.

Or what woman, having ten silver coins, if she loses one coin, does not light a lamp, sweep the house, and search carefully until she finds it? And when she has found it, she calls her friends and neighbors together, saying, "Rejoice with me, for I have found the piece which I lost!" Likewise, I say to you, there is joy in the presence of the angels of God over one sinner who repents (Luke 15:4-5,8-10).

When we're lost, God is relentless in His pursuit of us. The Shepherd leaves the flock to find the wayward sheep. How relentless? The Bible tells the story of a woman who, when she loses one of her ten coins, turns her house upside down to find it.

You've been there when you've lost your jewelry or car keys, right? I know I have. Jesus reveals that God is precisely that way when even one person is lost; He will relentlessly pursue that soul until he or she is found. This is something that's hard for many of us to understand. Why would a responsible shepherd leave his entire flock to find one sheep? It's like asking yourself why you would spend the better part of your busy day looking for a set of keys when you have duplicates hanging on the wall in the foyer. Why would you turn your house topsy-turvy looking for one small coin when you have nine more? It's because they are important to you, they belong to you.

Jesus insists (however irrational this seems to us) that God pursues us because we are His; we belong to Him, He lays claim to us; thus, He refuses to leave us wandering, confused, abandoned, misguided, lost, or alone.

The shepherd rejoices upon finding the lost sheep and the woman rejoices when she finds the silver coin. The angels and all of Heaven rejoice!

"Even so, I tell you, there is joy among and in the presence of the angels of God over one [especially] wicked person who repents (changes his mind for the better, heartily amending his ways, with abhorrence of his past sins)" (Luke 15:10 AMP).

GOD SUPPLIES OUR PURPOSE

Oh how that excites me! If you're lost and found by Jesus, all of Heaven sings hallelujah! You probably know by heart Psalm 23 that starts, "The Lord is my Shepherd" (Ps. 23:1). It's time to stop thinking that Psalm 23 is only for funerals; it is about trusting God for everything you need to live an abundant life! It's really about God's amazing power and His relationship to us. As the Shepherd, God supplies what we so desperately lack in ourselves.

What are those things? Well to start, something that I yearned for was "purpose." A shepherd always has a goal in mind for his flock, whether it's a reason for leading skittish ones to still waters, hungry ones into mountain pastures, wayward ones into valleys, obedient ones into wilderness, or some

even *into* the *midst* of wolves. Likewise, Jesus, our Good Shepherd leads us to these places because that's where He wants us. He supplies our purpose.

A person without purpose is depressed or angry! How many people have left suicide notes citing that they "have no reason for living"? They miss purpose in their lives. Victor Frankl, a Jew imprisoned in a concentration camp in World War II, survived the holocaust for the most part, because the Nazi's appointed him as personal physician to several SS officers. Trained to save people, in his doctor's mind he tried to figure out why, even though all of the prisoners suffered similar horrors and hardships, some survived and others gave up the will to live. He discovered that those who gave up the fight to live had no sense of meaning or purpose in their lives, perhaps no one to survive for or nothing to go back to. Many who made it never gave up the hope of reconciliation or reunion with their dreams.

The apostle Paul, also a Jew, had the same revelation about purpose but perhaps deeper and wiser: that the hope and purpose to live with is "Christ *in* you, the hope of glory" (Col. 1:27). Yes, the triune God with us is hope enough, but how much more so when Christ is *in* us!

Someone can have *everything* but not want anything he or she has because those things don't provide anything that makes life worth living such as purpose does. That's precisely what God supplies, a purpose, destiny, a reason for being, and the promise of something beyond this life that makes it all meaningful and worthwhile for living, Christ *in* us! Christ in you!

*A person without purpose is
depressed or angry!*

CAST ALL YOUR CARES

In the process of living out your divinely inspired purpose, He assures you that you can cast all of your anxieties, your worries, your concerns *once and for all* on Him because He cares for you affectionately and endlessly watches over you.[35] Perhaps that's why John Newton, the former mean-spirited, cruel ship's captain turned mighty man of faith, wrote in the hymn *Amazing Grace* about the safety and grace he found when led "home":

Thro' many dangers, toils and snares,
I have already come;
Tis grace has brought me safe thus far,
And grace will lead me home.
Amazing grace how sweet the sound
That saved a wretch like me.
I once was lost but now I'm found
Was blind but now I see.

Blind, lost, and hiding—that's where you can end up if you're empty of God's Word in your life. You'll lose vision for the destiny that He sets before you. You don't want to be filled with the flowery stuff that fades away because it's a long way from the field of dreams of His purpose. Without that purpose, it's almost impossible to have the spirit of an overcomer.

I needed to have the spirit of an overcomer for what lay ahead. Yes, I'd need to be close to God and trust Him to knit my body back together.

LIFE CURVES AND CRISES
FOR TRANSFORMATION

"As bad as the physical pain was, I don't know that the emotional torment and the pain of seeing my dreams dashed was any less extreme. Like a knife stabbing me in the gut and twisting a little deeper for good measure, failure pierced my soul—the very heart of me."

*I*T'S *a miracle you're even alive...* The words of the man at the scene of the accident, while on my way home from Kansas City, still resonate in my heart. In my spirit, I clung to the hope of that miracle as the ambulance driver wheeled me into the emergency room of a hospital that, thankfully, was less than 30 miles from the accident scene on I-70. I had no idea what the extent of my injuries were—but the pain was immense each time I flitted into consciousness.

People told me that I'd cry out, "Don't let me miss that pageant...I can't miss it...don't call them." Understand that I'd worked *so* hard for this opportunity—it was a single-minded pursuit that identified who I was. This accident—I'd lost my identity. Without, at the least, the chance to show that I could make it, I would just be the old Leigh—the one who seldom followed through on things.

"Honey," my father said during one of my more lucid moments, "I *have* to call your pageant director and tell him what happened. You're not going to make Miami...the pageant...."

Incoherent and deliriously in pain, my father said that I begged him not to call Robert. "No dad—they'll fix my leg so I can get out of here...I'll make it...I have to...don't call them...please Dad, don't call them...."

The stabbing and throbbing pain was unreal—screaming, crying out in agony for relief, I continued to plead, "Dad...I'll make it...you're not stopping me...they'll send my runner up..." and finally bliss—medicine to make me sleep.

My doctor father knew just by looking at me and by what the doctors told him, that I might never walk normally again. Indeed, it was a miracle that I hadn't worn my seat belt; otherwise I would have been trapped in a rolling, crashing steel grave, decapitated, burned alive, or worse, if that's possible. Much later, my brother and father went to see my damaged Corvette. The remains of the car resembled a gnarled old sardine can.

The police were concerned by the accounts of the witness who had seen the vehicle seemingly purposefully hit me, and especially so when a threatening call to my hospital room came from a man claiming to be responsible for the accident.

"I tried to kill you once, Leigh, and failed, but I won't fail next time." I didn't know about this until much later, but they placed a security guard by my door for awhile and prevented visitors until they could investigate. They decided that someone may have been trying to prevent me from participating in the Miss U.S.A. pageant, but the investigation didn't yield any further leads.

Daddy arranged for the best of care through his medical contacts. I would need a burn specialist, an orthopedic specialist, physiotherapists, psychotherapists, and a host of other medical experts after I was stabilized.

My face was OK, surprisingly, but I had third-degree burns up my lower back and along my left arm. My leg's femur bone protruded 3 inches through my hip socket, which shattered my hip. My pelvis was crushed and I had internal bleeding. I was in agony.

REPAIR WORK

For four grueling hours, the surgeons did what they could to stop the bleeding, fix my shattered bones, and tend to my burns, but they weren't in any way certain of a favorable outcome. Even with the surgery and traction, we could only wait to see the outcome. The doctors said I probably wouldn't ever walk normally because of the now mismatched length of my legs, and that arthritis in my limbs and hip area would probably require multiple hip replacements. I would later need skin grafts for my burns, and later had the procedures done at the University of Missouri.

Days dragged into tormenting weeks as I lay in that hospital bed drifting in and out of consciousness. Hooked up almost constantly to intravenous, I thought I'd go crazy if I had to lay there immobile for much longer, and yet I didn't want anyone to move me. That was the worst part. It took six nurses to lift and turn me over to change my bedding, and when they did, the pain was unbearable. I would cry out in agony, such that when I even saw them coming to change my sheets, I'd beg them not to. "I don't care if they're dirty, just leave me alone."

I had no choice though, or my bedsores would worsen. Bedsores develop when blood supply to the skin is cut off for more than a few hours. As the skin dies, the bedsore first starts as a red, painful area that eventually turns purple. Left untreated, the skin can break open, get infected or worse, extend deep into the muscle. Once developed, they are very slow to heal and painful. Bedsores already covered my back, so I really had no choice but to be constantly repositioned and daily turned.

With the pain of broken bones, burns, bedsores, and painful traction, I needed pain medication. Even though I was in danger of addiction, they gave me high doses of morphine, which only made the pain bearable. To sleep at night, they'd top off the morphine with sleeping pills—the torment just too great to bear through the night.

As bad as the physical pain was, I don't know that the emotional torment and the pain of seeing my dreams dashed was any less extreme. Like a knife stabbing me in the gut and twisting a little deeper for good measure, failure pierced my soul—the very heart of me. I'd failed everyone: Mom, Dad, my brother, my pageant director, and yes, eventually I realized I had failed God too.

Just when everything seemed to be flourishing, my dream slipped out from under me as though I'd tripped on a banana peel on destiny's path. I'd sacrificed everything for this title—including my relationship with God, my Christian friends, and others. Still unable to prioritize rightly, I grieved most of all the fact that I couldn't win Miss U.S.A. and thus never realize the fulfillment of my dreams that would have most certainly followed.

A SURGE OF FAITH

Never did the twist of that knife hurt as much as it did on the night that the Miss U.S.A. pageant was televised. Well-meaning but unthinking people called. "Are you watching the pageant, Leigh? Do you see those girls? They can't hold a candle to you...too bad you didn't make it, Leigh—I know you would have won...!" Well, I wasn't there—I was lying in traction in a hospital with burns and feeling ugly and like a failure. What people were saying were the last things I needed to hear or be reminded of. I cried and cried and cried and withdrew into myself.

As the pain became more manageable, I experienced a new kind of throbbing ache—loneliness. Because the weeks had turned into months, people simply stopped visiting as they went back to their own lives. It was very lonely and scary when I was left alone with only my morbid and fearful thoughts for company.

GROWING IN LONELINESS

Perhaps that loneliness helped me grow to trust God, because one day, as I lay in my hospital bed, faith poured into my spirit and I began to read books about overcoming and about miracles. I had never heard much about supernatural living or the Holy Spirit, but feeling abandoned made me reach out and grow in my faith.

A nurse brought books to me and many times when she noticed me crying, she would pray for me, and she always had an encouraging word. What a beautiful feeling to realize that no matter the distance I had put between God and me, He was *still* on my side. I knew that I knew that I knew God still loved me! Whoosh! As this precious revelation dawned deep within my soul, I knew that Jesus was my Friend and that He would be with me through my grief, my pain, and through whatever the future held.

One day I felt the unction to turn on the television and flip through the channels for a Christian broadcast, finding the 700 Club and others. This I did every day, switching from station to station, hungering to hear the Word of God. One day, Pat Robertson seemed to look right at me from the television screen and said that there was a woman lying in a hospital bed who had lost all hope. He said, "God is going to heal you of that condition." I just knew that Pat was talking to me, I was sure of it.

With every Word of God about Christ's healing touch spoken from the mouths of the television evangelists, faith burgeoned in my spirit.

Then shall the virgin rejoice in the dance, and the young men and the old, together; for I will turn their mourning to joy, will comfort them, and make them rejoice rather than sorrow (Jeremiah 31:13).

Was God preparing me for a miracle? Why the flourish of faith? I began to tell everyone that I would be totally healed—I knew I would be. I learned that the apostle Paul told the Church in Rome that "faith comes by hearing and hearing by the word of God" (Rom. 10:17). I sought Him more and more and cried out to Him to send help. Yes! I wanted a miracle. Please God!

Pastors came and left though. They comforted me in my solitude and pain but not one ever gave me the word I desperately craved: that I would be healed. They didn't speak of Jesus the Healer, or of miracles. But somehow in my childlike knowledge,[36] I took hold of faith and without really realizing what I was doing, I pressed in for my miracle anyhow. He had to heal me! I wanted out of the bed, out of the hospital, and out of what was almost certain, the wheelchair! I was a jogger, swimmer, overachiever, and I couldn't believe that being in pain and immobile was God's plan for me.

THE BELIEVERS

I would not lend my ear to half a Gospel! I would not fall prey to the misconception that the miracle age was dead. I knew better. Mrs. Allen's life was proven testimony—the doctors told her she was filled with cancer, but when they operated there was no cancer. Jesus had performed His surgery the night before! God had already saved me once. He would do it for me again—of that, I was now certain.[37] I expected a miracle and cried out to God to send me another "Mrs. Allen," someone who had childlike faith.

The help God sent me this time was pint-sized and wore a habit. Unlike the nuns I'd come to know in Catholic school who were stern and constantly clucking and frowning, this nun glowed and dripped in love. There she stood in my hospital room doorway just looking at me, and then she was all smiles when she walked into the room boldly speaking in another language—a heavenly language in other tongues.

As she stood looking down at me, I said, "Sister, I have never met a nun like you, not even in the Catholic school my parents sent me to!"

"That's right young lady, I just got saved and born again and filled with the Holy Ghost in the Charismatic movement!"

My spirit stirred, soared. She went on to say, "As I prayed today, God told me to visit you and tell you that He would heal you."

"Well, who—who are you? How do you know me?"

She explained that she was president of the hospital (praise God for women in high places) and had been following my case closely since the day I was admitted. "I've seen God move in the children's wing of this hospital and totally heal children of multiple sclerosis, leukemia, and cancer; and if He can heal children, I know He can heal you! If Jesus can put their little bodies back together again, He can certainly heal Miss Missouri!"

We chatted a little longer and then she said, "You're going to have more visitors—they're coming to pray for you."

"They are believers,"

I immediately thought that priests and nuns would be coming. "Are they ordained ministers? Pastors? Who exactly are these people who are coming to pray for me?"

"Why, they're miracle workers!" she said.

"Yeah, but *who* are they? Preachers?"

"Uh...no."

"Well then...who?"

"Believers—they are 'the believers'!"

Believers! Suddenly I recalled that the Bible said somewhere that believers would lay hands on the sick and the sick would recover. Not *maybe*, but *will* recover (see Mark 16:18). Oh, my spirit soared with excitement as this revelation began to hit me.

"They are believers," she explained further, "who love God and volunteer their time to come to the hospital and lay hands on the sick."

When these believers were about to show up one night, I felt a lot of excitement, but I did not want them to see me in my dreadful condition. I looked terrible. Don't think me vain, but I had to think of someway to get my hair at least washed and some color on my pale and sickly looking face. I paid a nurse's aid $10 to bring in a bucket to wash my hair and put my make-up on. Why? Because I had a date with Dr. Jesus! When we begin to act out of faith and not from fear and doubt, we will sometimes do some crazy things. I just knew that I knew something great was about to happen...I had a date with destiny that night. I would meet the believers, but more importantly I would meet Jesus and I was ready! What a feeling to get fired up in anticipation of a date with Jesus! He is the Man whom I knew loved me and would never break my heart.

HEAVENLY HEALING ANOINTING

Finally "the believers" showed up just before visiting hours were almost over. Didn't they know I was expecting a total healing and I needed to get out of the hospital? To my surprise, the believers were an unusual group—two housewives, a lawyer, and an accountant. After the introductions, they pressed in around my bed. One of the members wielded a big bottle of Italian olive oil. *What is that* I wondered? He told me that it was in fulfillment of James 5:14-15 where the elders (servants) of the Most High God should be called upon to come, anoint with oil, pray the prayer of faith, and heal. He said that even more miraculous than healing, God would forgive sin.

When he opened the bottle and dabbed some on me, I thought he'd poured out the whole bottle! The oil felt hot and it was as though it literally saturated me. "Too much...too much oil, and it is too hot," I said pushing his hand away.

"Oh no," he said with a soft chuckle and a glint in his eye, "that wasn't the whole bottle...just a little dab will do ya!"

I relaxed and submitted myself to the heavenly healing oil anointing and the room filled with an electric-like Spirit of faith, as I was readied to experience the healing power of God. The more they laid hands on me and prayed and prayed, the more power of Heaven hit me full on and coursed through my body. I knew something miraculous was taking place. Healing warmth coursed through me, delivering me of my searing pain. My discomfort from lying in that hospital bed day after day, month after month, lifted too. Then God began His healing work on the ugly bedsores and the pain from burns on my back and arm.

The power of God was alive with healing power deep within and it almost felt as though He were rearranging my organs. I'd had internal bleeding, my pelvis was broken, but the healing balm of Gilead moved into my damaged hip area and I felt the warmth of His touch go into the socket as He knit the bones together again. Where the doctors had done all they could, the Great Physician was now operating on me as an all-consuming wondrous sense of His presence pervaded the room.

We all knew we were in the midst of miracles.

"The believers" had prayed loud and strong and now there was silence. They had their eyes closed and silently they stood around my bed as if to wait for more instructions.

There I lay, with tears of joy running down my face; for I knew I was unworthy of His touch—yet it was evident that He had touched me. I had been broken into pieces by the devil; but because of Jesus and the work of the cross, God didn't count my sin against me. He loved me so much and so deeply that He sent me these wonderful people, "the believers," to see me put back together again.

What amazing grace! What amazing power these believers had. I had never felt anything like that before, I just knew I was healed. The heat was too great to not be. I was free from horrific pain and I was comfortable. I was ready to walk out of the hospital because I knew my hip was better and I felt no discomfort. I was pain free without morphine and codeine!

As soon as "the believers," God's ministers, left my hospital room, I knew that I would walk again and more importantly, do something great for God and fulfill the divine destiny I now realized lay on my life. I was determined to remember that God was turning the tragedy that satan used to crush me into something for His glory. As long as I lived, the miracle that happened on this day would live on to the glory of my Father in Heaven.

PAIN, A SIGN OF LIFE

Physical and emotional pain, anxiety and fear, heartache and sorrow, turbulence and struggle are actually signs of life! God created us with the ability to feel these things. Have you ever wondered why? Perhaps because they lead us to Him. Ultimately, pain needs a cure or it will lead to death. When we come to God for a cure for guilt, for feelings of unworthiness, for the stains on our conscience, the most awesome thing it leads us to is a life of knowing He who created us, and to an identity only and ultimately found in Christ Jesus. These signs point us to the promises of Heaven because when you know who you are in Christ Jesus, when you root yourself in Christ, joy and delight in the knowledge of Him supersede and displace everything else. In light of seeing Jesus and rooting our identity in Him, we'll see amazing transformation happen!

One look at Jesus and your entire life paradigm will shift as it did for the woman who took her heart on a pilgrimage to Him and silently cried out as she poured her life savings on Him, "Lord, save me!" When you're in that place of being in His gaze, you'll see your debt, understand His innocence, and hear Christ say, "Do you *see* her?"

Then when our paths take us on sorrowful adventures, we can be sure that they will lead to the place where tears are no more and where, out of the infinite riches of Jesus, He giveth and giveth, and giveth again.

What does He give us? Confidence in Him most of all. Annie Flint wrote another beautiful poem:

God hath not promised skies always blue,
Flower strewn pathways all our lives through;
God hath not promised sun without rain,
Joy without sorrow, peace without pain.

God hath not promised we shall not know
Toil and temptation, trouble and woe;
He hath not told us we shall not bear
Many a burden, many a care.

God hath not promised smooth roads and wide,
Swift, easy travel, needing no guide;
Never a mountain rocky and steep,
Never a river turbid and deep.

But God hath promised strength for the day,
Rest for the labor, light for the way,
Grace for the trials, help from above,
Unfailing sympathy, undying love.[38]

Hold Onto Your Miracle

Like any good and wonderful thing from the Lord, though, the enemy sought to snatch my miracle away! The devil didn't waste any time challenging me! I encourage you not to give up. For every miracle that God does, the devil will send someone or something along to cause doubt or denial of the miracle. There are people who despise the things of God. They hate Him and they hate His people, and one such person was the nurse who came to tend to me shortly after "the believers" left.

"Honey," she said in a sickeningly sweet tone, "you've got to take your morphine shot, your sleeping pills, and oh yes, your muscle relaxants now."

"I'm not taking them—I'm not in any pain," I said with conviction.

A look of outright fury came over her that I later discovered was triggered by her anger at the believers for praying for me late into the night.

"You've got to, doctor's orders," she persisted as though I had no choice! This was to be the first of many spiritual battles. "Nurse, I don't *need* the meds anymore; and further more, you need to tell the doctors I want new x-rays taken! I have been healed tonight and those x-rays will prove it. I want you to put all of that down in your reports." Those who know me know that I can be a little spitfire when I truly believe in something!

She went off in a huff, but I expected her to do as I asked. Imagine my surprise the next day when a psychiatrist walked in instead of the radiologist to take x-rays. I was so ready for the x-rays to verify and prove to everyone I was truly healed. God had visited me and I couldn't wait to show my dad and everyone. I was in shock when it dawned on me he was there to x-ray my mind!

"Mr. Psychiatrist," I said, "no offense, but I'm not talking to you. You're a very nice doctor, but I know your kind—I've spoken to people like you during my problems in high school and college, and they never helped me, not one bit. What they couldn't do, Jesus just did!"

Exit the first psychiatrist.

Enter a new psychiatrist. "I hear we have a personality conflict with the other doctor."

OK now I was fighting mad, with a look that said, "Read my lips," I told him directly that all I wanted was a new set of x-rays, and that was that! Never one to be bullied or pushed around, I persisted. For Pete's sake, all I wanted was to confirm what I already knew happened—a miracle.

If ever there was a time to roll my eyes skyward in unbelief, it was when my father called shortly after psychiatrist number two left. "Honey, you are my favorite daughter, and I know you have been through great misfortunes and pain; however, I am getting a lot of phone calls that you won't cooperate with the staff. Are you all right? What's going on?"

"Daddy," I replied with a calm reassuring voice, "I've never been more sound and sane than I am right now! Jesus came into my room yesterday and now I want more x-rays taken to confirm what I know, that God has done a miracle!" *What was the problem,* I asked myself. *What's the harm in a few x-rays?*

CHOOSE YOUR REALITY

In the face of unbelief, you must stand strong when you know that God has moved in your life. Don't let the enemy or even well-meaning people defeat you! They will confuse you and cause you to doubt yourself and God.

There are two realities that we deal with while living in this world: the natural reality of what is happening to you or around you, and the spiritual reality of what God says He is doing in and around you. *You choose* which reality you wish to believe and stand in. I chose God's reality! I was sane and perfectly normal. I was not the problem!

The world likes to say that Christians are the problem. I once heard Led Zeppelin say, "We know who the problem is in this land. It's all those people driving around with little fishes on the back of their car!"

He couldn't be more wrong! We are not the problem; we have the Solution to the problem!

HAVE PREVAILING FAITH

God wants to prevail in the midst of unbelief; and God did prevail in my life and body. And yes, I finally had new x-rays taken. The doctors relented and sent me and my whole hospital bed and traction contraption to radiology for more x-rays.

I will never forget the day I received the results. I expected maybe one doctor, but seven doctors filed through my door. One of them held an x-ray up to the light of the window.

"Uh...um...we really don't understand this...these x-rays show significant differences from those first taken when you arrived. It appears that your hip has now turned and calcification has happened in the injured sites. Um...we did our very best in surgery when we rebuilt your shattered bones, but at the time held little hope that we could fully restore them as they were prior to the trauma."

What he said next just floored me.

"Obviously, our surgery is working faster than we ever anticipated!"

My silence was more effective than any retort I could give. Of course, "intelligent" jargon would try to analyze my condition, and the enemy would try to explain it away, but inside my whole being smiled. I had just received confirmation that God had healed me! I was convinced God's surgery, not theirs, mended my hip and pelvis.

> ## *I had just received confirmation that God had healed me!*

God's Special Doctor of Faith

Six left and one doctor remained—a dermatologist/burn specialist. He stood at the foot of my bed staring or pondering, and then he wept as the power of God struck him. It was awhile before he mustered the courage to speak.

"*They* may not believe that Jesus did this, but I have *never* seen a miracle like this in America. Only once in my life while on a missions trip in Africa did I see miracles like this." In remote parts of the world they do not have doctors readily available so they have to trust in a higher power.

This was a jaw-dropping witness to God's healing power, and my smiles bubbled to the surface.

"I know that what you said is true. God was here and He has begun a good work in you and I believe He will complete it," he said. Do not give up and do not let humanity's intelligence and book knowledge stop you from believing and receiving your miracles.

"ENOUGH IS ENOUGH, ALREADY!"

I'm still a cripple! Why is my leg so weak? Where's my miracle?

LITTLE did I know how desperately I would cling to that doctor's words, especially when things didn't happen as quickly as I thought they should have.

The hospital finally sent me home, but I would still be immobile for a long time. My family arranged for a special medical bed to put in the family room. The doctors placed me in a full body cast, and my left leg would have to remain elevated and with a bar uncomfortably wedged between each leg to keep them separated.

It was good to be home but I was still a burden to my family. They, and a daily visit from a nurse, were my caregivers. Thankfully, being home, people regularly visited me again, and Jeanne, Nancy, Bobby, Mindy, all my friends would stop by for short visits.

It was hard to endure for so long, especially during the humid St. Louis summer months, and I couldn't wait to get out of my full-body cast. "Please tell them to get this thing off of me now, Dad. I am healed. I can walk! Tell the ortho doctor, 'enough is enough already!'"

The Mississippi River steamed and the mosquitoes were everywhere—my body cooked in that plaster prison! I knew I was healed so why was I bedridden, still suffering, and sweating in this two-month-old cast? It was unbearable not to be able to walk myself to the bathroom—privacy would be nice for a change! It gets to a girl!

Finally and thankfully, the big day came to remove my body cast. My brother and friends lifted me out of the bed I'd laid immobile in for two months after I came home from hospital. They loaded me flat out in the back of the station wagon. The smell of fresh air exhilarated me and it was so wonderful to breathe it all en route to the doctor's office.

The orthopedic surgeon prepared me for what he saw as the inevitable, according to his expertise and other patients' recoveries from similar injuries. He counseled that I would be in a wheelchair for at least nine months and then dependent on crutches. My damaged leg "would always be three inches shorter" than the healthy one, and I would have a noticeable limp. His forecast certainly wasn't very pretty.

I didn't want to hear that. Why did he have to be so negative? I refused to accept what he was saying. Jesus healed me. I'd be OK. I couldn't wait to see my leg. I was now going to prove it to the orthopedic surgeon. Just cut this body cast off so I can breathe and walk.

WOE IS ME!

Nothing could have prepared me for the pitiful excuse of a left leg that confronted me with the unwelcome reality that my problems hadn't ended. There it was, bearing no resemblance to the once shapely limb I remembered. It had shriveled up like a prune with no ligaments or muscles evident and certainly a whole lot shorter than the other one. Horrified, I couldn't believe what I saw. It was still so short. I mean, noticeably short. Like about 3 inches shorter than my other leg.

Fear and anxiety gripped me—was it true that I would always have a serious limp and maybe an artificial hip in my 20s? *Jesus, what's going on here? I thought You healed me..."*

Trembling, I tried to listen to the doctor's instructions.

"Don't put weight on the leg for at least six months—that would be until December, Leigh. You'll need a wheelchair and you can only use crutches when necessary. I warn you, Leigh. Do not put any weight on the leg. Do you understand?"

Did God heal me completely, or didn't He?

As I was wheeled out of his office, I couldn't stop crying. *Why...why...why* and more cries of *why? I'm still a cripple! Why is my leg so weak? Where's my miracle? Why God? I cannot take any more of this. I've told everyone that I'm healed and now look at me. I have to go back to Stephens College in a wheelchair? Why? Lord, why?*

I pled over and over—questioned Him. "Please help me....help me Jesus. Help me Jesus.

He has begun a good work in you and I believe He will complete it, the other doctor had said. I believed what this doctor had said too, but this stretched my faith. Will I be crippled forever? I'd be in a wheelchair for six to nine more months—this leg couldn't support a feather, much less my full body weight—things just didn't appear to be as I had hoped. When I was in the hospital I had read the story of Joni Erickson, who had become a paraplegic after a diving accident. One of her favorite verses was:

being confident of this very thing, that He who has begun a good work in you will complete it until the day of Jesus Christ (Philippians 1:6).

Miracles come in phases, don't let the enemy shake your confidence.

It's easy to think that once in God's will, everything will fall into place and we'll get from one point to another without any problems. But that's not really how things always work—there are often curves along the way. This doesn't mean that God isn't doing the work. Consider David whom God chose to be king and yet David spent much time running and hiding from Saul. The chances of David becoming king looked slim many times during the journey to the throne.

So too, as I looked at my leg, the chances looked slim that it could ever be even half-normal again. But God hadn't stopped the process of David's kingship, it just went a little different than expected. David did indeed become king, and I had finally to determine that God had healed my leg—the healing just wasn't yet complete. There were still a few layers of gift-wrap left to open in the process, that's all.

Sometimes our miracles come in phases, and during the unfolding of that process the enemy will inevitably try to shake our confidence in our God, to cast dispersions on His character. "Did God *really* say...?" It is during those times when we must hold fast to the love of Jesus because natural reality is not God's reality. Miracles come in phases, don't let the enemy shake your confidence.

YOUR CRISES FOR GOOD

While I don't believe that God caused the car accident, I do believe that I opened the door through my disobedience and distancing myself from Him to allow satan to *cause* a crisis. However, it's vital to understand that God may use a calamity, even a devastating one such as I experienced, to help us understand His purpose and will, and often to help us make a U-turn in the direction He desires for us. God cares deeply for our suffering and will extend to us His fullest mercy in every crisis or tragedy, even ones that we cause by our wrong choices—if we ask Him to. This applies individually and corporately as the Body of Christ. It's critical that we ask Him how He wants us to grow in light of crises if we want fully to realize our potential in Him and for Him.

These times, in fact, as you'll see in my emerging story, sometimes yield the most treasured revelations about God's intentions for our lives, and often these revelations speed emotional, physical, or spiritual healing considerably and open the door for understanding of our calling, of what God has created us to do, and whom He has created us to be.

The prophet Isaiah's near-death experience may be the reason why he so clearly grasped the call on his life. His were traumatic circumstances as his own mortality faced him as well as sorrow over King Uzziah's unfortunate downfall. "Woe is me, for I am undone," he exclaimed under conviction as he met God. God cleansed him with fire, and then, when God said, "*Whom* shall I send, and *who* will go for Us," Isaiah was quick to respond, "Here I am, send me!"[39]

A WILLING HEART

How strange of God to ask the question at all, "Whom shall I send..." (Isa. 6:8), because God certainly has all of the answers! In a heartbeat He could have commanded angels to carry out His will, or created some other being, or done it Himself, but instead He asked for volunteers. Why? Because He desires willing, surrendered people who don't have to be forced to serve Him, and Isaiah was at that stage where he knew that he knew finally, and wholeheartedly that he wanted to serve God with everything He had. No room for compromise. Isaiah *wanted* to be the answer to God's question.

An accident, a doctor's bad report, a sick loved one, a lost position or relationship, a crisis of any kind has the potential to create that willing heart. In the midst of your darkness and darkest hour, something spectacular can happen. As Isaiah, when you're in the presence of God, your heart will know its own sinfulness, and bring you to repentance and you'll know that your heart has been touched by God's cleansing fire.

So too, your crisis may take your heart through a radical shift in thinking about Jesus and your destiny, just as it did for Saul of Tarsus (later known as the apostle Paul) after God blinded him on the road to Damascus.

Not all crises result in life-changing transformation or dreams and visions, but they can build new foundations for breakthrough as they topple existing paradigm blocks of independence so that we learn to trust in Him for provision of all things. Sometimes a crisis will knock out only a block or two, immediate obstacles to God's best for us, the fullness of His blessings.

OPPORTUNITIES

Have you missed important appointments or meetings because you didn't feel good about yourself, or smart enough, or beautiful enough, or important enough?

God wants us to seize the opportunities He presents for us; the greatest of these opportunities is the gift and privilege of life. Opportunities disappear quickly, and we have to determine to grasp God-given opportunities as He gives them to us.

Take the opportunity in your crisis to take note of the resilience God has placed in you. Look back on past situations and see how He strengthened you as you picked up the fragments of your life and moved on. The Holy Spirit can work miracles, signs, and wonders in you through all of your heartache, healing your pain, bringing life to your weary bones, and birthing new life from the ashes. Many times we don't understand how certain situations could have even been a part of His plan.

Above all else, our brokenness in a situation has great potential to strengthen our relationship with Jesus as we seek His very great and tender comfort, and in our helpless resolve, seek His aid and direction.

The very week I had my cast removed, my brother, Robbie, bought a newspaper and cut out a little article about a Bible teacher and healing evangelist who were coming to our downtown St. Louis auditorium. Ironically, even though my brother was backslidden at the time, God used him to get me to my destiny encounter. He believed in me and somehow he believed that I had to get to that meeting. We decided to go with a group of Baptists who had received the Holy Spirit (I affectionately call them "Bapticostals"), and we were eager to hear the evangelist.

Many times we don't understand how certain situations could have even been a part of His plan.

Don't tell God how to do His business!

As we entered the meeting, we saw thousands of people who seemed hungry for God. The visiting minister was a well-known healing evangelist, Kenneth Hagin. I must have been in a daze because I don't remember the content of his message, and I don't recall feeling much emotion, probably because I was very tired. This was my first time out in five months, and I felt almost disjointed—delirious and weak what with the crowds and the sudden headiness of having to breathe and be around so many people.

After the message, he invited people to come up front for prayer. My brother wasted no time and quickly pushed my wheelchair to the altar area. The helpers aided me up on my crutches from the wheelchair and I balanced myself as I waited for the Bible teacher to come my way. He began to pray for each person he passed by and I cannot say that I felt anything special—I didn't feel a tangible presence. To my shock, people fell to the floor as the man prayed for them. It was only the second time I'd seen this strange phenomenon.

"Please God, don't let me fall," I whispered in prayer. "We've come too far for me to have more problems."

Here's a vital lesson: You don't really want to tell God how to do His business! If He wants to knock you down like He did the apostle Paul on the road to Damascus—then just let Him do it. Under His power, He's gonna knock you down! Don't tell God how to do His business!

Of course as soon as he laid hands on me in the healing line and prayed, I fell despite my fear and resistance to falling. One minute the crutches supported me, and the next, *plop*! I was doing serious floor time. Hot waves again went through my body and washed over me as I prayed and cried out to the Lord. His power was weighty and all over and through me, and I lay

there for what seemed like ages. At one point I wanted to get up but I could not. I tried to get up but I couldn't. Suddenly two ushers lifted me upright and I went in search of my brother and the others.

Feeling different and a little embarrassed by it all, I made my way back through the throngs and found my seat and sat down. For some reason, Robbie was weeping and our Bapticostal friends were too. I had no idea what all the gushing was about except that perhaps God had touched them. I felt strange and very light-headed.

A moment later one of the head ushers found me. His eyes had so much kindness in them.

"Excuse me, ma'am, do you think you'll need these anymore," he said, pointing to my wheelchair and crutches.

It only then dawned on me that I had *walked* back to my seat on my own! That was impossible! I was too weak in the natural to walk. I couldn't walk just an hour before. No wonder all the commotion and tears—ah ha! Those gushing tears were tears of joy, awe, and thanksgiving to God.

SUDDENLY, SUDDENLY

Suddenly I looked down at my legs and they were the same length. I raised them up from the floor and stared at them. Was this a dream or for real? It was as though I was seeing my legs for the first time—I was in utter awe. I put them down and then raised them again. God had stretched my damaged left leg until it matched my good one. My left leg grew 3 inches in the blink of an eye.

There was no explanation except a total miracle. Even the circumstances surrounding my being at the meeting—it was just too amazing. Even in my doubt and unbelief—my cries of, "Why me, God"—He performed a second miracle and truly touched me.

My left leg grew 3 inches in the blink of an eye.

Only Jesus Christ can do such a miracle! When the doctors can do no more, Jesus can! I would still have had to use a wheelchair, a walker, or crutches to this day, but God had other plans! He made me whole. Six months later, (when according to the doctors I would still be in that wheelchair or walking with a great limp) I skied down one of the highest mountains in Vail. Not long afterward, while attending Rhema I ran my first marathon.

God is no respecter of persons. What God has done for one He can do for another. What do you need from God? Do you want to walk and maybe even run? Are you crippled in some way? God can heal you. He can help you through your misfortune...whatever it is!

One day, while I was sitting in a large class in the Rhema auditorium with a thousand other students, Kenneth Hagin walked in to teach the faith class. Nothing unusual in that, but suddenly he stopped and said, "My brothers and sisters...just look up here."

"I want to teach you all today that certain people have certain gifts and anointings for specific miracles and healings. For instance, I have a special anointing to pray for the sick in several areas but one in particular is in the area of hips...especially hips hurt in accidents, not so much birth defects."

Wow, I just about came out of my chair when he said that! He didn't even know who I was and here he had been the one who prayed over me

back in St. Louis. The biggest revelation then confirmed to me, was that the Spirit of the Lord had supernaturally brought me to the exact healing crusade where He knew I was destined to be healed. I didn't even know this man Hagin, had never even heard of him when he laid hands on me for healing. Now only a few years later I learn that he has a special gift for hip healing such as mine. Chance? Coincidence? No. God-incidence. Divine favor to the max!

Even as you read this, remember the God who created you can direct you and bring you to the exact place you need to be...if you'll let Him! God taught me a very powerful lesson. What if I had given up all hope for a full and complete miracle? Sometimes God takes us step-by-step. Deliverance and healing are a process. For clarity on this, just start reading your Bible and you'll find God moves when we obey. Thank God I went to that healing meeting. He honors obedience. Every situation is so different. What you need is different from what someone else needs. Sometimes the enemy has assignments on our lives and it doesn't become clear until we see patterns develop. My last year in high school, at a Catholic retreat, a priest tried to molest me. In college, I experienced attempted molestations twice more. After I became a Christian, the Lord showed me how to break this assignment against my life by binding up the devil and breaking this curse off my life. I've never had even close situations since.

Just ask the Lord to help you and to reveal the patterns. Open your heart to Him. Pour out your heart. You say, "My problem is too much for even God to handle." Or perhaps you say, "My need is too insignificant to bother God with it. He has world issues to worry about so why bother Him." Please stop thinking that way.

That is not His will, and if you read His Word, you will learn that God likes it when you ask Him about the little things *and* the big things. He wants *all* who are weary, tired, and weighed down to come to Him, and He will give each one rest. Sweet rest.[40]

Hear this truth. All needs are small in the Father's eyes. He can heal arthritis just as well as He can make the lame walk. He can heal bronchitis just as He can heal cancer or any kind of disease. He raised Lazarus from the grave, but He didn't stop there. He said, "Loose him, and let him go!" and the grave clothes came off (John 11:44). Jesus healed an ear on the soldier and he healed blind eyes and opened deaf ears. God can heal you. Just ask Him. God has a miracle for you.

Possibly, you've given up hope. Don't. Please don't.

Whatever your situation, whether it is physical, mental, spiritual, or financial, God loves you deeply. Faith begins when you ask Him to show you His will for your particular situation. Just ask Him. He wants to help you, but some never enter into the blessings because of hard heartedness and rebellion. God loves you unconditionally and desires to heal you and bless you.

YOUR PAST CAN'T STOP YOUR FUTURE

Your past cannot stop God's future for you, unless you let it. Often, when you're in such turmoil that it seems as though your life is in a tailspin and you can see no good coming of it, it's at this time when the good you can't see is about to happen. No matter where you are in your life right now or the condition of your life, it's nothing compared to the glory that you can experience.

God has flung open the doors and is preparing you to walk through them. Perhaps you've been struggling. The enemy may have caused you to

lose your focus. Trust that God may be trying to birth something different in your life. Surrender and yield to it.

I learned not to get caught up with my circumstances but to be caught up with the Lord and open to His way of doing things.

This is a time of reversal in your life when God will reverse your misfortunes for His glory. Whew! Yes! What a time of reversal. It's a transformation. What you've lost cannot be compared to what you will gain and more. Raise your expectations for total restoration. Believe and declare that even in the face of every kind of devil and opposition, trial and setback, that it's your turn to make it. You can only succeed if you flow with God's plans. It's your turn to flow with His plans for you!

Chapter 12

COME AND SEE

"Hidden inside the desires of my heart, in the linings of my lists, is that desire to be loved, to be cherished, to be championed, to be accepted, to be beautiful in the eyes of another—that other, being Jesus."

━━◆━━

My leg was healed but because of the cast that had encased it, it was skinnier than my right leg was and it still took several months for muscle tone to return. Although I had regained some mobility, it still felt stiff when I returned to Stephens College to finish my last semester in fashion merchandising and business administration that fall.

Imagine my surprise when the department administrators asked me to model in their autumn fashion show. *Would I even be able to stand on a high heel,* I wondered. Unbelievable, when I thought about it. Here it had been less than seven months since I was hurled out of that car at 70 mph, burned, broken, bruised, told I might never walk normally again, and now God had healed and restored me such that I could balance in high heels down a runway as normally as anyone else.

Truly, this was a victory walk and a testament to God's healing, loving power! God in His wisdom knew just what I needed—confidence to walk through the doors He was opening in my life. These doors would lead me into His plans of restoration in my walk with Him. I may have thought I was walking toward *my* dreams, but God was readying my feet in those towering heels to walk in some pretty high places.

COME AND SEE!

QVC and other home shopping networks sell tons of exercise equipment, beauty products, and organizational resources in the month of January because every New Year people spend time thinking about how to be more successful. They think about what they want, and write resolutions. Some want to lose a dress size, others want wealth, some seek to be more organized, and some, perfect health. Marketing executives leap at the chance to tap into these renewed motivations and advertise things to make you skinny, to increase your muscles, to earn you a million dollars, and dozens of ways to organize your life.

We all hope that tomorrow will be better than yesterday. Perhaps we won't be as lonely if tomorrow we meet our soul mate. Maybe we'll fit into that new dress or suit by summer, or it's possible that dream job will open up.

If Jesus had said, "Leigh, what are you looking for" as I prepared for the Miss U.S.A. pageant, in all honesty, I'd probably have avoided His question. How could I possibly answer that if I didn't even know who I was. At that point in my life I equated my identity with the things of the world—with "belonging." If He had asked anything of me before He planted the desire in my heart to preach to the nations, I would have said, "Uh...I dunno, Lord."

God's destiny for you is to be discovered. This comes about by sincerely asking what your destiny is. He will show you your gifts and calling.

Perhaps when Jesus asked the disciples what they were looking for, they were caught off guard because they responded to His question with another: "Where are You staying?" Jesus responds, though not with an answer, but an invitation, "Come and see."[41] The disciples followed Him, and along the journey introduced Jesus to their friends, and to their brothers. Of each, Jesus extended the same invitation, "Come and see." It wasn't long before all those who followed Jesus to see, learned that He was everything they ever wanted or hoped to find. He had everything they needed, even though they didn't know what that was. But Jesus, well, He knew what they needed and how badly they needed it. He knew where they had been and where they were going. He knew the deepest longings of their hearts. He saw their hidden dream lists. He knew them, and He longed to satisfy their true yearnings by being in relationship with them, by "staying in their hearts" and He calls to each one of us, "Come and see My heart for You!" In fact, a woman's heart should be so hidden in Christ that a man should have to seek Jesus first to find her![42]

GOD PLANS TO PROSPER YOU

God has plans to prosper you and not to harm you, plans to give you hope and a future (Jer. 29:11). We can take hold of this promise of greatness for our lives because God's desire for us is always for good. Whatever the destiny God has for you, that is where the blessings will be.

Many equate divine destiny with ministry, and then success with size or prominence—but this just isn't so. God calls all believers into ministry wherever we are and in everything we do. God wants everyone to fulfill his or her gifts and callings. You have a special gift from the Lord and He expects you to use it, and walk in your gift and calling. God treasures the quiet achievers, for they are the true backbone of the Church. Destiny isn't only for the Billy Grahams. It's not just for the Donald Trumps and the Bill

Gates of the world. Destiny isn't only for the youth, nor is it only for the elderly. There is never an age or a qualification—just a willingness to serve the Lord in whatever capacity He chooses, no matter what position you hold in life, no matter the career. I would rather be a doorkeeper in the house of my God than dwell in the tents of the wicked (see Ps. 84:10).

You have a special gift from the Lord.

JESUS LOVES YOU FROM THE INSIDE OUT

Only a person who sees us from the inside out, can know the intimate details of our lives. Throughout the New Testament, Jesus encountered people and told them things no one who wasn't deity could ever know. In John 4, He encountered the woman at the well. An outcast, she was there to draw water in the heat of the day to avoid people. But someone was there—Jesus! He revealed areas of her life that only she knew. Then Jesus told her that He was the Messiah, the Christ. She ran back into town and told everyone that Jesus had told her everything she had ever done. Her testimony was a call to "Come and see," and many did and believed.

Our desires for healing, deliverance, or accomplishments should always take second seat to pursuing Him all out. When He infuses us with Himself, when our hearts meld with His, suddenly our desires align with His and then He is faithful to give us all that we hope for. Only when we let Him in to the secret places of our hearts can we truly expect tailor-made answers to our cries.

Now that I think of it, almost every time God did a miracle in my life it was because He'd drawn me unto Himself first, planting His desire of wholeness in me.

Just as the woman at the well, and the woman who poured out her costly oil on Jesus, I want to be known by someone from the inside out. I want to be beautiful in the eyes of another. Hidden inside the desires of my heart, in the linings of my resolutions, is that desire to be loved, cherished, championed, accepted, and beautiful in the eyes of another—that other, being Jesus. The only place I can find peace is in that "Come and see" place that is the very heart of Jesus, the love of Christ, the yearning of Christ to be intimately connected with us.

In answer to Christ's question, "What do you want me to do for you? What are you really looking for?" I now have an answer: "I'm looking for heart change and restoration for all the places I missed. I am looking for a life of child faith in which I can trust, humble myself, love everyone (even the unlovable) and truly forgive those who have broken my heart. I'm looking for my heart to be totally fixated on You and You alone so that I can experience the peace and joy that sings, that sears, that heals all the scars. I'm searching for my future to be like no other because of the love blazing within me for You and others."

God doesn't promise that we will be problem-free, but I'm convinced that nothing will separate me from the love of God that is in Christ Jesus!

READY YOUR FEET TO GO

When your feet are ready, God will ceremoniously roll out the red carpet for you. He has a special path of righteousness for you where the Word will be a lamp to your feet and a light for your path.[43] Your path is walking with God moment by moment, day by day; that is your destiny. Hearing God's voice moment by moment is your destiny. God's plans and purposes for your life might lead you to being a stay-at-home parent, into the marketplace, or into ministry. The most important purpose is to follow Jesus—to become a follower of Jesus. It's not by your works that you're saved (thank You Jesus!) but by His grace; therefore, there's nothing more that God desires than for you to follow Him faithfully—in all that you do. That's what success is, as Mother Teresa knew when asked by a reporter if she thought her work would be successful. "Young man," she replied, "the Lord doesn't call me to be successful. He calls me to be faithful." Faithfulness *is* following Him. Mother Teresa was able to help the unloved in devastating conditions. She let God's love flow through her, and as she was faithful to the mission for her life, God helped her, protected her, and blessed her as she fed and cared for His children.

He raises up the poor out of the dust and lifts up the needy from the ash heap, to make them sit with nobles and inherit the throne of glory. For the pillars of the earth are the Lord's, and He has set the world upon them. He will guard the feet of His godly ones... (1 Samuel 2:8-9 AMP).

Come unto Me, all ye that labour and are heavy laden, and I will give you rest. Take my yoke upon you, and learn of me; for I am meek and lowly in heart: and ye shall find rest unto your souls. For my yoke is easy, and my burden is light (Matthew 11:28-30 KJV).

The truly exciting part of following Jesus into His plans for your life is that He never sends you into any situation, and that includes career or ministry, with a faulty plan or a plan to fail. God nurtures and matures us with a different pattern of growth in each of our lives—each pattern being unique to the individual. Therefore, success might not come as quickly as you'd like it to, but trust and have faith! He also knows the future and what you can handle and what you can't at any particular time of your life.

Be ready to move and switch gears fast. God values nimble feet. In the Old Testament, *nimble footedness* was an image applied to a life of righteousness and obedience to God–a confidence that the feet would tread and "slip not."[44] This means being in the will of God and instant willingness to go in the direction He leads us, even if it's out of our comfort zones, trusting Him and His protection and care. Another way to demonstrate our faithfulness is in spending time in the "secret place of His presence." Simply, that means spending one-on-one communion time with Him, in quiet and stillness, in prayer and quiet worship, in the Word and in hearing Him speak to your heart. It's about just being in His presence and coming to know Him as Moses knew Him; as Mary of Bethany sought to know Him; as John, the one whom Christ loved, knew Him.

In short, faithfulness is all about our resolution to accept God as our Keeper and there's no care better than God's care! David, in Psalm 91,[45] gave us a great example of God's faithfulness in caring for us, particularly as it relates to protection and favor as we abide in His care. We have a promise that we'll remain stable and fixed. That's important, especially these days with our seesaw economy, the country's sudden vulnerability, with the pull of the world toward self-sufficiency, political and religious unrest, natural disasters, and terrorist threats, for starters. Stability is important in upcoming days and we have to fix our eyes on Jesus if we're to see them through without fear.

Here are some additional promises that will help you to "slip not":

- You can always lean on and rely on Him. (See 1 John 4:16.)

- He will be your Refuge and your Fortress. (See Psalm 31:2.)

- You can triumph over your enemies with His power. (See Psalm 118:7.)

- You have His angels to accompany you, defend, and preserve you in all of your ways. They will carry you "lest you dash your foot against a stone" (and even lift a car off of you, as in my case!). (See Psalm 91:11-12.)

- You'll walk on even ground. (See Proverbs 4:12.)

- You'll be a special favorite of God's. He'll favor you because you have a personal understanding of His mercy, love, and kindness; because you trust and rely on Him knowing that He will never ever forsake you. (See Deuteronomy 31:6,8.)

- You will be delivered as you honor God and walk with Him. (See Psalm 107:6; 2 Corinthians 1:10.)

- Your life will be filled with His saving grace. (See John 1:17; Acts 15:11.)

YADA, YADA—
FACING RELIGION

"Our relationship with God isn't 'one-size fits all'..."

RELIGION will kill you. As part of the college graduation curricula, I had to do an internship, and the school sent me to Marshall Fields, a department store in Chicago. Actually, I planned to go to the windy city because Michael lived there. Since the time we had come to know Jesus through Mrs. Allen, he had fast-forwarded his walk with the Lord, which caused us to somewhat drift apart. However, I still loved him and desired a relationship with him; he called me every day and encouraged me to study the Word. Michael was extremely controlling, but he did have a heart after the Lord, and me!

For a time, everything went very well. Michael, with sights set for ministry, enrolled for leadership training with a well-known Bible discipleship ministry and the plan was that we would eventually marry and do ministry somewhere. We actually got engaged and I moved in with some girls from his college while I worked at Marshall Fields and he attended his classes. On

Sundays, we attended a great Assemblies of God church in South Chicago—*Maranatha*, with a wonderful pastor. We both loved the open worship and how the Holy Spirit so beautifully led the services.

However, in those days the training ministry he was involved with was quite legalistic and eventually Michael seemed to lose that "freedom" in the Spirit that I so loved. His acquaintances at the ministry weren't quite sure what to make of his "high fashion" seemingly "worldly" potential soul mate. The pressure to conform to their expectations of a ministry leader's wife mounted. Their mindset was that I was only good enough for Michael if I did this, or didn't do that, or if I memorized 300 odd Scriptures, or dressed ultra conservatively, or spent half of the day in the Word. The condemnation was horrible.

Soon it all rubbed off on Michael and thus he hounded me—though I believe he did it with good, though misguided, intention: "You're not spiritual enough, Lisa," or, "You don't read the Bible enough" or, "How much time did you spend memorizing Scripture verses today," and so on. Feeling a nervous wreck I screamed, "Help me Jesus!" What could I do? We couldn't even hold hands to pray in a group or lift our hands in worship without someone raising an eyebrow, and I couldn't take one moment alone for myself without Michael trying to organize my time as he saw fit.

YADAH! YADAH!

One day while attending a prayer meeting with him, I just wanted to worship the Lord and so spontaneously and without thinking, blurted, "Well, let's all hold hands and then lift them to the Lord," and everyone looked at me as if I was from a lost planet. Suddenly a fellow there explained, "We don't *do that* because it might be taken wrong and as too charismatic...."

I was so embarrassed and frustrated because I got excited and gave it my all when I prayed and worshiped God. I loved to glorify the Lord that way, and I still do! When we worship and the Holy Spirit touches our hearts, thankfulness, surrender, and sometimes just the desire to glorify God compels us and even causes us to lift our hands. Biblical people did it all the time! *Yadah*, a Hebrew verb used often in the Old Testament in the context of praise means *to use, hold out, and extend the hand. To revere/worship.* The opposite meaning is to *bemoan*, or *the wringing of hands.*

The psalmist says, "So will I bless Thee as long as I live; I will lift up my hands and call on Thy name" (Ps. 63:4 RSV). Worship this way feels great and is a physical act of acceptance and receiving what God has for us. It's also a demonstration of humbleness, of surrender, of finally letting go of the junk in your life that acts like a barrier to God so that you can embrace His greatness.

The Bible tells us to love the Lord with all of our heart and our entire being (heart, mind, and soul[46]) and with all of our might![47] In other words, we are to love with *all* that we have! If you take a read through the Bible, you'll see lifting of hands before the Lord in many circumstances:

- As an act of thanksgiving to God (see Exod. 17:11-16).

- When crying out for mercy and God's help (see Ps. 28:2).

- When in agreement with the Lord (see Neh. 8:6).

- As an act of sacrifice (see Ps. 141:1-2).

- As an act of obedience (see Ps. 119:48).

- As something His people could do together in unity (see 1 Tim. 2:8).

- As something we can do in the temple (church) (see Ps. 134:2).

So, worship by the lifting up of hands is biblical. Not only that, worship is vital to our walk with God. Whoa. I'm happy to report that this ministerial organization that Michael attended has since lightened up a lot, and today continues to do great work; but back then, religion threatened to quench the fire of God in me. Try as I did, I just couldn't memorize Scripture from those little cards or live up to their expectations—I didn't measure up. That rang true especially after I held a huge birthday party for Michael. I decided to go big, and with some of the insurance money from the car accident I bought a ton of food and decorations. For days I cooked, prepared, and planned, inviting everyone we knew from his school to come. On the night of the party though, Michael acted embarrassed and annoyed. The boiling point came when one of the leaders took me aside and said, "You know, Mike is to be trained for the ministry and is one of our key leaders. We just don't know, Lisa, if you and he are going in the same direction."

Worship is vital to our walk with God

"I think the problem is that you just don't like me...that I'm not good enough for you or for him," I said with pertness. I sensed this was true but even more so on the part of Michael. He wanted me to conform to *his* way of thinking about my relationship with the Lord, but that wasn't God's way for me. Our relationship with God isn't "one-size fits all," just as one person's relationship with someone is different from another person's relationship with the same person.

We remained engaged and never officially broke it off at that point, but we eventually drifted further apart. I'm sure through love and concern he tried to tell me what to do, but I needed Christ to show me who I needed to be. I didn't need the "should's" and "should not's," but a love relationship

with the living God. Additionally, I needed unconditional love from Michael and it seemed as though he didn't approve of me.

After the end of my internship at Marshall Fields, I went to work for Carson's (Carson Pirie Scott & Co.) in downtown Chicago, where I sold cosmetics first for Frances Denney Cosmetics, and then for Revlon.

Revlon later asked me to interview for a corporate job as a national beauty consultant which was unheard of for someone my age and just out of college. To my surprise, and by God's great favor and grace, they hired me, and before long I was traveling all over the country, though still with Chicago as my home base. So what with all of my traveling, I saw less and less of Michael. I still loved him and we both lived in a beautiful, ritzy high-rise in downtown Chicago—my condo was on the 53rd floor and he was on the 4th floor. It was there in the clouds looking out at the Sears tower and Michigan Avenue where my life would ever be transformed.

GOD'S PURPOSE UNFOLDS

God's purpose for my life was something I still had to discover, and for the most part up until this point of my life, I wasn't sure what He had in store for me. Until my healing at the hospital and my resolve to follow the Lord, I'd opted for the world's dreams for me, my dreams for me, and the devil's dreams for me. Those yielded some success as far as the Miss Missouri pageant was concerned, and any one or all of them may have yielded *great* success, but I'm a living, breathing, walking (praise God) testimony that they simply didn't bring me God's intentions for my life—that I prosper, have a future, and especially, a hope. Now I wanted what God had for me, and I wasn't so sure if Michael was to be a part of that or not.

As one whom the world and satan wounded, and at times as one who even wounded herself, I didn't want to be controlled by my negative past, nor did I want to be controlled by the negative things of the present. Now with these healing miracles, the surge of faith, and the awareness of newness in me, hope for a successful and purposeful future was a reality.

There is nothing impossible for God, and nothing so ugly that He would turn His eyes away. He saw my withered leg and made it whole. No heart is so mutilated that it's beyond His ability to heal. He saw my wounded heart and started the process of mending it. He'll take what the world has stomped on, messed up, and make it new again. He'll take wounds and cleanse them tenderly. According to God's Word, I was a new person in Christ Jesus, a beautiful new creature, and I had to believe, therefore, that all of the old destructive and hurtful things had passed away.[48]

GOD OF CHOICES

Jesus never forces His will on us and He doesn't insist that we love Him, but He patiently waits for us to accept all that He's done for us so that we can be all that He created us to be. He will whisper words of love and encouragement to us and never release His grip from us, but the choice is ours, whether we choose to hang on or let go.

I had no idea what God would have in store for my life beyond the healings—but I knew I wanted to hang on and find out! *Where would He lead me?*

I can be a very impatient person, especially when I know something belongs to me and yet God is taking His time to reveal it. The Father's plan sometimes takes awhile to become real in us, and it's possible that we can face great opposition as satan tries to pluck it from our hearts. Hey, the enemy tried to take me out physically, spiritually, *and* emotionally—more than once. Often, before the big picture becomes real to us, we enter into a valley of decision; a humbling time where, before our parched ground

becomes a pool (see Isa. 35:7), God shapes us, sometimes painfully into a vessel capable enough to carry out His purpose. Those "Help me Jesus" times gradually opened my spiritual eyes to see the reality of that purpose.

The water that the woman at the well drew for Jesus,[49] I believe metaphorically was God's intentions for her. Just like her, I had first to draw out those intentions before I could learn God's plan for my life and then start to walk in His purposes—a life filled with significance and vision.

TAILOR-MADE DESTINY

God says, "*I know* the plans I have for you...."[50] They're His! They aren't your plans, or anyone else's. Nix the devil's plans too. God had a vision for you before He flung the stars in the sky. He created you in a way that He created *no other being* on earth, with His unique vision for you implanted right into in your spiritual DNA.

In the physical realm of things, scientists often refer to DNA molecules as compared with a set of blueprints, since they contain long-term storage of information and instructions needed to construct other components of cells.[51] This spiritual DNA component works in a similar way and contains blueprints for the rest of your life that are filled with information and instructions that you need to walk successfully in Him.

When Christ redeemed me and I accepted salvation, the seed of vision that He sowed inside of me, constructed (birthed) anew too, and I became a product of God's own vision.

For we are God's [own] handiwork (His workmanship), recreated in Christ Jesus, [born anew] that we may do those good works which God predestined (planned beforehand) for us [taking paths which He prepared ahead of time], that we should walk in them [living the good life which He prearranged and made ready for us to live] (Ephesians 2:10 AMP).

As His masterpiece with a dream and purpose that He set for me before time began, I automatically and uniquely "fit" into His plans. Just as He told Jeremiah that before he was born He set him apart and appointed him as His spokesman to the world[52], so He told me that I would speak to the multitudes and that He would give me visions, purpose, and favor to get the job done.

As His appointed one, *you* have great favor too! God has a destiny purposed for you, and don't think for a second that He didn't knit you with that very thought in mind. Listen, I have a *need* to live for a higher purpose or calling because God designed me that way. He designed you, too, to *need* to live a higher purpose than just eking a living day-to-day. I don't want my tombstone to read, "She lived, she died, nothing significant to report." I hope it reads, "Leigh loved God, and fulfilled her call to the nations" because those words infer that I followed Him to the ends of the earth.

I've said it before and I'll emphasize it again: God created in every human being, the need to know what his or her purpose is, an endless thirst, a desire to be filled, and the need to know.

When my son, Joshua, was a toddler, he endlessly asked, "Why?" I ask "why" too because our need to know doesn't stop as we mature. However, often we search for the answers to our "whys" in the things of the world— fame, physical gratification, alcohol, work, even religion. But our longings are infinite. And who is Infinite? God! The fact that our longings are infinite reveals that only Someone who is infinite can truly fill that longing. However, often we look elsewhere. There we might find the thrill of success in a career, school, or the public eye, but we never get enough success, and we're always searching for more. Sometimes we become a success overnight,

but then it vanishes or wanes and we're left empty, hungry, looking for love, looking for approval—looking for that one thing that will fill the void.

The pains in our life are signals that something has to change—that we're on the wrong road and we need to veer off. Yes we have suffering, yes things go wrong, yes there are disappointments, but we who walk that road of glory learn that suffering has meaning.

You Can Walk Victoriously

When the apostle Paul was close to dying in prison, he summarized the walking out of God's plan for His life in an epitaph-type letter to Timothy. Paul didn't fear the future and he didn't regret the past either because he knew he had walked victoriously; his longing was that all believers would be triumphant in their walk. He recognized that his was a spiritual struggle worth battling for a noble cause! Thus, he recognized how vital it is for all of us to treasure the time we've been given on this earth to walk in His ways and to hold firmly to our faith in all that God has entrusted to us.

For I am already about to be sacrificed [my life is about to be poured out as a drink offering]; the time of my [spirit's] release [from the body] is at hand and I will soon go free. I have fought the good (worthy, honorable, and noble) fight, I have finished the race, I have kept (firmly held) the faith (2 Timothy 4:6-7 AMP).

Inspiration in the Word

We run the course by treasuring Jesus who *is* the Word, we stay on course by abiding *in* the Word, and live and have our being tasting of and partaking of the Word! In short, we have to become *desperate* for the Word of God in our lives, and *cling* to it.

Kiss the Word, keep it close, and see the visions God has for your life

A French missionary once told a story about a little girl who became a believer. Although she'd been blind from birth, she knew how to read Braille. Someone gave her the Gospel of Mark in Braille and she loved and treasured the words so much that by and by she developed calluses on her little fingers from so much "reading" and could no longer feel the Braille to read.

Hoping to make her fingers more sensitive, she peeled the skin off their tips, but they developed scars such that she lost sensitivity forever. Believing she would never "read" again, she planted her lips upon the book to give God's Word a farewell kiss. As she did this she discovered that her lips were far more sensitive than her fingers ever were and before long she could lip-read God's Word!

What a fantastic story! We should be *that* desperate for His Word, because the Word keeps our dreams alive. Kiss the Word, keep it close, and see the visions God has for your life that will bring you into the fulfillment of your God-planted destiny.

VISION FOR LIFE

God wants to satisfy the needs of your heart. Every human being wants to be able to say, "I finished well—my life really counted." That's why my heart cried out to God in Chicago, because in my spirit I felt so strongly that

He had something more for me than what I was doing. Throughout my life thus far, God had drawn me to Him, but now it was time that I drew from the well what He'd placed there.

What do You want me to do Lord? What have You got for me? I felt that I'd missed His mark somewhere, yet at the same time as if I were on the edge of something incredible. I couldn't quite place what that was. He'd already transformed my crazy-quilt existence into workable tapestry, but now I felt Him weaving His thread through and gathering the fabric to shape it into something. Unsatisfied, I wanted to see what more He had for me.

Where there is no vision [no redemptive revelation of God], the people perish; but he who keeps the law [of God, which includes that of man]—blessed (happy, fortunate, and enviable) is he (Proverbs 29:18 AMP).

Purpose motivates us and if we're not motivated, we risk having a sick heart because where dreams come true, there is life and joy.[53] God had visions for Paul, David, Esther, and many other biblical greats, *and* He has visions for you too, because divine pictures planted in our hearts of what could and should be are for every believer. We're all ministers of the Gospel, like it or not; and no matter what job or role we're in, we must learn to be open to what God has for us because this is the key to transforming us from apathy and lethargy to purposefulness and boldness. We can't risk living life haphazardly or we risk falling prey to unhealthy emotions and hardening of our spiritual arteries. You *don't* want that, because that's when misfortune happens.

BREAKTHROUGH!

"I never expected, though, that God also had plans to expose and deal with another diabolical scheme of the devil to take me out early in the process of my destiny. In fact, this was something I had struggled with for many years and it threatened my life because I'd tried to hide it for so long."

"WHAT do You want me to do Lord? What have You got for me" was a question I wasn't about to stop asking. Determined to know, I never let up. God gradually unfolded His vision for me, leading me to the right people at the right time, and indeed, the paths led me straight to my answers!

I will bring the blind by a way they did not know; I will lead them in paths they have not known. I will make darkness light before them, and crooked places straight. These things I will do for them, and not forsake them (Isaiah 42:16).

I had the first glimpse of His plan while spending a few weeks in Boca Raton with my University of Tampa roommate, Leslie. She introduced me to the person who lived across the hall from her apartment and right away she asked, "You're a Christian, aren't you?"

Nodding yes, I wondered why she asked.

She left the room, returned a few moments later, and handed me some tapes and a book.

"I want you to read and listen to this material by Kenneth Hagin," she instructed.

This Kenneth Hagin was the same man in whose meetings God healed my leg, but it hadn't clicked yet and so, finding myself with lots of free time while Leslie had to work, I played the tapes and read the book. His teachings I found hard to understand and I wondered, *What does it mean, faith to move a mountain—why would I want to move a mountain, what would I say to it?* However, the more I listened, the greater I understood and suddenly, while in a teaching about healing, revelation hit...this teacher was the very same man who had prayed over me! Coincidence or God incidence? Was this God creating a common stream for me to follow so that I would go in the right direction and know that He was leading me?

The Planting

Suddenly, the teachings of faith drew me in with insatiable hunger to learn more as I connected faith with miracles. I would fall asleep listening to the tapes and awaken in the middle of the night to listen again. Something about it all excited me deep within, and I felt as though puzzle pieces were fitting together in my life to complete a bigger picture. I had experienced this same hunger for knowledge before my first healing miracle in the hospital when flipping through television channels for Christian programming to learn about faith and the Jesus who heals.

Destiny unfolds day by day

The next "piece" that would reveal more of God's plans for me and start to interlock for a bigger picture surfaced when I traveled home to St. Louis at the request of my brother, to visit with and to pray for his 25-year-old girlfriend, Connie. They'd met at Bible school and had fallen deeply in love, such that I believe he would have married her. A cheerleader and quite athletic, Connie went to see Doc, our father, about some back pain, but he immediately sent her to a specialist who diagnosed her with an advanced stage of cancer. I and a few others prayed over this precious girl. One of the women later took me aside and prophesied, "You have a call of God on your life," and then she told me about the Rhema Bible Training Center in Oklahoma and about their "camp meetings." [54] She encouraged me to look into them. I'd never heard of this Bible school and put it in the back of my mind to check it out someday.

Have you ever considered that you were born for "such a time as this?" God has a definite appointment and plan for you. Some of us miss the appointment and we don't fulfill the plan because we follow paths of our own choosing. Often, we question things that happen; for instance, the people we meet who speak God's rhema Word into our lives,[55] or career opportunities. Could it be that God had these divine contacts or opportunities for you set up from the foundations of the earth for this time in your life and in God's big plan? I tell you the truth, God's biggest plan for me was in my divine appointment with my teacher Mrs. Allen, the day Jesus saved me. I am so thankful to her for pressing in with me.

Destiny unfolds day by day, just as it did for me, and as it will for you. Each day is pivotal to the next.

STIR TO HUNGER

After returning to Chicago, I was devastated to hear that Connie died and this news weighed heavily on my heart. Also, the death of my relationship with Michael was apparent—we'd drifted too far from each other and we broke off our engagement.

Reluctantly at first, I started to date again; and I found a new church that I loved instantly: Faith Tabernacle, "Where Grace Meets You on the Broadway of Life," pastored by Al Smith. Certainly, grace had found me there in the middle of an almost 80 percent African- American and Latino congregation where I felt loved and accepted—welcomed! God was alive and real in that place!

One week some missionaries ministered at the church, a husband and wife team, Doctors T.L. and Daisy Osborn of Osborn Ministries. They had an international ministry headquartered in Tulsa, Oklahoma. Daisy (1924-1995) preached that evening, and she wowed and motivated me in a great way and stirred in me a hunger for the nations. An evangelist, author, businesswoman, soul-winner, and true ambassadress for Christ, this was the first time I'd ever heard a woman preach. She ministered with such passion that I suddenly realized that this is what I wanted for my life—that same hunger for souls, the fire and fervent desire to follow and serve Christ Jesus. The Lord definitely stirred something in me that evening, and I felt something seed-like deposit in me—something that wasn't there before. Desire! Passion!

Some time later, in November 1981 during my mother's visit, I had heard about a female evangelist in town, Sandy Brown.[56] So we went to the convention center—this dynamic impassioned woman of God was unbelievable! The room was full of business people and ministers and many were crying and going to the altar, falling on their knees onto the dirty convention floor.

At times when she spoke no one moved. While there, I felt the Lord drop into my heart that I was called to preach. Sandy Brown stirred up the gift in me to bring people to Jesus—a real evangelistic gift to get people excited about the Lord. Sandy told the audience not to follow religion or man, but to follow God. She was full of fire, as was another minister who was there with her, Elizabeth Prewill. This was the first time I felt the call to tell others about the Lord. Sandy made it seem so simple to reach out to others.

I purchased some of Sandy's testimony tapes, and as soon as I got home I put them in the player and listened to them over and over again. Something arose in me as I listened: desire, excitement—a yearning that compelled me to want to fall at the feet of Jesus and totally submit to Him. If it was true that God was calling me to be an evangelist, I wanted to know for sure.

"Oh Lord," I prayed, hoping to fan such a flame as this preacher woman had in my heart, "I don't know what You want to do with my life, but I'll do anything!"

And I really meant it!

I FEARED A FEAR

To ready me for my destiny of stirring people for Jesus, I had to face my enemy—bulimia. This eating disorder was something I had struggled with for many years and it threatened my life because I'd tried to hide it for so long. The problem started in junior high school and its root cause was fear. My mom had a terrible fear of gaining weight, and I admired her for watching her weight. But she encouraged me to go on all kinds of diets, everything from the cabbage soup diet to the apple cider vinegar diet. Because my dad was a doctor and worked with patients about their weight, there was never a shortage of diet pills at my discreet disposal. I first started on prescription diet pills when I was only 16, because I had a fear of becoming fat. Even though I was the member of a swim team and swam backstroke and freestyle competitively, I was so afraid of becoming fat, especially when I was 16, 17, and 18, that I was consumed with fear.

For the thing which I greatly feared is come upon me, and that which I was afraid of is come unto me. I was not in safety, neither had I rest, neither was I quiet; yet trouble came (Job 3:25-26 KJV).

In other words, "I feared a fear and it came upon me." I remember seeing the photos of three models on the cover of some magazine with the headline, "Famous Models, Dangerous Diets," and the subheading, "Fear of food drove them to abuse their bodies."

The photos shocked me and I thought, *There's no way I'd ever do that or get that way.* But that's exactly what happened...subtly.

As a young teen, I was super skinny, maybe because I read many of the Hollywood teen magazines and in my mind I wanted to look like those girls on Malibu Beach. I wanted to have a model's figure like the girls in the photos. During my early teen years I wore braces to straighten my crooked teeth and a cumbersome back brace to correct a spinal deficiency called Sherman's Disease. When I was 15, the back brace came off and I became even more concerned about how I looked.

Slimming down like the models wasn't hard because my mother was often concerned about her weight and went on crash diets all of the time; so I'd sometimes join her. Later, when I started to enter beauty pageants and the modeling industry, being thin became an obsession and my favorite line was, "You can never be too skinny or too rich."

Binging and purging became my life. I'd eat and then I would force myself to throw up, over and over again. Or, I'd eat and then take diuretics and laxatives to rid myself of what I had eaten. Some weeks I'd be super skinny and a scant month later swollen, puffy, and 10 pounds heavier. Bulimia, like anorexia, is a life-threatening disorder. The doctors confirmed that what I was doing was serious and if not corrected quickly, I could die.

I had an eating disorder, but in some strange way, it drove me deeper into the cycle of fear. Sometimes I would eat so much food at one time that it would make me ill without even having to force myself to purge. If the food didn't purge, I'd take more laxatives and diuretics, until it all came out. I would pig out on whole cartons of Haagen-Dazs ice cream, bags of Pepperidge Farm cookies, pizza, hamburgers, and other junk foods. I couldn't stop. Then I'd awaken several pounds heavier and go crazy with the fear of being fat. Consumed with thoughts of food and craving sugar all of the time, I'd awaken in the middle of the night and drive or even walk alone in the dark to wherever the nearest store was without even considering the danger. My torment was indescribable.

Sometimes I thought I was having a heart attack because the amphetamines and weight loss drugs were so hard on my heart and body. I kept thinking, *Why can't I just be naturally thin like other people.* This fact made me extremely depressed such that I would call my mother and cry over the phone to her.

When out on a date, I'd just pick at my food pretending to be a light eater so that my date wouldn't comment that I ate like a horse or something. I always binged in secret, never wanting anyone to suspect anything. Once home I'd raid the refrigerator and like a vacuum, consume anything I could find.

The bulimia problem had worsened when I moved to Chicago, and for a time I hid it well. However, my best friend Jill, a Jewish believer, (we went to Jews for Jesus Bible Studies with Jan Masquowicz all the time and hung out on Rush and Oak Street where her million-dollar art gallery was located) noticed something wrong and confronted me.

With lots of hutspa she said, "Leigh, I'm really concerned...what's happening?" But I denied her suspicions and lashed out at her.

One night she cut out an article from the *Chicago Tribune* newspaper. "Read it," she demanded, thrusting it into my hand.

Later that night in my room, I cried myself to sleep because the article was about how this insane eating disorder behavior destroys the digestive system—it terrified me. Jill was right; I needed professional help.

THE DEVIL'S TENACITY

I tried two years of analysis with a Christian psychologist, without success. Overeaters Anonymous didn't work either—in the group I attended, the people were too oppressed and depressed and I'd leave the meetings feeling worse.

Desperate, I'd heard on a Christian radio broadcast about a deliverance ministry at a church on the South Side of Chicago. Although not the best neighborhood, I was determined to go and seek help. I should have checked out the ministry first because it turned out that it needed more help than I did!

Seeped in religiosity, self-righteousness, and piety, the ministry was full of religious zealots looking for quarry to wreak havoc upon. No doubt I looked like great prey in my nice worldly-looking business designer grey suit, chunky earrings, and lipstick. I should have bolted as soon as I saw those dour women with tight hair buns, no jewelry, make-up, or adornments of any kind except for white kerchiefs on their heads.

A hard-faced woman tossed one on my head before I spoke to the pastor. Sensing something wasn't quite right, but frantic to be made well, I pressed in for healing. "Pastor," I said, "I am tormented with fear about my weight, and I need help." He motioned the women to minister to me and like vultures swooping on a lifeless victim they surrounded and attacked. They didn't even know why I was there and it was almost as though they thought I was about to seduce the pastor or something similarly as far-fetched. Their eyes were filled with animosity, disdain, and jealousy—no kidding. Imprisoning me with their barely concealed judgment and religious spirits they screamed, "You spirit of a harlot, come out of her! You spirit of a harlot, come out of her!"

I could sense disgust as they stared at my long red polished nails, and said, "We do not wear that here." In reality, I looked like a young professional businesswoman ready for success. Then again they prayed in a disgusting tone, "You Jezebel spirit, come out of her now! Come out of her right now!" Half an hour later, I mustered the courage to run—I'd had enough—something was wrong, very wrong with all their letter-of-the-law ministry and judgment. In tears, I handed them back the hanky off my head, said thank you so very much for your time, but I must get back to my condo in downtown Chicago now, and raced out the door and jumped into my car.

I had come seeking help—depressed, in need of compassion, understanding, and unconditional love—and all they wanted to do was get me religiously cleaned up. *Religion stinks!* Hurt beyond reason and feeling hopeless, I could barely see my way home. "Lord, Lord," I cried out to God. "That pastor—on the radio...it seemed he understood and I thought he could help. He said on the radio that he would help people who are struggling...but when I got there...oh Lord, there was no power, just religion and judging. There was such a weird spirit...not the Holy Spirit. Help me, please! I don't know what to do now." If deliverance is the "children's bread" where can it be found? I cried out for God to show me.[57]

CRY FOR BREAKTHROUGH

It was irony that I sensed the Lord telling me to fast and seek Him, especially in light of my eating disorder. However, indeed, He called me to fast on just water and pray for seven days.

So I spent a week in my condo on the 53rd floor in the sky fasting the only way I knew how: by eating nothing and drinking just water. Day after day I pressed in without food—crying out to Him, yearning to be made well and to birth whatever it was I felt was about to explode in me. The weather had been overcast for days. I couldn't even see the Sears Tower from my window, and so it appeared to me that I was alone in the clouds for seven days with the Lord, crying out to Him for life and purpose, seeking His will in my life, waiting to receive a revelation from Him.

Hindsight is 20/20, and when I started the fast, I had a whole lot of zeal but not a lot of wisdom—I dove full steam ahead with no pre-fast preparations. I went cold turkey—no coffee, caffeine, sugar. I consumed only water with lemon and fresh beet juice to help cleanse my liver. By the third day I was crawling on the floor to get around. I was so toxic and had lots of headaches. But I was determined to hear from God. I had to have a release from this eating disorder, but more importantly I had to know what God wanted me to do for Him. I was desperate!

I took Joel 2:13 to heart which says, "Rend your hearts and not your garments and return to the Lord, your God, for He is gracious and merciful, slow to anger, and abounding in loving-kindness; and He revokes His sentence of evil [when His conditions are met]."

The breakthrough you might need in your life too is the knowledge or at least a sense of where God wants you to be, of His direction; for not only the present or future, but also for your life overall. If you yearn to know God's purpose for you here on earth, then get motivated to fast. God likes

it for some reason—He ordained fasting to help us break the bands, which means fasting gets the devil off of us! I highly encourage you to pray and fast to seek God's will for your life *now*—don't wait.

Determine to breakthrough for anything that lines up with the Word and will of God, whether it's spiritual, emotional, or personal, or in the areas of health, finances, career, relationship, or family. Periods of fasting and prayer produce incredible spiritual results as you seek to draw close to and move the heart of the Lord. If you think that something is impossible, fast and pray! If something hasn't worked in your life, suddenly it will. If you need a promotion, fasting and prayer is effective! If you struggle with a habit, fasting will help you break through.

Whatever you need breakthrough for, fasting is the biblical answer. Fasting and prayer move God and help us to focus deeper on Him. Believers of the Bible often fasted before they made important decisions[58] and it's as much for believers today as it was for the heroes and heroines of old.

Biblically-guided fasting helps us focus deeper on God and is often vital to spiritual growth. It isn't about the lack of food or a way to punish our flesh or a drastic way to lose weight. It is an opportunity to take our eyes off the flesh and the things of the world that obscure God so that we can focus on Him better. It's a way that many show God and themselves the commitment and seriousness of their relationship with Him.

We don't only have to fast from food. Fasting can be anything we temporarily give up—television, coffee, sugar, meat; things we eat or regularly do. The fast has time limits; it can last for simply one hour a day for a week, or as much as a 40-day fast. Fasting and prayer usually go together.[59]

If you think that something is impossible,
fast and pray!

The Bible admonishes not to advertise what you are doing to the world as you're going through it. Why? Because it is something between you and God, and in fact His Word takes it a step further and says when you fast you should not "look gloomy, sour, and dreary" and vie for attention like a hypocrite "that their fasting may be apparent to and seen by men" (Matt. 6:16-18). Fasting should encourage humility and moves God's heart.[60]

I needed breakthroughs many times as I matured in Christ, and I still do, not only for my personal life, but as I intercede and fast for the needs of others, for my city, for the nation. If fasting and praying are means to a breakthrough that God has for me, I'll do it! Everyone needs breakthrough in some area, and I'm no exception. I needed understanding of what God had for me, understanding of this drawing that I had been experiencing. Today I fast for breakthrough in understanding situations, answers to problems, breakthrough for creative ideas and solutions, breakthrough for the yokes of bondage to be broken, and breakthrough for the release of God's manifest presence and power in my life.

Then shall your light break forth like the morning, and your healing (your restoration and the power of a new life) shall spring forth speedily; your righteousness (your rightness, your justice, and your right relationship with God) shall go before you [conducting you to peace and prosperity], and the glory of the Lord shall be your rear guard (Isaiah 58:8 AMP).

GOD'S VOICE

At the end of the week of fasting, a doctor friend called and said, "Leigh, you need to get out in the sunshine. Why don't you let me take you

out on the yacht? I've hired a captain, so we can just go somewhere out on the lake and soak it all up." Although he wasn't a Christian, he added, "You can bring your Bible if you want."

A day in the sun sounded good and it would be nice to relax, so I agreed and packed a day bag. Just as I was about to shut the door to head downstairs and to the waiting Rolls Royce, I heard the small inner Voice of the Lord tell me to bring my journal and pen. I felt very much impressed by the Holy Spirit to go back in and grab these things in spite of the fact I was running late as usual.

Lake Michigan is the third largest Great Lake and the sixth largest lake in the world. At 22,300 square miles, it's about half the size of Tennessee, and stretches 307 miles by 118 miles averaging 279 feet deep and reaches 923 feet at its deepest, so it's very much like being out on the ocean. The captain cut the engines once we were out of sight of land and I found a comfortable, peaceful place to soak up the warmth of the sun. Thankfully, the doctor and the captain found their own space and soon they were dozing off leaving me alone in my thoughts. The waves lapped against the boat's hull and I decided I was glad for this short daytrip getaway.

Suddenly the quiet broke, and like thunder I heard my name, "Leigh...Leigh!" Bolting upright, I looked around but the captain and the doctor were still dozing. Instantly I knew it was God. Then very audibly, He said, "Leigh, don't you know that you are chosen and called by Me? Get the notebook and pen and go below."

I headed into one of the staterooms all the while trembling. He started: "Leigh, I've been calling you and I've been trying to talk to you but you haven't been listening. You forget things you know to be true and the enemy comes and tries to steal those things I've spoken into your life. From now on, I want you to write the things that I tell you. If you leave the things of the world behind and follow Me, you will see My plans happen in your life.

I have called you to ministry and I will take you to the nations of the world. You will preach and teach My Word, and you will be a prophetic voice."

What did that mean? I didn't know what a prophetic voice was, but He expounded on everything, giving me Scripture verses, reassurance, words of love, and He spoke destiny into my life. He kept saying I would bring many unto Him. Many from all walks of life. Many rich and many poor. They would come to the Lord from all backgrounds and walks of life.

I wrote and wept, wept and wrote and soon I had an entire page filled with His words and instructions to me. Trembling, I came undone because I knew I was in the presence of the Most High God, my Father in Heaven, the Creator of the universe, and it just broke me. Who was I that He would speak to me in such a manner?

At home, I poured over Scriptures and everything He told me lined up with the Word. I had every confidence, therefore, that the destiny He had spoken into me would come to pass.

The Spirit of the Lord God is upon me, because the Lord has anointed and qualified me to preach the Gospel of good tidings to the meek, the poor, and afflicted; He has sent me to bind up and heal the broken-hearted, to proclaim liberty to the [physical and spiritual] captives and the opening of the prison and of the eyes to those who are bound (Isaiah 61:1 AMP).

A few days or so later I set up an appointment to see my pastor, Al Smith, to tell him about what God spoke into my life. Honestly, at that time in my life he was the most awesome pastor, but in those days women just didn't do much preaching and I thought he would say that perhaps I had misinterpreted things, or perhaps that I was called to something else. When I read my notes verbatim from what God had given me, I was afraid to look

up and into his eyes to read his thoughts; however, to my amazement he said, "Yep, that's God!" and then gave me much wise counsel for the days ahead.

When my father found out that I planned to go to Bible college, he was upset and said, "You can't do that Leigh Ann...you have a *great* job! How can you leave all that?" I tried to get a word in but he continued, "You mean I paid for your education in the finest colleges for five years and now you want to go to a Bible school that's not even accredited? To be a minister? This is absurd; this is stupidity on your part."

"Dad," I explained, "I've been talking to God a mighty long time about all this and...."

He lightened up a bit. "Well Hon, I hope you didn't charge all of those heavenly long-distance calls to my office—if you did, my bill will be out of control!"

HOW GOD SPEAKS

God speaks to His people today through the Bible, through supernatural (audible voice of God, angels, visions, word of knowledge, the prophetic, for examples) and through natural means. The most common way the Holy Spirit speaks today and reveals Jesus is through the Bible, which is the inspired Word of God. Apostle Paul explains it so beautifully in Second Timothy 3:16-17:

Every Scripture is God-breathed (given by His inspiration) and profitable for instruction, for reproof and conviction of sin, for correction of error and discipline in obedience, [and] for training in righteousness (in holy living, in conformity to God's will in thought, purpose, and action), So that the man of God may be complete and proficient, well fitted and thoroughly equipped for every good work (2 Tim. 3:16-17).

Jesus often took people to the Scriptures to reveal God's heart and more of Himself. On the day of Pentecost, when the Holy Spirit brought the mighty winds and tongues of fire, many thought the 120 assembled there were drunk. However, God opened Peter's mind to understand that these things were the beginning of the fulfillment of ancient prophecy, spoken of in Joel 2:28-32, and Peter explained the Pentecost that was going on to the inquisitive and startled onlookers.

The Holy Spirit teaches, reminds, testifies, guides, and tells us the truth about the past, present, and future!

The advantage that Peter and the others had and that we have in interpreting the Scriptures, is the Holy Spirit whom Jesus called "the Spirit of Truth." The Spirit of Truth would teach them of all things, remind them of all the things Jesus taught them, would testify of Jesus, guide them into all truth, and tell them what was to come.[61] So the Holy Spirit teaches, reminds, testifies, guides, and tells us the truth about the past, present, and future! The Holy Spirit is the Key to unlocking the Scriptures. The Psalmist wrote, "*Open my eyes that I may see* wonderful things in Your law" (Ps. 119:18 NIV) and such that Paul told Timothy, "Reflect on what I am saying, *for the Lord will give you insight* into all this" (2 Tim. 2:7 NIV). Surely, the Holy Spirit is the only Person powerful enough to break through the darkness and hopelessness of our hearts with a conviction of sin that leads us into repentance.

God speaks audibly to people especially those whom He is raising up as leaders. He often spoke audibly to His Son, Jesus. Paul heard the audible voice of God on the road to Damascus. Ananias heard the Voice in a vision telling him to minister to Paul. Peter heard His voice in a trance, and John heard the Voice giving him revelation of the last days that we read about in

the Book of Revelation.⁶² Often those biblical people (and people today) heard from God audibly at a turning point in their lives, at the beginning of ministry, when something was hard to accept or believe, or when the task itself required great effort or even suffering.

Although rarer than other forms of God speaking into our lives, His audible voice usually happens when we're praying to Him, drawing close, and communicating with Him regularly.

Sometimes God speaks to us in an internal audible voice that we hear internally, when we don't actually hear Him speak with our ears. We'll hear the Holy Spirit speak to us in complete sentences, and then relay it back.

There's also an internal audible voice that we can hear, where God speaks to us internally—we don't actually hear Him with our ears. At the same time when we hear His voice in this way, our emotions kick in, stirring our heart radically because this usually happens when there's something significant or life-changing about to happen, whether it's for one's own life, or for speaking into the life of another.⁶³

FREEDOM!

For all of the labor pains I'd been through those past few years, for all of it, I sensed a birthing of my true life coming forth. I could see the thread of events that had unfolded previously that were pointing the way to this very day. I recalled the young woman telling me to look into the Rhema training center, so later that day I called my mother and said, "Mom, we're going to a Rhema camp meeting in Tulsa—get ready!

We arrived at the July camp meeting eager and hungry for the Word of God and rich teaching, but I never expected that God would expose and deal with my bulimia at the same time!

My mother and I were in Jerry Seville's session and I was diligently listening and taking notes when I suddenly had a craving for Haagen-Dazs ice cream. It was so strong I couldn't shake it off so I left mid-meeting and headed out to the hotel in search of some. Wouldn't you know it, the gift shop had the exact flavor I loved—and I royally pigged out. However, in true cycle, I punished myself for the next three days by only drinking diet shakes and sodas.

I suddenly had a craving for Haagen-Dazs ice cream.

As God would have it though, one day a woman approached my mother and said, "Is that your daughter? I have a word of knowledge about her from the Lord: she needs to be set free in a certain area of her life...do you think she'd be open to it?"

When mom shared this with me I said, "Where is she...of course I am...," and when I met the woman I had no misgivings. I must confess that I liked that she wore a little makeup and jewelry and her eyes oozed love and glowed with the compassion of Jesus. My spirit too bore witness that this was a divine appointment—that I'd moved God's heart through prayer and fasting for such a time as this—freedom!

We met in my hotel room and she began her prayers softly but firmly, assertively commanding the demonic powers to come out of me. *Wasn't I supposed to feel something?* I thought. "This isn't doing any good," I said. "Let's just forget it."

"Leigh, the devil has to leave when we use our authority in the name of Jesus! You are a Spirit-filled Christian, aren't you? The devil has no right to stay in your body or in your mind. He has to go in Jesus' name."

"OK," I said hopefully yet nervously. "Let's pray some more, try again, I need help."

She raised her voice a little more purposefully, and my mother joined in too: "In Jesus' name, we bind you devil and command you out of Leigh! Out, in Jesus' name!"

After the fifth or sixth round of this, I felt warmth—like a fire rise first from my stomach and then all through me. It was such a hot and burning feeling that I squirmed in my chair and wanted to escape it, but suddenly I had a vision of a black snake coiled around my stomach. It was huge and ugly and inscribed on it were the words, "fear" and "anxiety," and other words I couldn't decipher. Then in the vision I saw the snake uncoil itself and flee out of me. I began to cough and then I fell almost lifeless on the hotel bed next to my mom. I was very weak; yet I felt free, different, and lighter...not so heavy and nervous. Freedom!

When the torment left me, I fell limp onto the bed—light—burning with desire for all that God had for me—hopeful! Because of my cries to Him, I moved His heart and He sent me a faithful servant to do His will, and through her faithfulness, He set me free. What a great and humble woman of God she was, with not one ounce of religion in her—just relationship with Him—what a great example to me.

He set me free.

From that day until now, I have never ever struggled with my weight again. Nor have I binged or purged, nor have I taken diet pills or gone on crazy fad diets. Rather, I stay thin, trim, and healthy by eating healthy food and by the power of the Lord Jesus Christ; and I'm at the weight He wants me to be! Never since have I had a craving that would cause me to eat in secret and I have no problem eating in front of people. No longer do I fear weight gain, because it just hasn't happened. God is so good and His mercy endures forever!

If you're struggling with an eating disorder, the root cause is fear. This spirit of fear also causes other problems. There are still several areas of fear that attack me periodically, but I have great hope as I walk with the Lord that He will complete the work He has begun in me. Nothing is too difficult for God. I'm a living, walking testimony that you can come out from beneath crippling bondage and be set free by the power of God. To help you through struggles, have at least three Scriptures that you can stand on while you seek help from a reliable Christian. (Please turn to the back of the book for recommended Scriptures in the Prayer for Overcoming Fear.) Let the gifts of the Spirit in your life flow.

The Holy Spirit has the answer for you personally, and it may be different from how He set me free. I don't have all the answers because your situation may be quite different from mine. You are unique and special to God and He wants to bless you. Trust the Holy Spirit as your Administrator and let Him direct you to the right place for personal prayer and ministry. My precious mom smoked for 23 years, 2 packs a day, but one day the Lord totally delivered her from a spirit of nicotine. How? She had a pure heart and asked the Lord to send someone to help set her free.

Of all people, God sent an Assembly of God lady who had never prayed deliverance over anyone. She put my mom in a chair in the middle of her living room and she asked God to use her in this way: "Jesus I need your help to minister to Mary. You heard her admit she is addicted to cigarettes and she can't stop smoking in her own strength, so I have never done this before...in fact I never even believed a Christian could have a demon...but I am stepping out in obedience to You to help Mary—set her free God." After

20 minutes of praying, my mom felt something and she began to weep uncontrollably when suddenly the spirit of nicotine come out of her.

My mom's friend saw what looked like in the spirit a small dark cloud that floated out of my mom. She saw it float out of the house through the corner of the wall. "Oh that is ridiculous," you might be saying about now, but my mom never ever smoked a cigarette again, and frankly the thought of it made her sick. Deliverance is real! Deliverance is for you. Deliverance is needed in all of our lives because of sin and generational curses and bondages from our past. If you were in sexual sin, demons entered you and their bondage must be broken.

Remember, he who joins himself to a harlot becomes one with them.[64] All sexual sin is against your own body and causes destructions. Demons can even enter people because of the movies they watch and video games they play. You open yourself up to demonic influence when you do things apart from the Lord's will. You must be in His will at the right time for your healing, deliverance, and victory. To God be the glory!

CALLED TO BIBLE SCHOOL

On the last day of the camp meeting, Kenneth Hagin's son, Ken Junior, called on those who wanted to give a monetary love gift toward the ministry to come up to the altar for prayer—or at least that's what I thought he said. So I headed up there for prayer, but discovered that he had called those *who felt led to attend the Bible school that fall* to come up for prayer! I'm not so certain that if I'd heard him right I would have mustered the gumption to go up there, but I think this was God's way of getting me out of my seat and moving me quickly with nimble feet toward what He had called me to do!

This cinched it for me—I was to start the semester at the end of the following month and that meant lots of packing and preparations back in

Chicago. Once home, I resigned my job, packed up, and headed to Tulsa to rent an apartment close to the school. Then, I secured a part-time job working as a makeup artist for Estée Lauder to help pay for school, and soon classes started.

I settled into the first semester OK although it was hard to get to know the professors and leadership. I soon made friends and in particular, Bobby Valentine. He was so dark and handsome and very charming. Italian, he reminded me a little of Michael. Bobby sang Gospel, seemed to really love God, was a good listener, and pursued a relationship with me, so I began dating him. Our first date was going to McDonald's in his real beater of a car that he had to kick to make the headlights turn on! This was part of his charm and it didn't bother me, even though I was used to being wined and dined in more style. Whether in my heart I felt that since he was a Christian it would be in God's will, or whether it was my yearning for acceptance, I don't know, but I know that I didn't really hear from God about being in relationship with Bobby. In fact, I ran way ahead of God and married him within the year. Hence, we finished the rest of the two-year program as a married couple.

FEAR OF PUBLIC SPEAKING

Especially in the first year or so of classes, I really struggled with getting up in front of people to speak—a fear I'd had for a long time but had never sought to overcome. Every time I had to go up front or say something, I'd break out into a sweat, my notes would go blank, and fear of what people might think of me would smack me in the face. *How could I ever preach,* I asked myself.

This spirit of fear hindered me much, but it didn't just start at college. When I was six, my mother was being honored at a sales event attended by

thousands of people. It was held at the famous Fontainebleau Hotel in Miami Beach. I wasn't feeling good that night, but my mom literally pulled me right up on stage thrusting the microphone at me. "Say a few words, Leigh," she said. I just couldn't, and burst into tears because I was so embarrassed, and especially upset that I let them down, that I didn't perform well. Ever since that night, I've feared getting up in front of people, even though I was an extremely outgoing girl.

Fear was there during the pageants too. My acting agent and pageant directors were often concerned about my fear of getting in front of the camera or people because it was restraining my talents. In those earlier days, I tried pills or alcohol as band-aids, but nothing gave me the confidence I needed; the "fear of man" always seemed so prevalent. Of course it followed me to Bible school. Here I was a Spirit-filled Christian, sold out to God, desiring to minister, and yet I feared an audience.

One day in evangelism class, I had to get up and preach for ten minutes in front of my classmates. My teacher was also the college dean whom I admired and deeply respected, especially because he showed me much mercy when I flubbed up things. However, this day in particular I remember because I was terrified. Dean Moffat walked in and I was first up to preach. My face I'm sure was white as chalk as my carefully prepared notes went blank before my eyes and when I looked up, everything was a blur. As I was about to burst into tears and give up, the Spirit of God came to my rescue through my best friend—a beautiful dark-haired girl with brown eyes, nodding encouragement to me. The Lord remembered me in my time of trouble, and out of my spirit, I preached as hard and as fast as I could—enough to impress the teacher and the students. I aced it.

However, I still don't know how I managed through it, and I knew something was terribly wrong. I needed help. The gift was there, the call too, but I was all bound up and it wasn't right!

A precious woman at work one day invited me to speak at an upcoming Christian women's group, *Women Aglow,* which met in Bartlesville, Oklahoma. The moment I said "Yes," I wanted to change my mind, and actually got physically ill just thinking about it. God's Word says, "Fear hath torment," and this truth reared firsthand. *How do preachers do this without fear...they do it though, all over the world they get up to the pulpit—are they afraid,* I wondered.

Though I knew I was called, I didn't see how I could ever fulfill that call because of the enormous fear lurking inside, so I didn't confirm the invitation. "For ye have not received the spirit of bondage again to fear..." (Rom. 8:15 KJV) kept surfacing in my mind—but still I felt the spirit of fear hindering the Word from exploding from me.

Running late as usual one Monday night for a prayer meeting, a beautiful blonde lady smiled at me and said, "Hi there!" Then she gave me the biggest hug, just like that! Love just oozed out of her—so I asked around, "Who is she?" Someone told me who she was and that she was an intercessor, someone who prayed for people at length. In my heart I thought, *Wow—maybe she can pray for this fear of mine.* She seemed trustworthy.

To check her out a little more, I called my brother Rob and asked him to join me at one of her prayer meetings. He came from Oral Roberts University where he was studying to join me. She actually prayed and prophesied over us both, much to our surprise and said, "I see you working together alongside of each other helping many!"

It was so powerful that Rob and I just smiled and smiled.

Little did I know how effective the prayers of this mighty intercessor would prove in my life in the coming months as I entered into a new dimension of my spiritual walk—bolder and stronger.

Chapter 15

FEAR, THE GREATEST OBSTACLE

"As I think through it, I realize that my biggest fear wasn't rejection but being alone, friendless. Truthfully, even today, even with my faith, I sometimes sway to the fear of rejection, the kind that leads to loneliness, and that's exactly the enemy's plan."

———◦◦◦———

ONE day I mustered the courage to ask the intercessor for a private prayer session because I knew how powerfully my life had changed when God delivered me from bulimia and the fear associated with it. This time my fear was of public speaking and I knew that this would affect my future in whatever line of work I chose to do, if I didn't deal with it. At Rhema, we were supposed to be people of faith and power and I was afraid to admit weakness to a teacher.

"I'm so scared to get up in front of people," I confessed, "that's why I never really pursued acting I think...I get so...fear grips me! Sometimes I can press through it like for the Miss Missouri pageant but it was a miracle because I couldn't remember a word I said afterward...please help!"

"Honey! That's a spirit, and we're just going to get that little spirit right out of you!"

"I...I was so afraid to tell you what's going on in my life."

"Well," she said in her thick Southern belle drawl, "that's just like telling me you ate peanut butter and jelly for breakfast—it's no big deal! Jesus can take care of you."

For you did not receive the spirit of bondage again to fear, but you received the Spirit of adoption by whom we cry out, "Abba, Father." The Spirit Himself bears witness with our spirit that we are children of God (Romans 8:15-16).

I confessed my sins, she prayed, and I felt that spirit of fear lift as the presence of the Holy Spirit filled the room; then she ministered the life of God to me and I felt so free. Freedom so great that I felt 50 pounds lighter. With all intimidation gone, I was ready to go through any doors the Lord opened for me. I was so ready!

What are you personally afraid of? Inquire. Are you afraid of what the Lord might ask you to do? Corrie Ten Boom who was imprisoned in a Nazi concentration camp during the Second World War made a list of ten things she needed to get done for the day. Suddenly the Holy Spirit came on her and said, "Corrie, give me a blank sheet of paper."

"Why," she asked?

"Because I'm going to give you the things I want you to do for Me and none of them are on your list."

We need to give the Lord a blank sheet of paper and let Him fill it in with His desires and plans for our lives. What have your fears crossed out from God's list for you? Don't let fear abort your dreams!

LET GO OF PRIDE

Don't let pride keep you from being free from fear. It is a big problem in all of our lives today and even in leadership. People hide behind false fronts: religion, education, knowledge, or puffed-up righteousness—but God wants humble people. We should all be able to receive correction from someone who sees something not right in our lives, or at least when that happens, we should go to God and ask Him to expose what's not right. There's no way we can fulfill what He has for us unless we take care of those things because we leave doors open to the enemy to set us up for a fall.

It's vital to control fear. Open up and be honest with yourself and others about it. You must remove the mask that you wear and come out in the open. Recognize and acknowledge your fear and then get serious about dealing with it. What you don't acknowledge, you can't deal with! You must come to a point where you refuse to continue to coexist with fear. Sadly, too many people have grown accustomed to living with fear and see it as a way of life. They erroneously accept that this is just the way life is and always will be.

Some seek to anesthetize the pain of pervading anxiety with alcohol or drugs. Others turn to psychotherapy or hypnotism in an attempt to find peace. Still others seek relief by burying themselves in their work. What I have discovered is that there is only one real way to overcome fear, and that is by the power of God.

Here are some vital keys that I've used to crush the power of fear in my life:

1. Ask the Holy Spirit to show you the root causes of your fear.

2. Admit you have certain fears and ask God to forgive you.

3. Stop the "cover-up" and face fear head-on with friends you trust.

4. Humble yourself and turn your heart and mind toward God.

I caution you. Before you allow anyone to pray deliverance over you, look for spiritual fruit in his or her life and family. You only want a minister who is truly walking with the Lord to minister to you. Certainly God sent this godly woman along my path because my fear could have caused me to abort His plans for my life. Because of her intercession and prayers, I was set free from fear of man and fear of public speaking. Today, I appear on television to as many as 80 million people at a time, and I have no fear. I'm bold enough to talk on any platform that God calls me to. Thank You Jesus!

The proof of the pudding is in the eating. I confirmed the invitation to speak at the Women Aglow meeting, and from the moment I stepped behind the pulpit, I was a preaching machine! Fear wasn't there and the gift of God was released in my life. Transformed, I was astonished at His quick work in me and was totally a different person.

Driving home, Bobby turned to me and said, "Leigh, how did you do that?" He was in such shock that he pulled the car over to the side of the road and said again, "What happened to you? How did you flow in the gifts of the Spirit like that?"

I explained what God had done in my life—it was supernatural. Joyful tears flowed as I explained to him what had happened.

"Let's thank God for the great things He has done. He's truly set me free and I will preach to the nations. He truly set me free and I will speak wherever and to whomever God sends me."

From that day forward to this day, I don't care if I'm sharing or teaching 100 or 100 million people via international television, I can honestly say, "I have no fear" of speaking in public, and I have been to many nations. God is no respecter of persons—what He has done for me, He will do for anyone who wants help and deliverance.

DOES FEAR CONTROL YOU?

Probably the greatest deterrent to enjoying and succeeding in life is fear. Baseball Hall of Famer, Babe Ruth, said, "Never let the fear of striking out get in your way of hitting a home run."

What a ruthless tyrant fear is! Let me expose fear for you. Fear paralyzes, sabotages, sickens, suppresses, terrorizes, inflicts, exaggerates, lies, oppresses, and is just plain nasty.

Loneliness can be a byproduct of fear brought about by feelings of insignificance or unimportance for instance, that lead us to feel afraid of being laughed at or ignored. I can attest that loneliness is one of the most profound and disturbing experiences and so too it is for the majority; for loneliness echoes in the deepest chambers of our hearts. It's hard to believe that anyone on a planet of about six billion people could be lonely, but it's a reality. Mother Teresa described loneliness and the feeling of being unwanted as "the most terrible poverty." According to Mother Teresa's statement, I was dirt poor.

"Never let the fear of striking out get in your way of hitting a home run."

Former news anchor Doris McMillon said that she "used to think that success meant getting the big contract with a television station, becoming famous and making plenty of money...." She had all of that, but those things don't "satisfy our longings for significance."

Many people who are alone are not lonely, but for the most part, humankind fears loneliness—and the leading cause? Rejection. The nub of loneliness is the fear of rejection.

Fear of rejection may underlie many feelings of loneliness. I recall that fear of rejection at school. At 13 I was diagnosed with Sherman's Disease (curvature of the spine), and had to wear a back brace 24/7. In those days back braces were quite cumbersome, which meant I had to wear specially made outfits that would fit over the brace—the antithesis of cool for an adolescent! A healthy social life is vital to a young teenager, and all I could think about was how my classmates and peers reacted.

As I think through it, I realize that my biggest fear wasn't rejection but the thought of being alone, friendless. Truthfully, even today, even with my faith, I sometimes sway to the fear of rejection, the kind that leads to loneliness, and that's exactly the enemy's plan. He wants us to feel fearful of rejection, and thus distance ourselves from God. He wants our esteem to nose-dive. He wants to shroud who we are in Christ Jesus. He wants to take the surety out of our faith. To kill, steal, and destroy. Sadly, without the covering of praying, Christian parents or guardians, children are an easy target.

Fear paralyzed a woman I knew because earlier in her life she'd suffered physical abuse. Satan replayed this in her mind over and over like a cassette tape until she feared going outside, feared people, driving, and being in any situation that could possibly be an open door to "attack." Hers was an irrational world of "what might happen," and she was a mess! Personally, I know what it's like to suffer and live in such a prison because for months after that man assaulted me as a little girl, I was afraid to go to sleep, to go outside where he might see me, or even to be alone.

Please don't let fear stop you. There is hope! All of God's promises are for you. He can deliver you from your prison of abuse and feelings of hopelessness and failure. He did that for me. You can experience Christ's healing touch and be delivered from every manifestation of fear.

A friend of mine, a young woman in Tulsa, died at an early age of cancer. Prior to her illness, she'd lived in constant fear of not pleasing people, especially her mother and then it passed to her husband. She couldn't even think for herself. Fear begins in the mind, but it's a proven medical fact that if it's not dealt with, it will eventually affect one's body. A *psychosomatic disorder* is a physical disorder brought on by or made worse by one's emotional state. Researchers believe now that debilitating bouts of fear, stress, or anxiety can bring about serious disease. Fear can kill you physically as well as spiritually, and the only fix is to turn wholeheartedly to God and embrace the deliverance that only He can offer you.

IDENTIFY/EXPOSE FEAR

The feeling of fear is a natural reaction to unknown, uncomfortable, or dangerous things or circumstances. God gives every living creature the "instinct" to fight or flee these things and the temporary fear triggers an internal alarm that alerts us to the presence of danger and primes us to deal with it. In an emotionally healthy person, this fear is momentary until the brain decides what to do about it: fight or flee.

However, some people don't process the fear right away and that's when irrational fear invades their mind and fear mounts to terror, dread, or worse, causing depression, anxiety, heart palpitations, hyperventilating, and many other outward and inward detrimental manifestations. Webster's

Dictionary defines *fear* as "painful agitation in the presence of, or anticipation of danger; anxiety, loss of courage, and dread." It usually includes the idea of intense reluctance to face or meet a person or situation.

The good news is that we can survive in the face of fear. The Prince of Peace can guide you through the dark alleys of anxiety and alarming situations, as Paul so aptly pointed out to believers:

> *Finally, brethren, whatever things are true, whatever things are noble, whatever things are just, whatever things are pure, whatever things are lovely, whatever things are of good report, if there is any virtue and if there is anything praiseworthy—meditate on these things* (Philippians 4:8).

The Authority of the Believer

My story so far is typical of what many people have been through and suffered as the consequences of evil being done in their lives, whether that evil was done unintentionally or on purpose. So many Christians have lost part of their destiny because they're still in darkness. Jesus said that He came to set the captives free and release us from darkness. Luke 4 quotes from the Old Testament in my favorite Scripture, which says that right before your very eyes—today—right now you're in the reality of the fulfillment.[65] That very day, Jesus took those words to preach the Gospel to the poor, heal the brokenhearted, preach deliverance, restore sight to the blind, and set people at liberty. That's deliverance! God will restore the years the locust has eaten—those very things that are vital for a healthy, joyful, prosperous life, for He comes as Healer and Restorer, to set us free from the powers of darkness and to release us from our prisons, to give us back those satan-stolen

years. Yes, salvation secured our eternal destiny to be sure, but we still have to live on earth, and that's why He gave us deliverance and taught the disciples deliverance too. He told them to go out and do the things He taught them to do: preach the Gospel, heal the sick, cleanse the leper, cast out demons: *set people free* to see life restored. He gave them *His authority* to do so and they were amazed how that authority He gave them transformed the multitudes. But Jesus pointed out, "Don't rejoice at the authority; rejoice that your names are written in heaven!" (See Luke 10:17-20.)

Some argue that deliverance isn't biblical. Well, I believe that the Lord's Prayer that Jesus prayed is a prayer for deliverance. It is a blueprint for how we are to pray for ourselves and for others. It's perhaps the best-known prayer in the Bible and the most recited. Guess what? Smack dab in the middle of that prayer is: "Deliver us from evil" (Matt. 6:13; Luke 11:4 KJV). Now why do you think God would tell us to pray like that if deliverance wasn't something we should seek? Jesus was revealing to us that there's an ungodly dimension in the spirit realm—an evil realm that can cause us to suffer—but that Jesus can heal and deliver us from that evil.

Have you struggled with something that you just can't shake loose? Perhaps you've wrestled with it and you've tried everything: prayer and fasting, cures and remedies, or different physical or spiritual exercise regimes, yet you haven't experienced victory. Maybe poverty hounds you and you can't break free. Many fight battles but don't realize that they're spiritual battles. Paul tried to help us understand this when he wrote to the Church at Ephesus and told them that we're not wrestling flesh and blood (people), but spiritual powers (see Eph. 6:12). Thus, when we seek to walk in obedience and in relationship and step with Christ, the spiritual opponent tries to rob us of it. Although spiritual warfare is just one of many weapons we have, Jesus knew how vital it was for us to engage in spiritual warfare so that we could walk free.

Yes, we must pray faith-filled prayers, but we also must pray with understanding or else that faith can be misguided or not applied to the right problem. People perish without knowledge and understanding, and that's why many of us struggle today, for lack of knowledge of all that the Teacher taught concerning healing and how He came to set the captives free.

Deliverance won't get rid of all your problems, but it's not something to fear, either. You can engage in spiritual warfare in your life yourself or have someone else pray with you. It doesn't have to be loud or scary—it's not exorcism. Spirit-filled people are not possessed by evil spirits—it's impossible because the Holy Spirit possesses us. However, these spirits can torment us and oppress us, and that's what Jesus knew and came to release you of. A third of the healings that we know Jesus carried out were done in the ministry mode of deliverance.

Just casting out a demon isn't all there is to it though. There are fundamental issues to deal with as well as the strongholds of the mind (conditioning) that we have to re-learn—we do that by daily putting on the mind of Christ. We must also pray for outer and inner healing and deal with what God wants to deal with in our lives. Guaranteed, that can come through close relationship with Him. Walk with Jesus!

God doesn't only want you to pray when bad things happen, but to be in relationship with Him always so that when trouble nears you're already strong and strengthened in the Lord. Faith is active and should continually increase. When you're in daily relationship with Him, if something happens you'll be able to stand firm, even if you feel like fainting, because you'll know that you know that you know that in Christ and through Him you have victory.

A pattern that I had and that I still struggle with at times is that I can become so consumed with my problem or circumstance that I'm unable to see God's promises of provision in it. Do you recall the promises of God in

Psalm 91 listed in a previous chapter? Those are just some of the great things that God promises to those who abide with Him. If you're dealing with something agonizing or painful, something that causes you to be anxious or afraid, don't give up on Him or question His love for you. If you do, you'll tire in your faith. Ponder how big He is! He's more than you could ever imagine in your human mind. Surely the Creator of the universe can make your situation right. Remember Romans 8:28? *"And we know that all things work together for good to those who love God, to those who are the called according to His purpose"* (Rom. 8:28).

God assures us that He shares in our labor and that everything that happens will ultimately work into His plan for the good because we love Him and He has called us according to His design and purpose.

TAKE DOMINION

Real freedom from fear comes from an inner connectedness to the Father and a sense that we exist for a higher purpose. It is this awareness of our destiny that gives meaning to life and the ability to conquer fear when it raises its ugly head. We live in a dangerous world and times, and too many people—even God's people—have taken on an escapist mentality. They want to get off the planet and go home to Heaven. They see no relief from the fear of looming threats. But that is a myth. *Living free of fear is a choice.* You either choose to let fear wrap you in its tentacles or you make the decision to refuse to allow fear to control your life. Take the leap and move beyond fear. Recognize that the world's placebos are only temporary wound dressings that will not significantly help you in the end.

Fear makes you forget that you are an eternal being! Although you are just passing through this world, God created you to use your years here enjoying it and enjoying Him. Your outlook will determine how you live your life. If your focus is on all the temporal things surrounding you, you will live anxiously, consumed with the worries each day brings. But if you live with the daily realization of your connectedness to God who lives outside of time and circumstances, you will be filled with peace and purpose. Remember, He is the Way...the Truth...and the Life. And we are hidden in Him.

You are almost guaranteed to fail in life until you break the chains of fear. You cannot become wealthy without sorrow until you cast away your fear of failure. You cannot be a hero without facing the enemy and making the decision to stand and fight. You cannot get a college degree if you are afraid of exams. You cannot win an Olympic medal if you are afraid of the race. Courage, not caution, will bring you victory. And God will gift you with courage. If you ask and believe, it is yours. You must ask and keep on asking until each and every chain of fear binding you is broken and falls away. It will happen!

Part III

CAN YOU SAY "AWE"

RESTORING THE GLOW

Rejuvenate: To make young again; restore to youthful vigor, appearance; to restore to a former state, to make fresh or new again; to *return to life;* get or give new life or energy.[66]

OVER the years, I have successfully developed a line of skin care products. Many of these products help rejuvenate the skin through cleansing, exfoliation, moisturizing, hydrating, soothing, and calming the skin for a healthier, more youthful-looking glow. Later, you'll learn more of the creative wisdom God gave me for the creation and distribution of these products; nevertheless, right now I want to say that nothing works better at renewing and restoring the "glow" than Christ in you, the hope of glory, because Christ is the Morning Star, and the Restorer and the Repairer of the breach. In fact, He *is* the antidote to your outward countenance, as David attested saying, "God is the *health* of my countenance" in Psalm 42:11 and again in Psalm 43:5 (Ps. 42:11; 43:5 KJV). The key to a healthy countenance is Jesus who resides in the inner sanctuary of your heart.

He is alive, and if you've accepted Jesus as your personal Lord and Savior to rule and reign in you, to sit upon the very throne of your heart, then even when you mess up, and for all that the enemy seeks to destroy in your life, God will restore to you the joy of your salvation and renew your vigor. The key to building your life around what's *wrong* with your life is to build your life around what's *right with Him*! You've sinned and fallen short? Yes, we all have , but Jesus is your Defense Attorney! The devil is the prosecuting attorney and he demands execution of the Law, but Jesus went to your defense and He paid the price of your pardon so that God the Judge could set you free. When the devil reminds you of your past, all you have to do is look to your Defense Lawyer![67]

The blood of Jesus Christ cleansed you from all sin.

Jesus looks to the Father and pleads your case: "Father, forgive her. She's another one of Mine, Father, who has received Me and who has believed in Me as her advocate. She has received My defense and My sacrifice in her place and believes that I took her punishment for her. Therefore, Father, pardon her." God hands the pardon papers to Jesus and Jesus hands them to you as your accuser slithers away, defeated.

BARRENNESS

No matter what you've done, when you are repentant and seek forgiveness, God pardons you because Jesus took your place and died on Calvary's cross so that you could live. The only sacrifices He needs are a broken spirit, a broken and contrite heart. The blood of Jesus Christ cleansed you from all sin (1 John 1:7). His blood healed your diseases. His blood delivered you. His blood defends you. His blood lifts, firms, and restores!

Restore to me the joy of Your salvation, And uphold me by Your generous Spirit. O Lord, open my lips, And my mouth shall show forth Your praise. For You do not desire sacrifice, or else I would give it; You do not delight in burnt offering. The sacrifices of God are a broken spirit, A broken and a contrite heart— These, O God, You will not despise (Psalm 51:12,15-17).

Jesus can birth something new in you and change everything overnight. If you want peace, love, joy, forgiveness, freedom, or healing...if you want a relationship with your father...if you want the foundation right in the lives of your children...if you want your wayward spouse to come home, Jesus can restore these things to you. If you need anything restored in your life, Jesus is the answer.

For about six years, my husband, Bobbie Valentine, and I tried to conceive. Dearly wanting a child, I went to five doctors all over the U.S., and they didn't offer me much hope given the severity of my injuries from the car accident and other medical conditions.

"I'm sorry," the doctors said.

Let me tell you something—you will never hear those words from God! He won't say, "I'm sorry Leigh, but I cannot restore your womb." He says, "I *can restore*." He's God of the impossible! In an encounter with God, He told me, "Leigh, I want you *to believe* Me for a son," and I stood on the promises of "yes," and "amen!" So be it Lord, so be it!

I got pregnant, and God gave us a healthy boy! The doctor said it couldn't be done, and satan confirmed it, but God kiboshed those facts and negative thoughts and restored my womb. Today Joshua is a 15-year-old mighty young man who serves God. He wants to sing and preach for God—hallelujah! A mother couldn't ask for more! The gates of hell will not prevail against you. He can take a barren physical or spiritual womb, restore it to health, and fill it.

The enemy wants to deplete both. He doesn't want children raised up in God's way because this coming generation will be an army generation, with faces set like flint, radical obedient soldiers bent on destroying the works of darkness. Satan doesn't want you to birth your spiritual destiny either, or even get near the pangs of labor. In fact, he is hell-bent on preventing you from conceiving a God-given vision—but listen, when God wants to restore, He will restore!

PASSION DRIVES TRANSFORMATION

The enemy wants to blind you to what's available for restoration because he knows that once you're restored, you will go about speaking life into others. People will want transformation, but more importantly, the Transformer. They'll see your transformation and say, "It must be God."

Transformation happens when you have passion. The enemy hates passion in God's children! Passion awakens us from the slumber of indifference to pursue the scent of the impossible! It's the fire of life and the energy of the soul! It is the wind that gives loft to the eagle, lifting it above the masses locked in the drudgery of apathetic inactivity. It is the fire that warms the heart in the midst of the coldness of a culture set adrift. It is a person's friend in the dark hours of the night when others abandon him. It is the inner support that keeps us awake in the night seasons when others are fast asleep. It is the power for the race, the propulsion for the jet, the spark for the fire, the wind for the sail, and the contractions for the birth!

Have you experienced the transforming power of passion? Passion brings forth a harvest of dreamers and visionaries. It is the dynamic link that connects a dream to its reality. A dream is not enough; it always must be accompanied by the intensity of passion and prayer that drives one into the impossible and often invisible.

Passion is what separates the famous from the millions who only dream of success. Passion is what keeps an athlete going back to practice on the days when his or her knees and muscles scream for time off. Passion is what helped Victor Frankl and Corrie Ten Boom and sadly only a few others survive the horrors of the Nazi concentration camps. Passion kept Thomas Edison on task when he failed over 150 times in his quest to create electric light.

Without passion, your dreams will fail. Passion is one of the greatest keys to success and it will unlock the door to incredible possibilities. God might have to create a storm or two to get your attention before He can get you into that place of restoration and passion. Listen, when Jonah ran away, God sent a storm to reveal his sin and to separate Jonah from the innocent crew aboard the ship bound for Tarsus. God saved the crew and then sent a whale to save Jonah from drowning after the crew tossed him overboard.

God could have just wrung His hands, shaken His head and said, "I'm done with you, Leigh! Over you go, and there won't be a whale this time to save you. I've tried to teach you My ways, but you just haven't listened!" He didn't do or say that. God didn't even try to find someone else to fill the high heels of my divine calling. Instead, He extended His great grace to me and of course, I kicked off my heels and on bended knee cried out in repentance. Then I put those puppies right back on and passionately set out to pursue high places with God.

THE CRIPPLING SPIRIT

There was a time when I got it right, but I lived it all wrong. I understood, but I didn't apply what I knew to my life and therefore, I lived in defeat. This defeat caused me to withdraw from the presence of the Father in secret shame. There were areas of my life that desperately needed rebuilding, but the enemy blinded me and tried to keep those things hidden. I had alienated myself from God because of the sheer mounting weight of these burdens. These became crippling yokes that caused weariness and lack of resolve, and if I had recognized those places of pain and cried right away for healing, I wouldn't have suffered as long as I did.

In the story of the woman with a spirit that had crippled her for 18 years (see Luke 13:10-17), the Bible doesn't reveal what particular disease, disorder, sickness, or other infirmity; it simply says, "...there appeared a woman with a *spirit*..." (see Luke 13:10)—a spirit of an evil nature. Jesus walked into the room where she was and discerned something diabolically oppressive—such that its weight caused her to stoop under its burden. This is what happens to us when we're under the weight of a crippling spirit. We can't walk upright! But guess what? The woman didn't ask Jesus to heal her; she wasn't in that frame of mind. Rather, Jesus called her to Him, laid hands on her, and said, "Woman, you are *set free* from your ailment" (see Luke 13:12). Immediately she stood upright and began to praise Him.

He was right there, she was in His presence, but still she didn't ask Him for His help, just as we sometimes don't because of the crippling spirit that takes all hope for healing out of us. It can cause depression such that you can't even imagine God in the situation. If you don't look to Him as soon as possible, the crippling spirit will bleed expectation right out of you and even cause you to fear your own transformation with thoughts as *How can I live without that man...even though he's an alcoholic, he pays the bills. What if I go hungry?* These are irrational thoughts when you are confident enough in the Creator of the universe who can heal and restore anything; but they are rational thoughts to someone so stooped over by depressive and oppressive spirits that he or she doesn't recognize that Jehovah Rapha (God the Healer) is in the house!

GOD MAKES IT UP TO YOU

God wants you to be free—and He'll lead you into freedom. That's why He's so worthy of our praise at all times. All Jesus had to do was take one look at this woman and He knew that it was time to get her free and standing upright.

Not all of us will ask for healing because although we get it right, some live it wrongly. Jesus then steps in and tears down the obstacle, in this case the crippling spirit, for us.

When bulimia controlled my life, I assumed I had to hide it in the shadows. Shamed by it, I actually believed that if I couldn't handle that yoke on my own, something serious was wrong with me, even my relationship with Christ. This is how the devil manipulates us, and sometimes we get to that point of not even being able to recognize our burden or cry for help from someone. We don't ask because people will think we're weak.

There's never shame in asking for help! Jesus says, "Cry to Me and I will answer you!" That's a promise!

Call to Me, and I will answer you, and show you great and mighty things, which you do not know (Jeremiah 33:3).

He shall call upon Me, and I will answer him; I will be with him in trouble; I will deliver him and honor him. With long life I will satisfy him, and show him My salvation (Psalm 91:15-16).

The enemy may even use people to hurl accusations at you like, "What will people say if they find out you're suffering torment?" or "If you can't control this part of your life, how can I ever trust you?"

Rejoice! That means you're on the right road to healing because the devil will try to stop you any way he can. When you are weak, then God is strong! Transformation: restoration and rebuilding glorifies Him! God will deal with the devil as Jesus lays His hands on you and calls out that crippling spirit so that your light rises in the darkness making the gloom as noonday!

What has crippled you? What's affecting you right now? An eating disorder? Alcoholism? Guilt from having an abortion? A failed marriage? Broken body image? A void left by a loved one? Financial woes? Poor health? A runaway child? Family dysfunction? Job loss? Depression? Wayward children? Physical or sexual abuse? Lack of self-esteem? Feelings of unworthiness? Has the church hurt you? Do people ostracize you? If anything hunches you over, let Jesus lay His hand upon your shoulder and then lean into freedom and experience restoration. Then, as the woman did in the Bible, praise and give honor and glory to the Creator who made you whole and upright.

Had I not eventually accepted the grace of God's mercy, healing, and forgiveness, I would have never been able to walk upright again. The point is that I had to get up again! The process of tearing down and building up was necessary to build character, to mold my heart as His, to smooth out my tattered edges so I could be the voice in the Ninevehs of earth, shouting God's love and grace for all to hear. His forgiveness and restoration wrecked me, and it will wreck you for the right reason—Jesus!

This is what the Word of God says will happen when you call to Him to remove the yokes.

What has crippled you?

...If you take away the yoke from your midst, the pointing of the finger, and speaking wickedness, if you extend your soul to the hungry and satisfy the afflicted soul, then your light shall dawn in the darkness, and your darkness shall be as the noonday. The Lord will guide you continually, and satisfy your soul in drought, and strengthen your bones; you shall be like a watered garden, and like a spring of water, whose waters do not fail. Those from among you shall build the old waste places; you shall raise up the foundations of many generations; and you shall be called the Repairer of the Breach, the Restorer of Streets to Dwell In ...Then you shall delight yourself in the Lord; and I will cause you to ride on the high hills of the earth, and feed you with the heritage of Jacob your father... (Isaiah 58:9-12,14).

Do you know what this means?

1. You will have answers.

2. The darkness will lift off you.

3. You will be guided constantly!

4. He will satisfy and strengthen you!

5. You'll have good health and strong bones.

6. You'll flourish!

7. You'll have great favor!

8. You'll have restoration.

9. You will walk in the blessings.

The enemy will try to prey on your wasted years. How much of your life did you permit the cankerworm to eat? Of course we all wish we hadn't squandered the time through our sin and rebellion that we could have spent walking in the blessings—God knows our hearts on that matter. The closer we draw to Jesus, the more broken we become, the more shame we feel, the more unworthy: *How can I live with myself knowing how much Jesus loves me and yet still sin? How could I have hurt Him so badly? How come I didn't trust Him enough to give Him my yoke right away? He said His yoke was easy and His burden light, why didn't I listen? Why did I covet money more than I did God? How can I make it up to Him?*

Honey, it's not about making it up to God! He makes it up to you! He says "I will restore...." As long as there's breath and life in you, there is still hope for God to save you. As long as there's still breath in your children, there's still that hope. The Lord says, "Don't fear but be glad and rejoice and I will do great things in your life."[68]

Listen, there's a lot of dirt and debris in our lives that God has swept away, but the accuser will try to tell you differently. Paul said to forget the past and reach forth to Jesus; press toward the mark for the prize of your high calling of God in Christ Jesus.[69]

Don't trip in the dust of your mistakes! Ensure the enemy eats that dust! Kick your heels, shake it off, and move forward!

CONSIDER HOW YOU RESPOND...

We may not be able to prevent hardship, but we can change the way we respond in a situation. We often give the devil more credit than he deserves. How often have you said something like: "The enemy is attacking me so badly right now," instead of, "Wow, another opportunity for God to show Himself strong?" Immediately take it to God and give it to Him and then watch the devil tremble!

Most human suffering is caused by people wronging others.

Not everything bad is directly attributable to the enemy; sometimes we bring things about ourselves, and sometimes things are a result of living in a fallen world. The world now is not the way God created it but is the result of sin, which brought us suffering, disease, sickness, disasters, and accidents.

We have choices to make. Sometimes we make the wrong choices and open the door to consequences. Many of the people that I counsel wonder how they get into such messes and why there are so many consequences in their lives. We can't rebuke consequences, but we can beg for mercy. God created us with free will to choose. Wrong choices affect others and us. Most human suffering is caused by people wronging others.

Listen, if you eat a high fat diet and then have a heart attack, who's to blame? If you drink and drive and then cause an accident, or get caught driving while under the influence, who's to blame?

Repentance is vital. God is more concerned about your soul than He is about the enemy of your soul. He says, "If you would just humble yourself and pray and seek My face and turn from your wicked ways, then I will hear you and will forgive your sin...."[70]

Daniel understood the need to be humble and repentant. He prayed and confessed on behalf of God's people who were in captivity. He admitted that they had been out of alignment with God, that they had rebelled and turned away from His commandments, and had not earnestly begged for forgiveness or fervently sought the favor of the Lord that they might turn from their sins and learn and grow from them.[71]

Surrender and obedience freed the Israelites from bondage. It was only when Daniel sought repentance through confession of the sins of the people that God quickly sent the archangels to battle the prince of Persia.

Being in the will of God means safety, hope, health, and prosperity. When we're not in His will, we set ourselves up for making wrong choices and then the consequences. This creates also a void that becomes a place for the enemy to establish footholds because we are out of the center of God's will, which gives satan access. As soon as you find yourself away from God, repent, confess, and get back into His presence, practicing what He teaches in His Word.

When God does deliver us out of something brought about by a wrong choice, He does it to get us back into His will and moving forward in His plans and purposes for our lives. In light of His deliverance, we would do well not to venture out of His will and into the sin, because it may not be as easy to get out of trouble the next time. God is full of grace and merciful, but like any good parent He sets His boundaries and limits.

Ask God to help you discern your situation. Is it a spiritual attack or a consequence of your action? Did you open a door to the enemy? Did you make a wrong choice? Have you been away from God? Examine yourself and then see what's not lining up with His Word. Get in right agreement with Him, and when He shows you where you made the wrong turn, ask the Holy Spirit to help you get back onto the right path.

It's a walk of faith whereby you go to the throne of grace and ask God for what you need by faith, and then wait upon Him with the knowledge that you are His child, whom He loves and will not let down.

You can tear down the darkness through confession and repentance and the forgiveness of others and storm the gates of hell, reminding satan that Jesus is Lord.

Trust too, that once you're back on track satan won't like it one bit and will try to prevent you from pressing in. He'll fight your finances, relationships, health, peace and joy, and the battle may come through people you love. But remember all of the good that God will bring out of it, and learn how to employ the greatest weapon in your arsenal—the Sword of the Spirit, the powerful Word of God. You are more than a conqueror! You are an overcomer, not one overcome, because Jesus overcame the world. Remember that the next time you cry out to God. If possible, through your tears, try not to complain, "Oh woe is me," and instead praise Him for Who He Is: the Great I Am, the Beginning and the End, the First and the Last, your Creator God who is bigger than your problems. He's on your side!

FROM PIT TO PALACE

"Peter, this is Leigh Middleton and I'm calling because I know that I am the right one for this position."

———◇———

RECOGNIZING OPPORTUNITY

WE can be abounding with passion, talents, and giftings, but if we aren't looking for open doors whereby we can demonstrate and use these things we might miss the boat! A Roman philosopher, Seneca, said that luck is when preparation meets opportunity, but I don't believe in luck. It's *divine favor*!

Favor will come to those who are walking in the pathway that leads them to their purpose.

Now therefore, listen to Me, My children, for blessed are those who keep My ways. Hear instruction and be wise, and do not disdain it. Blessed is the man who listens to Me, watching daily at My gates, waiting at the posts of My doors. For whoever finds Me finds life, and obtains favor from the Lord (Proverbs 8:32-35).

Lance Wallnau, life coach to many successful people in the business and political worlds, describes favor as the affection of God toward you that releases an influence through you so that other people are inclined to like, trust, and cooperate with you. Favor creates an atmosphere around you where opportunities become realities.

The problem with opportunity is that it is sometimes hard to recognize. Most of us are waiting for the "big one" to come along, something recognizable and undeniable! We expect opportunity to come at us with beepers and billboards. Little opportunities often lead to big opportunities. If we are unwilling to seize the little opportunities and be grateful for them, we may not be entrusted with bigger opportunities.

Back when I interviewed for the plum job with Revlon I wasn't quite sure that I even had the necessary credentials for the national beauty consultant position. The opportunity was incredible and would involve travel every month between St. Louis, where my parents and brother lived, and Philadelphia, where my good friends Joel and Mindy Chernoff lived. I prayed, "Jesus, please, please, let me get this position...please give me this job, I need Your favor Jesus."

The first interview with Peter, a representative with Revlon, went great but in the second step of the interview process, I'd have to meet with other consultants to see if they liked me. *Oh Jesus, please help me now!* I started having doubts. *I'm too young...I'm only 22.* I thought about my lack of experience. *Because I had won the Miss Missouri pageant, I knew something about beauty,* I thought. I also knew a little about sales from what my mother taught me, but I was insecure. Suddenly I felt ugly and stupid. Would they

think me naïve? Every insecurity from my past reared as I stepped into the interview room, into what I saw as a den of wolves.

My future was at stake. This was my chance to significantly advance my career and a great opportunity such as this wouldn't come around often. The beautiful and bright woman I would be replacing had suddenly accepted a higher profile job with a competitor. This was only one position for which many girls, much more qualified and beautiful than me, were flying in from all over the U.S. for the interview. It was a prominent, exciting position that also required credible and professional references.

Still young in the Lord and with not much of God's Word yet buried in my heart, I did recall that the Lord loves to give His children the desires of their hearts and I clung to that promise.

Michael prayed with me and then reminded me of the favor that was upon Joseph when God elevated him to the second highest position in Egypt. For weeks I prayed throughout the day believing God's favor upon me with Revlon; believing God could cause me to stand out in a crowd as Joseph did.

A month went by after the interview. Nothing happened. Peter interviewed many women. Through the grapevine, finally I heard it was down to three. Oh wow! I felt the urge to pray and fast and I did that that with all my heart. I prayed as I awoke, as I went to work, as I fell asleep.

One night I felt the Lord impress upon me to call Peter. I mustered the courage, not wanting to bother or annoy him. My adrenalin ran high as the phone rang. His wife answered and said he was on the road and out of reach. *Could this mean the job was taken…maybe he was there but just didn't want to tell me I didn't get it.* Despair festered in me for a second, but then I thought, *Hey, this job belongs to me. I know God wants me to have it. I'm not giving up.* I prayed once again and reminded God that He loves to give good things to

His children and then I picked up the phone and dialed Peter's number again.

"Please forgive me," I said to his wife. "But may I call Peter at his hotel, I must speak to him." Once I explained why I needed to contact him, she kindly relented and gave me his hotel phone number.

"Peter, this is Leigh Middleton and I'm calling because I know that I am the right one for this position."

"I tried to reach an applicant all last week to offer her the job," explained Peter, "but haven't been able to tee up with her. I really need to hire someone quickly and I was hoping she would call. Listen. I like your personality and your persistence. You're not experienced, but you light up a room when you walk in—the job is yours."

Thank You Jesus for the new car, the big base salary, the awesome contract with bonuses, the stock allowances, *and* the expense account! The blessings of God overwhelmed me!

Thank God that I heard the Holy Spirit tell me to call when I did, and am I glad I listened. For almost three years I worked for Revlon and got to fly home every month all expenses paid to be with my family. My mother and I drew very close at this time and had fun when she'd accompany me to my stores. While I met with the cosmetic executives and sales people, she'd shop, eat lunch, and sit and have a coffee in a roadside café. This was Mary's favorite thing to do.

FAVOR AND DOING *YOUR* PART

Sometimes we create our own opportunities by our own efforts that are strengthened by God's power. If opportunity doesn't knock, we might have to prayerfully build a door or we might miss the opportunity because we are sitting around waiting for something to plop in our lap. Opportunities come to those who seek them, who put themselves out there in places where they can be found. Thomas Edison said that most people missed opportunity because it is dressed in overalls and looks like work!

> *Thomas Edison said that most people missed opportunity because it is dressed in overalls and looks like work!*

Whether you've built a door or if God provides the door, if we do our part, He will do His. We really have to be in tune to His voice and listen to His direction without asking, "Why?" We need to react immediately to His voice.

Many of us wish we could start over, go back and do things differently; but if you're to start a brand-new life of victory you'll have to be in that place where you expect God's favor because success depends on it. Divine favor opens the right doors and attracts the right people into our lives.

Favor will take you from the pit to the palace. As God's child you are of royal blood—the King's kid—and He can raise you up to high places.

The story of Joseph is a great example of how God's favor works. Joseph's favor with his father angered his siblings, and one day they attacked him while he visited them at work in their father's fields. They threw him into a pit and had every intention of leaving him to die.

A caravan came by and they sold Joseph into slavery instead of leaving him to die. Imagine the rejection Joseph must have felt. Just the grieving and a broken and wounded heart could have killed him. Imagine losing your entire family, and now you're in a strange country with no worship or acknowledgement of your God. But God's hand of mercy, grace, power, and favor was upon this young man because he refused to look back and be offended by his circumstances.

Favor will take you from the pit to the palace.

I can relate to Joseph because I have experienced the same rejection that I'm sure he felt in that pit when his very own brothers turned their backs on him in his time of need. I've had that happen before with friends, even close friends, family members, colleagues in ministry, and even business associates, where someone has believed an untruth, has pre-judged, or even become resentful, alienating me or throwing me into a figurative isolated pit. The pain of some of these situations has been almost more than I could bear at times. But the last two years, especially, the resultant pain has drawn me closer to the Lord. In some instances, especially where believers were concerned, I still find it hard to believe that I could be treated so cruelly and judged so harshly. Thankfully, not all of my friends, sisters, and colleagues are like that!

We have to be resilient, as Joseph was. He didn't allow despair and disappointment to rule his life.[72]

God has blessed me with a successful skin care business. He creatively gave me formulas and brought the right professional people into my life to help me develop them. The resultant products have been a huge success in my business, *Valentine Spa Collection.* Surely there were scientists with tons more scientific training and better able than I was to come up with what I did, but God showed me favor.

Why did God choose me for these great things? Why did He choose me as a worthy vessel? For the same reason He chose Moses the stutterer to be a great leader! He loves us and gives us divine favor when we submit to Him, die to our desires, seek His direction and guidance, and willingly obey Him. Don't think for a moment that it has anything to do with luck! Take that word right out of your vocabulary, because God's divine influence in your life will get you to the place of prospering.

Not one of us deserves God's favor. We certainly don't merit it. He favors us when He knows us to be faithful to use what He gives us to do His will, and that often takes knowledge and wisdom. Seeking God's wisdom and knowledge in pursuit of Him will place you in position for advancement and promotion.

Favor is also about divine appointments; that is, meeting the right people at the right time and doors of influence opening as a result. When God's favor is on you, trust that supernatural empowerment will get the job done! It's transference of the ordinary to the extraordinary things of God. God sets us up for success.

AWAY YOU GO!

Ask yourself if you are aligned with His will? Are you willing to listen and go?

The heavens declare His glory and the skies proclaim the work of His hands![73] The sun is one of the smallest stars in the galaxy and yet big enough that if hollow, would hold more than one million planet Earths inside of it! That said, there are stars big enough to hold a half billion suns with room to roll around inside. There are 100 billion stars, give or take a few billion, in our galaxy alone, and there are thought to be over 100 million galaxies in just our universe. That's just for starters. God created all of that! Some CEO we serve!

When you're rooted in Christ Jesus—when you're in daily fellowship with Him, you will grow to know greater measures of the width and length and depth and height of His love and greatness. You will learn to grasp just how mighty, willing, and able He is to turn your circumstances around.

Apostle Paul, full of the fullness of God, wrote to the Church:

That He would grant you, according to the riches of His glory, to be strengthened with might through His Spirit in the inner man, that Christ may dwell in your hearts through faith; that you, being rooted and grounded in love, may be able to comprehend with all the saints what is the width and length and depth and height—to know the love of Christ which passes knowledge; that you may be filled with all the fullness of God. Now to Him who is able to do exceedingly abundantly above all that we ask or think, according to the power that works in us, to Him be glory in the church by Christ Jesus to all generations, forever and ever (Ephesians 3:16-20).

When you get filled up, (which doesn't mean you're satisfied, just filled and desire to get more and more full), you'll be just as fervent and full of awe and zeal as Paul was in writing this passage of Scripture. When you're full of God you're full of His love, His power, and His favor!

You have glorious privileges, riches, and blessings as the Father's child. How can these things, so far above our own ability ever become a reality? God. Only He is able to do exceedingly abundantly *above and beyond* all that we ask or think, or hope for.

In 1984, and after our graduation from Rhema Bible Training Center, I attended a special information fair on campus where we could interview with churches in need of leadership. When I got home I said, "Oh Bobby,

maybe we can get a church in Washington D.C. or pastor Virginia! Wouldn't that be something!"

At the booth that the Holy Spirit had led me to, was a young, attractive couple, Randy and Cherie Gilbert who pastored Faith Landmarks Ministries church in Richmond, Virginia. After chatting for a while, they said that they would love to meet my husband and take us both out for dinner.

At dinner, they shared more about their church outreach and then said, "The church we'd like you to consider is not our Virginia church, or one in Washington, but an outreach church in New York City."

"New York City! Did you say 'New York City?' " That's where I'd hoped to become an actor. I was in shock. Never did I think I would ever pastor there, much less be there. Excitement stirred in my heart. But how could we afford the move? We didn't even have two dimes to rub together.

"But first we'd like you to come out to our church in Virginia and preach."

We did and everyone seemed to like us, so we were placed as pastors of their New York church located in Manhattan. We called the ministry, Heart to Heart World Outreach Center. At the time, the church didn't have a permanent location and met in various hotels. Our greatest challenge was finding an apartment that we could afford because everything was so expensive. We had no money to speak of, just a credit card and our personal belongings packed into the trailer we towed behind the car. We were like real missionaries because we had to believe God for money—every day, even for subway fare. We had to completely trust him for money, for food—we barely had essentials. We arrived with nothing.

At first we stayed with Bobbie's relatives on Long Island, and then with a wealthy acquaintance on Park Avenue until we finally found a place to live–a quaint, old apartment on the upper west side. At first it seemed out of reach because there was a three-year waiting list and they required a big rental deposit. "Lord, You know what we need to do Your work," was the cry of my heart.

The morning following the day we viewed the place, the fellow, Abraham, who owned the property whom we'd only *spoken* to on the phone, called. "I don't know why I'm doing this or why I'm even saying this, but I couldn't sleep all night thinking about you two and I haven't even met you!"

"That was God keeping you awake," I said to this nice Jewish man while praising God under my breath.

"Listen," Abraham said, "I'm going to give it to you and bypass the waiting list and waive the deposits—just move in!"

Favor, favor. The favor of God.

Because the church only met on Sunday and Wednesday evenings, I had to supplement our income, especially because Bobby spent most of his time at home studying and preparing for sermons. Within the first 15 minutes of walking into the store, I got a job at the Estée Lauder counter of Bloomingdales.

"Lord," as I often prayed, "We've got to make more money—You have to bring in more finances."

Enter a woman who stops by the counter to purchase makeup. "You know, you'd be perfect—so perfect...!"

"Perfect for what?"

"Well, I'm a talent scout and I think you'd be perfect for our new Slim-Fast commercial."

It was one miracle after another in New York!

Later that evening and after I had a chance to talk it over with Bobby, she called and I told her I was interested. This was something I'd wanted to do before my accident. The following morning a beautiful limousine stopped by to pick me up and the doorman said as I left the building, "Wow...you're really moving up in the world."

At the studio where I was to interview and then audition for the role, I thought I was back at the Miss Missouri pageant—there were two other girls auditioning for the same role and the battle for the "title" was on. We went through multiple screen tests and grueling shots in front of the camera. Finally, at 11:00 P.M., the producer pointed to the two other girls and said, "You can go home now, thanks for your time." Then he turned around to me and said, "You're our new Slim-Fast girl, congratulations."

So here was God, fulfilling a desire of my heart I had as a young girl, while getting me ready for even greater dreams to walk in. Now we had income from the commercials, and I also became a member of the Screen Actor's Guild. Whenever I was on set, I took the opportunity to witness to the members of the set crew, and to the various actors that I met, such as Brook Shields, Tony Bennett, Diana Ross, and others. Thus, everyone knew I was a Christian. One day as I went to film, someone said, "Hey Leigh, some of your people will be here today."

What people? I thought.

They'll be serving us lunch, in fact," he said.

"My people?" What people?

Just as I walked off set, I saw the gourmet catering service truck: *Brooklyn Caterers—Caterers for Jesus Christ.* Wouldn't you know it—these were first-class caterers on *my* set and they served the most incredible food you can imagine.

IN DUE SEASON

Sundays and Wednesdays I spent being the pastor's wife and my life comprised day-to- day things of the church as well as acting, modeling, and fulltime work. By and by, we both felt led to start a church as well in Connecticut that would feed the hungry and provide a Bible School. We birthed "Heart to Heart Ministries" there. My heart was to preach though, and I kept asking God and Bobby, "When can I preach?"

"You put everyone to sleep, Leigh..."

One day Bobby unexpectedly said, "OK Leigh, I'm giving you a chance. Next Sunday is your day."

I poured into the Word, made copious notes and prepared like crazy to be organized so when Sunday came all of my papers were neatly stacked and organized atop the pulpit—more as though I was about to teach rather than preach.

"You put everyone to sleep, Leigh," Bobby said. "It was the most boring sermon I've ever heard." Oh how his words broke my heart. I could hear from the tone of his voice that I should just go and do my modeling thing because "you're just not called into the ministry—that's obvious."

"God, what's up?"

"Why are you trying to teach, Leigh?

"Well," I told Him, "I've got to teach the Word, don't I?"

"Yes...but that's not what I've called you to do!"

"What *am* I called to do, then, Lord? Please tell me." I mean, I just couldn't figure it out!

"You're called to *preach*."

OK, and praise the Lord, but still I was confused. "How does that look? I mean, I've only ever seen a few women preach and when they did they always had tons of teaching notes with them."

"Just trust Me and preach!"

I seriously doubted I'd ever be called upon to preach again. But one Sunday morning Bobby woke up feeling ill. "I'm too sick to even lead praise and worship, Leigh, so you'll have to do that and preach as well—but don't go longer than 20 minutes, and we'll make up the rest of the time praying for the sick or something."

Help me Jesus! I wasn't prepared and I ran and hid behind a popcorn machine that was in the theater-turned-church and said, "Oh Jesus!—I don't know what I can speak on—I haven't got even one note—how will I possibly handle this? I'm not prepared!"

No notes, not even a scrap of paper and no time for a scribble. I had no message. Praise God, I got up there and the power of God hit me and I preached my heart out. Never having experienced that before, it was the most exciting moment by far in my life! Bobby just sat there looking dazed and shocked as people shouted, "Amen," and excitement mounted as I pressed in with God's anointed message. Twenty minutes? Naw. God had me go for two whole hours and then just as I closed the meeting, the power of God moved mightily among the people.

"Why don't you let your wife preach more often," people said to Bobby and no one was more shocked than I was! But you see, I couldn't get to that point or any significant point in my life if I didn't first start off somewhere, and I did that by humbling myself and submitting myself to God, and He exalted me in due season. This was my due season; trust that He will promote you in your due season.

Bobby wasn't altogether overjoyed by my success, and it saddened me that he didn't receive the gift God had given me very well. He still didn't think I was called, but in my spirit, I could see it! I had a vision that God had planted in me, a vision so clear that I could see the people and the souls I would preach to!

People may come against God's call on your life for a variety of reasons; but as you cry out to God and begin to walk in the things of Him, He will bring the very ones who agitated you together because iron sharpens iron. The enemy will try to separate you from your brothers and sisters in Christ because he loves to stir disunity, agitation, and strife, and likely, he'll cause division between you and someone God has sent to you. Fight for the relationship and don't let the enemy steal those friends who are friends because of God.

It wasn't long before God moved me into preaching more regularly, but not only at my church. The launch of my worldwide ministry took only 30 days! Yes, in 30 days, the windows of Heaven opened unto me!

One day upon returning home to our tiny New York City apartment, we got a call about a request that had come into our church to host an upcoming prosperity and prayer breakfast with author/speaker Norvel Hayes.

Although Norvel had met me before at a Rhema Camp Meeting, and another time in Dallas where revival had broken out at Bob Tilton's church, he wouldn't have remembered me, although he did know my best friend.

As I washed our dinner dishes, I overheard Bobby talking to someone from the church on the telephone about how we somehow needed to do a phone blitz of all of the pastors, ministry leaders, and business/marketplace leaders in the area, to ensure a good turnout for the early morning breakfast. Something irked Bobby in the phone conversation, and things heated up. I heard him say something like, "Well, they can just find someone else to do the work!" and then he slammed down the receiver.

At that moment, the Holy Spirit spoke to my heart. "That someone, is you, Leigh."

Uh oh. That would be difficult—I was busy enough as it was what with working full time at Bloomingdales and church obligations. I had little available time available, and I only had 30 days to put the whole thing together! Nevertheless, I knew it was the Lord's heart that there was a good turnout. I sensed that not only did the Lord want to bless Norvel with a full house, but I "saw" the bigger picture—God bringing unity and a coming together of different denominations. I worked the phones every free minute, encouraging ministers and their wives to come into the city from Long Island, Brooklyn, Staten Island, Queens, the Bronx, and surrounding outlying areas for the early morning breakfast.

There was so much to do!

On the day of the meeting at 7:00 A.M., it was better than we could have ever hoped—we had a packed audience and Norvel, as he always does, had the crowd on the edge of their seats as He taught from the Word of God. The anointing was so strong as he encouraged and motivated leaders to keep "fighting" the demons in New York City, for breakthrough.

At the end of the breakfast meeting, as Norvel thanked the business people who had contended for him to come to New York to speak, he said: "Now where is this blond-headed girl I've heard about who worked so hard to push all of you out of bed so early, to come hear me speak—she deserves thanks for all that she's done!"

As I stood up, the room thundered with applause, and later Norvel .asked us to lunch at the famous Oyster Bar Restaurant in Grand Central Station. Bobby and I had some time with Norvel to talk about our church, Heart to Heart World Outreach Center, and then Norvel suddenly asked, "Honey, tell me a little about yourself and what Jesus has done for you."

What followed I'll never forget. The power of God hit the table as I gave a brief version of my testimony. Then Norvel invited *me* to *preach* at his Bible school in Cleveland, Tennessee! Praise God—in 30 days God had launched me in my speaking ministry.

The first time I preached was during a week-long camp meeting, and I preached in the afternoon services when the crowds weren't large. But word got out about the anointing upon my life and the crowds grew and grew. Before long, Norvel invited me to share my testimony at the larger night-time meetings when he taught, and eventually to teach, speak, and preach at functions with him all over the U.S., including Chicago, St. Louis, Palm Springs, and Miami. People by the thousands attended these meetings, My ministry exploded overnight. After consulting with Bobby, I quit work and traveled full time to preach all over the world, and eventually, was able to bring my baby son Josh along on the trips. I couldn't keep up with all of the invitations. Suddenly I was everywhere—flying all over the U.S. and the world, with appearances on Christian television like TBN and the 700 Club. I also released my first book, *Overcoming the Sprit of Fear.*

At first, Bobby didn't like the thought of me being away, but then he felt the Lord tell him to release me into what He'd called me to and he relented. Again, he was content staying home to study and pastored the church in Connecticut. We had secured my brother Rob Middleton to assist with leadership, and a great couple, Marcos and Nydia Manrique to pastor the New York City church.

HOW BIG IS YOUR GOD?

Maybe your God is too small. Do you know Father God, the One who cannot only do more than you ask, not only more than you think, but exceedingly abundantly above all that you think or ask? God not only was able in the beginning, but beginning right now in your life He can do the impossible, all that is above your own ability because it is according to the power that works in you, right now. Paul prayed that we would be strengthened in might according to His riches and let me tell you, God is rich! He has an enormous, endless, eternal storehouse from which to draw. Paul also prayed that strength would come through the Holy Spirit and that it would be deposited into your inner being.[74]

GOD'S POWER, STRENGTH, AND MIGHT

You need power, strength, and might in your life! I need power, strength, and might in my life. *We all need the power, strength and might of God* in this Christian life. That's what sets Christianity apart from all of the world's religions. To call ourselves Christians and not walk in power but rather in a set of legalistic rules, is not to follow Jesus, because Jesus walked in power. He preached the Gospel and healed the sick. He preached the Gospel and delivered the captive.

Christianity is not about knowledge of the power of God. It's not about knowledge of His love. It's about *experiencing* His power and love in your life and that's when you'll truly understand and start to grasp the very dimensions of His love that Paul wrote about. The first part of our experience is going to the cross. You've done that, haven't you?

You are blessed and highly favored! This took me some time to get used to because of my insecurities, but it is truth. So often I would look at what other people had and think, "Why wasn't I born as blessed as they are...everything they touch turns to gold...has God overlooked me?"

God has blessings for you that you won't be able to contain and favor that can catapult you to greatness. Even if your circumstances don't *look* good, don't let the conditions fool you, because you are favored! We have to change our conditioning from a poverty "woe is me" mindset, to an "I am blessed and highly favored" attitude. When you declare this with confidence because of who you are in Christ Jesus and the authority He has given you, the demons will scatter: poverty, timidity, fear, insecurity, and the likes. Your mind, will, and emotions will become as living streams that bring life and power wherever you go.

More Than Just Enough

You may know the story about Naomi and Ruth in the Book of Ruth.[75] Ruth was a widow woman with no hope of a future. A Gentile in a foreign land and society, she wasn't even in covenant with God. She worked in a field gathering the wheat and the owner of the field, Boaz, saw her and sought to meet her. He asked everyone, "What's her name...who is that...I want to meet her," and then he told the workers, "Give her the very best—not the leftovers." In those days in ancient Israel, a farmer couldn't cut the corners of the fields because that harvest was left for the widows and orphans.

"Give her sheaves of wheat," he commanded, and they supplied her with armfuls of the crop from the very best part of the fields.

Later, at midnight, as Boaz slept on the floor of the threshing house with those who separated the chaff from the grain, Ruth came in and lay by his feet. Long story short, he became her kinsman redeemer—they were married and her debts became his and all that he had belonged to her too.

Favor brings sudden blessings.

Boaz was a representation of Christ; Ruth, a Gentile, represents the Bride of Christ. Our Kinsman Redeemer is Jesus and He provides for us through His blood. "Now I am your Provider. All of My wealth is yours. Your debts are mine. I've adopted you into the family of Abraham, Isaac, and Jacob. You are royalty—rejoice! Be joyful! I'm tired of you living on just enough. I want to give you more than you can carry. You don't have to pick it up strand by strand, but by the bundle...more than enough. I want you to live on more than enough. You're about to live the life of a king's child!"

Favor brings sudden blessings. You may think that you're a nobody or not important, but with God's favor you can be a somebody overnight. God will pick you out of a crowd and give you favor that will astonish people, and they will say, "It has to be God!"

Now for a story that hits even closer to home with me, check out Esther[76] who had to be one of the first beauty pageant contestants ever— competing against 400 women. I've mentioned her before. This sweet Jewish girl prepped for months to be presented to the King. As the long procession of women entered the banquet hall, King Ahasuerus (Xerxes) pointed to Esther and said, "That one—that's who I want to be my queen."

He didn't know she was Jewish and made her Queen of Persia (modern day Iran) instead of Vashti. Suddenly Esther had clout and was privy to all sorts of secret things and affairs of the king's court and kingdom, but she'd need courage for what was ahead.

One day she learned of a plot to kill the Jews. The leader of the gang was Haman but he didn't know she was a Jew, nor did any of his henchmen. Therefore, Esther planned what she would do. She would tell the King that she had a petition for him but that she would ask it at a feast she wanted to hold for him. This would put her into even greater favor in his eyes. Then she'd spring the details of Haman's diabolical plot on him. However, first she had to get him to agree. Getting an audience with the king would be risky because in those days, she had to get his permission to speak to him and if he didn't raise his scepter signifying favor and all systems go, they'd chop her head off. Eweee.

She approached the throne; he lifted his scepter (whew) and said, "Esther, what do you want? I'll give you half the kingdom."

She told him how she wanted to hold a banquet in his honor and he agreed. The banquet went so well that she made plans for another feast. Chancing another favorable audience with the king, he lifted his scepter. "What do you want now, Esther?"

"Another banquet, Xersus—I want to hold another feast."

He agreed but this time at the banquet Esther made her petition. "There are people in your kingdom who are planning to kill me and all of my people."

"Who would *dare* do that to the king's wife?" he roared.

"That man, right there," she said pointing her finger at Haman.

"Kill him...and hang his sons too," said the King, and the fate of her people was secure.

God will give you favor to go where others can't, to do what others can't, to see what others can't, and to experience what others can't! His favor is better than all the silver and gold in the world.

Esther saved an entire nation because of being in the favor of a king, and so can you by seeking the favor of the King of kings. He asks, "What do you want?" and rest assured that if anything steps in the way of your receiving what you ask for, He'll crush the enemy!

Favor brings sudden blessings and may save your entire family, your business, or a nation. God will favor your family, your business, and all of your undertakings. You have association with the Greatest One of All to supply all of your needs and more. See a plentiful harvest in your life through the eyes of faith. God's favor (His goodness and mercy) is *permanent*. It will follow you all the days of your life, and you shall dwell in His courts forever. His blessings and goodness never wear out. He'll anoint you, invite you to feast at His table of abundance, lead you into still waters, along level paths, and cause every good and wonderful thing to be like an endless waterfall pouring over and into your life.

BLESSINGS OF GOD'S FAVOR

Take time to study the following passages of Scripture and learn more about the many benefits of living as one highly favored of the Lord. These things can come about if you're living a life according to His will, His plans, His purposes, and His ways, and of course, falling under His great mercy and His protection. In all ways remember that your favor in His eyes is meant to glorify Him! This list is by no means exhaustive!

- Prominence (see Esther 2:17).

- Honor in the midst of your adversaries (see Exod. 11:3).

- Preferential treatment (see Esther 2:17).

- Restoration (see Exod. 3:21; Joel 2:23-27).

- Triumph when things seem impossible (see Josh. 11:20).

- Promotion when circumstances deem it unlikely (see 1 Sam. 16:22; Esther 2:7-9).

- Increased assets (see Deut. 33:23; 6:10-14).

- Favor and influence in the marketplace, government, judges— by people of authority (see Esther 5:8).

- Influence to change or reverse decisions for the good, i.e., rules, laws, regulations, policies. (see Rom. 8:28).

- Strength in battle for victory because God fights on your behalf (see Ps. 44:3).

- Supernatural increase and promotion (see Gen. 39:21; 41:38-41; 42:6).

- Favor upon your family for generations to come (see Deut. 7:9).

- Breaking away of hindrances to new beginnings (see Zech. 4:7).

- Release of blessings that the enemy stole (see Ps. 37:23).

- Guided steps, level ground, streams in your deserts (see Ps. 119:105).

- Rejections turn to approvals (see Rom. 8:1).

MANIFESTING HIS PROMISES

The most important step is to be in an attitude of gratitude and stop complaining. Thank Him for all of the promises He has spoken into your life and rest assured that He will never fail you. Believe for your break-through and for His favor in your circumstance; trust that even though you're from a foreign land and not of this world, His favor will give you influence when you need it. Worship Him with all of your heart, with your

body, mind, and spirit and spend time at His feet, and with arms extended toward Him. Surrender to Him and ask Him to reveal the motives of your heart and any hidden, secret sin. Confess, repent, and ask for His mercy and forgiveness, His grace to walk in obedience and in step with Him. Ask Him to baptize you afresh with the Spirit of favor and grace that He might cause you to receive favor in the sight of your enemies. "You prepare a table before me in the presence of my enemies..." (Ps. 23:5).

EARS TO HEAR

"I know that divorce pains God, but as much as He hates it,[77] He still loves divorced people and has a plan for their lives. Marriages are special to God but the people in them, even more so."

My marriage with Bobby was difficult—actually from the day after our wedding onward. I sought God's will, but I rushed into things before clearly hearing. I thought that because he was a Christian, a Gospel singer, and desired ministry that the marriage was probably God's will. It seemed almost expected to meet and marry at Bible college, as many young people do, but we can't suppose anything when it comes to specifically knowing God's will and exact direction.

I knew that marriage was a commitment and covenant, and I did everything I could to try to make things right. This book isn't a "tell all" and I value people's privacy, but I need say that things were very difficult with crippling challenges that were hard to overcome and became huge burdens. As time went on these weights became burdensome yokes to many aspects of both of our lives. So often I tried to salvage things but nothing worked; however, I kept praying to the Lord, "Please help us see this marriage through or else make it clear what we're supposed to do."

Things got worse especially while we were in Connecticut. Bobby wasn't always pleased that I was traveling a lot in ministry, yet at the same time he was comfortable and preferred staying home, and running the church. At that point, many leaders and ministries had invited me to preach, like Norvel Hayes, Dwight Thompson, Juanita Bynum, and Brother R.W. Schambach. God had supernaturally opened doors for me, and sometimes I think that He provided me opportunities to travel to escape discomfort at home.

I know that divorce pains God

In those days, I'd have an assistant or a singer travel with me—I was so on fire to see others on fire for the Lord, that they would be saved, healed, and delivered. Although I loved ministering nationally and internationally, I missed ministering and fellowshipping with our church congregation. They were so wonderful and warm— I loved the people there. But it was always hard coming home because things worsened with Bobby. It all came to a sudden end when Josh and I, with nothing more than the coats on our backs, went to my mother's house to stay for a while. When two needy people carry much baggage into a relationship, it's doomed unless both parties allow Jesus in for deliverance. The Lord was busy doing a healing work in me, but the agony of my marriage relationship burdened me greatly; Bobby had issues of his own that needed healing. Later in our marriage when my father was fighting cancer, I was suffering burnout, and for a short time had difficulty climbing out of it. It was only by the grace of God that I didn't crash and burn totally from going through a very painful divorce and much later, bitter child custody proceedings.

I know that divorce pains God, but as much as He hates it (see Mal. 2:16), He still loves divorced people and has a plan for their lives. Marriages are special to God but the people in them, even more so. His desire is that a husband and wife love and enjoy each other fully to the utmost, and many do. However, like Bobby and I, our marriage was like a lead weight that kept pulling us under for the umpteenth time. There comes to a point, especially in an abusive situation, when it becomes a too-long and unmeaningful sacrifice.

Abraham obeyed God and took Isaac, his only son, to the altar as a burnt offering. Just as he obediently was about to slay his only son, an angel of the Lord called to him from Heaven and told him to stop.[78] What if Abraham had missed the Lord's voice telling him to stop the sacrifice? Isaac would have died. God never did intend the sacrifice. So too, I don't believe that God intends us to become sacrificial victims in the marriage setting. It can go on too long and kill the very heart of those involved.

Jesus said, "...I desire mercy [readiness to help, to spare, to forgive] rather than sacrifice and sacrificial victims, you would not have condemned the guiltless" (Matt. 12:7 AMP). Though sacrifice was the crown of the Jewish rites, this Scripture passage shows that our rites and ceremonies are worthless before God unless we have kind and merciful hearts. Jesus quoted what had been told before, "For I desire and delight in dutiful steadfast love and goodness, not sacrifice..." (Hos. 6:6 AMP). "Go and learn what this means: I desire mercy [that is, readiness to help those in trouble] and not sacrifice and sacrificial victims..." (Matt. 9:13 AMP).

God doesn't intend us to become sacrificial victims in a marriage. Certainly, our marriage was the end of something intended for good but went bad. Afterward, I needed to rely on God's strength and power in my life as I went through the grieving process and stages of divorce. In the grieving and adjustment process of our divorce, there were several steps to get through. The first, *survival.* If you've ever gone through a divorce or separation, you'll know exactly how these stages feel and can play on someone's emotions.

I tried to survive in the marriage, but it was impossible, given the circumstances. Grieved that we didn't make it, nevertheless, I was relieved it was over. There was a stigma of shame for being divorced but I'm convinced God gave my son and me a way out. God sent a precious woman all the way from Switzerland, Hetty, who I'd ministered to in one of the Europe crusades I did with Lester Sumerall and Morris Cerillo. Another young woman, Patty, my spiritual daughter from New York City, also helped me and Josh and my mother in our quick move to Florida, where I rented the first house I looked at in Plantation, Florida.

The second stage was *grief*, when I cried out for a dying marriage and felt shame that I couldn't make it better. It was a stage of wondering why things happened the way they did and feelings of rejection and insecurity. The third stage was *identity*—a potentially dangerous stage of discovery when I was the most vulnerable. This stage is when major life changes take place that can have good or bad consequences. The fourth stage was *direction*, when I learned to cope and realized that I could make it on my own and formulate great dreams for my future. I was barely in the third stage, the identity stage, when I fell head over heels for Bob Tilton.

WAIT ON THE LORD, BE CERTAIN

I was so starving for love, attention, and identity, that I was totally not thinking straight. My dad was very sick with cancer and only had weeks to live, and I was plum worn out. My emotions were all over the map, plain and simple, and it was easy to be taken in or deceived by something that seemed to offer what I so desired for my life—to be loved, and to be able to pour love into someone who would receive love.

Bob was charming, attentive, funny, and very charismatic in character. He had these highs where he'd be over the top excited, and it was a contagious excitement. So much so that you almost think you can conquer the world. What can I say? He was like a knight in shining armor to me, handsome and well dressed in his Italian clothes, compassionate, and desiring to work in Israel and around the world in missions. This too was my lifelong dream, to help God's chosen people; anyone who wanted or needed help. Bob had such a heart for Israel especially, supporting a prayer center there and visiting the country often. Of course, these things were attractive to me in him, because it's all I ever wanted to do too. To be married to someone who wanted full time ministry helping people as much as I did, drew me to him—and was like a dream come true.

I'd not been looking for a relationship because I was still in the throes of a difficult and painful divorce and custody proceedings. However, Bob Tilton pursued me quite zealously, and frankly it felt good to be desired again. For the first time in a long time I started to feel happy in a relationship. Almost as a surrogate savior of sorts—he seemed so close to the Lord with a charismatic personality that boosted my spirits and helped me to get through my father's death.

Although my life was in such turmoil, Bob had a way of making everything feel better and promised me that all would be great if I married him. I should have waited for a word from God, but I was in the doldrums—still crippled spiritually and emotionally, wounded from all that had happened. Like a mother bear protecting her cub, I wanted Josh to feel secure and to get our lives back into some semblance of order. It seemed as though a long-lost piece of the puzzle had appeared to make things right.

At this point in Bob's life, he was going through a rough time because of all of the ministry issues that had gained limelight in the media a few years earlier. He seemed very repentant about his ministry's alleged financial misdoings, discovered when ABC's Prime Time Live launched an investigation. After that, his show, "Success N Life," was off the airwaves and church numbers had dropped.

We'd pray for hours on end together early on in our relationship, and he made me feel as though he really was searching for new answers for his life, restoration of his ministry, and God's call on his life. I sincerely felt as though I was in love with him and where others saw the flaws, I saw a repentant man who really wanted to serve the Lord. He would say things such as: We'll preach together all over the world...you can preach... with me...we can go on television together...we can merge our ministries...we'll be a great team.

As you can imagine I felt these promises lined up well with God's call on my life, further reinforcing things in my mind; but I spent little time consulting God and just assumed it was part of His divine plan.

At the time I thought everything felt right. But I should have waited before moving forward and agreeing to marry Bob because I was doing it based on my perceived needs: to be loved, accepted, secure, and for my son to have someone he could rely on, too.

Concerned friends warned me...begged me not to rush into marriage with him, reminding me of God's call on my life and the direction He had already taken my exploding ministry. I'd been ministering all over the world, had appeared on the 700 Club often, authored a book, and had invitations from huge churches, so there was much at stake to lose by a wrong decision. But I could only see what my needy mind saw—he was handsome, kind, financially secure, seemed to love God, and *wanted* me.

The day after my divorce with Bobby, my father died. Two weeks later, I flew to the Dominican Republic to elope. Bob wanted it to happen fast, and had heard that the process of getting married there was a quick and private one (Michael Jackson married Elvis Presley's daughter there). Only a few knew about our plans.[79] In my hotel room before the ceremony, though, something bothered me in my innermost being. Something didn't feel quite right; but in my mind, my only options were: a) go back home and be alone, or b) be with this man who seemed so exciting, passionate, and full of life and fun.

In hindsight I see now how deceived I was. God would have shown me had I genuinely sought His counsel before agreeing to this relationship. I'm sure He spoke to me through my well-meaning friends, but I sincerely felt the Lord was moving Bob back out into ministry and that this would be a natural course for my ministry to take as well. In fact, I received a warning from a woman apostle/prophet who counseled me to wait. But when I got to Santo Domingo, I allowed a false peace to take me over.

Bob was a sinking ship because of excess cargo and had I taken the time to really see and investigate things about him, I would have jumped ship long before—or never would have boarded. My association with Bob caused quite a stir and for all intent, it temporarily destroyed my ministry. Almost overnight invitations to minister all but stopped after we were married, and those that were extended to me, Bob blocked.

The first year with Bob, I have to admit, was wonderful—it was a whirlwind of activity and excitement. However, everything in the relationship started to sink that second year as Bob's personal problems bubbled to the surface of his polished exterior. What he'd successfully hid or suppressed inside suddenly manifested in disturbing ways, including mood swings. Reality set in and my life took a turn for a horrible worse. I'll not elaborate on the separation and ensuing divorce except to say that once again, I had little, and this time much less than what I'd entered into the relationship with.

I was at rock bottom.

After the divorce, Josh, my mom, and I had no place to stay, no furniture, or anything from the marriage. Unfortunately, I'd let all of my own things go when we moved in with Bob, at his insistence, citing that we no longer had need of those things because he'd provide us with everything we needed, for life. Bob also disposed of many of things I had acquired in the marriage. Everyone thought I had tons of money, but when the divorce finalized, we received nothing. Bob's attorney convinced the court that everything in the house, including my son's playmat, his bed, everything belonged to the church, and we weren't entitled to anything because the church paid for it. So we left with nothing but the clothes on our back—not even beds for us to sleep in. We moved in with my girlfriend from church who had worked as one of my housekeepers during my marriage to Bob, and we slept on her floor. Eventually I found a tiny apartment and even though we had no furniture, moved in. It was a little while before I could even find the wherewithal to search for work. I had so much shame and embarrassment, and just couldn't bring myself to ask family for help. One Thanksgiving, I had no food for Josh, so we stood in line at the food bank at church. They refused to give me food because I was wearing expensive clothes—the only clothes I had.

I was at rock bottom. People treated me as though I had a contagious disease. Here I was with two college degrees and a Bible school graduate, in my 40s with two lost marriages, a lost ministry, failing health, no security, with my precious little boy in tow. Everyone had turned against me because of my marriage to Bob—that association that made me guilty in their eyes—and I was pretty much ostracized from church circles.

How could God restore anything? I thought. *Would He?* I prayed that He would. I already knew of His forgiveness and His ability to restore my body—would He restore the ministry—would He restore what I'd lost by making wrong choices? Could He remove the weighty burden of my downcast heart? Even restore my name? Honestly, for a while I wasn't too sure He would, as I spiraled into pit of darkness.

ARE YOU LISTENING?

If you desire greatness or success, listen to God. Two-way communication is impossible if you aren't listening. Most of the successful people in the Bible learned to listen. If there's a common stream in my life history it is that I didn't listen to God, which precipitated many of my problems.

Moses didn't listen when God first spoke to him from the burning bush. The Lord tried to tell him that *He* would deliver the Israelites out of Egypt, but Moses assumed that he himself would have to deliver the people. "Who am I," Moses said in response, "that I should go to Pharaoh and bring the Israelites out of Egypt?"[80] Moses reverted to his own lack of ability on that mountain. In essence, God told him, "Moses, I said that I would deliver the people—*My* power would deliver them—*My* power will save them." But Moses kept arguing, "I'm slow of speech, and slow of tongue" (Exod. 4:10). His emphasis was on *his* stuttering, *his* lack of ability. God told him, "I made your mouth..." (see Exod. 4:11).

Every time God said, "I will," Moses countered with "I can't."

Finally after the ping-pong match, Moses' grand finale for emphasis was: "Send whom You'll send...like not me!"

Reading this passage of Exodus you almost want to shout, "Moses, Honey. Listen to God already!" Well, somebody must have because he finally listened and went on to be a great leader. Abraham listened. David

Listened. Samuel listened. Mary listened. Peter listened. Paul listened. All experienced greatness because they listened to God.

The best part of listening is that God listens to those who listen to Him.[81] To the children of Israel who didn't listen to Him He said through the prophet,

I will destine you [says the Lord] for the sword, and you shall all bow down to the slaughter, because when I called, you did not answer; when I spoke, you did not listen or obey. But you did what was evil in My eyes, and you chose that in which I did not delight (Isa. 65:12 AMP).

Now that's pretty harsh—but in essence God is saying, "Look, listen to Me and stay in My protection." Jesus said that those who don't *hear*, meaning *those who don't listen and act,* aren't from God (see John 8:47).

There are four elements to listening. They are to look, listen, comprehend, and obey, and when we do, we can expect healing and deliverance and favor—tremendous growth in our spiritual lives.[82]

When Moses finally got it and acknowledged God's words, he became great and successful–and so will you when you listen. You may not accomplish the great feats that Moses did, or Abraham, or any of the other great saints of old, but you will be just as great in the eyes of the Lord because you listened.

...look, listen, comprehend, and obey,...

To listen you must draw near to Him. You can't hear Him when you're far away! You can't hear Him when your thoughts are on your own inability.

You can't hear Him if your own thoughts distract you. You can't hear Him if you believe that you can do things without Him. It takes daily communion—conversation with God, talking and listening, listening and talking, and meditating on God's Word. It involves getting His Word deep down into your heart that you might understand what He's asking of or telling you.

God doesn't ask any less of us than He asked of Moses. He's saying, "Listen already!"

When we listen to Him we avert danger, disaster and we know how to avert sin.[83] Are you listening?

Chapter 19

DAYS OF DISTINCTION

"God told me that if I would release people who really hurt me and did me wrong, that He would free me from captivity, give me favor and open big doors."

DIVORCED twice, my ministry in shreds, broke, bad name, alone, how could I make it? God doesn't just have a dream for us but multiple dreams, purposes, and divine assignments for our lives. King David fulfilled God's purpose before he died, even though he messed up royally along the way. It's important to realize that we *will* make mistakes, but even so we shouldn't give up on God nor should we abort His plans for our lives. David committed adultery and murder along the way, but his ultimate intention was to fulfill the divine assignments God had for him and he did it. He didn't wallow in his mistakes or cop the "woe is me and the world has done me wrong" attitude—he forged ahead with the call on his life. We're all in a process of growth and development. If we lock in on our mistakes and let them define our lives, we'll never be all God intended us to be. David lived the dream despite his mistakes.

Beware of Bitterness

Bitterness is self-induced misery and unless we deal with it right away it can produce more sin such as self-pity, prideful ambition, and even unteachability. Bitterness is resentment you won't let go of, and I had to let go once and for all to break the chain and yokes that could have destroyed and killed me. For God to do what He was about to do in my life, I had to let go, forgive others, and most of all myself. If I hadn't, bitterness would have penetrated deep within my heart and made me very wary, mistrustful, defensive, and self-protective. These attitudes would have been devastating because of what God was about to miraculously do in my life.

I, therefore, the prisoner of the Lord, beseech you to walk worthy of the calling with which you were called, with all lowliness and gentleness, with longsuffering, bearing with one another in love, endeavoring to keep the unity of the Spirit in the bond of peace (Ephesians 4:1-3).

God told me that if I would release people who really hurt me and did me wrong that He would free me from captivity, give me favor and open big doors.

Walk worthy of the calling with which you were called.

We have to check our heart every day. Do you love everyone? If you don't, you will stop the blessings in your life, especially the financial blessings. It will make you physically ill as well. I found that whenever I harbor bitterness toward someone, my arthritis flairs up. As soon as I release them, it subsides again. We can't afford not to forgive. No matter what someone has done to you, you have to ask God to help you walk in love. That's the

only way we'll really know if we're truly saved and born again, if we have the love of God in our hearts for everyone. And I mean, everyone!

When I could release those who had hurt me, God started to do amazing things in my life and the blessings really started to come in. However, once again I had to go through the learning process of listening and waiting on the Lord and not getting ahead of Him.

DIVINE OPPORTUNITY KNOCKS

For a time I worked in sales but by and by, I knew it was time for me to move on. I'd had some success and some downturns, but God had more plans for me and this was a time of learning and preparing me for something incredible.

"Leigh," God said one day as I prayed and fasted, " I'm about to bless you and create something for you for a season that will enable you not only to be financially free but to bless others—to bless ministries in desperate need."

One day while working for an MLM company in Dallas that wanted me to promote products for them, I met a man in his 70s who owned a huge manufacturing company. At the time, he was marketing and distributing a joint cream through network marketing. I told him that I often made up formulations at home that would work for me. After my accident, I spent time studying the benefits of vitamins E and C, minerals, and often mixed ingredients into creams to apply on my burns and scars.

In fact, I'd done quite a bit of research with ingredients from South Africa, Switzerland, and the Brazilian rainforest that had strong antioxidant properties and anti-aging benefits. Because I had experience in cosmetics with Revlon and Estée Lauder, I knew the value of good ingredients. If the product worked on me, I was certain it could help others.

I felt it hit a sweet spot in the intended blessings of God for my life.

"Leigh," the man said, "why don't you develop your own line of products?" Just like that, faith and courage began to rise and I felt it hit a sweet spot in the intended blessings of God for my life. "Why don't you gather your information together—all that you've mixed up at home, and then I'll introduce you to my friend who owns a private research lab, and we'll see what we can do."

The owner of the lab and I really hit it off. He said, "Leigh, you have what it takes to build a multimillion dollar company with your products. It's just going to take more product research, development, and planning."

When he said that to me, I went back to a Mary Kay Ash book I'd read before and poured over it again. In it, she talks about how we can do anything—and she had worked with my mother years previously at Stanley Products. She started Mary Kay Cosmetics after working at Stanley. In fact, she told my mom that she was going to start a cosmetic company and she was going to run it. She wanted my mother to help or partner with her, but my mom didn't think that Mary Kay really had what it took to start and run a company! This was one of the few times my mother was ever wrong. I've often thought, *Wow, where would I be today if she had said yes.*

Immediately, I got busy with the research and development phase. For the next year and a half, I worked with chemists to develop a serum, a moisturizer, and my own exclusive, non-surgical face-lift. Back and forth I'd go to the chemist as he made up samples for me to try according to my formulations, and he would show me what products worked together and what didn't. We'd adjust consistency, scents, and ingredient measurements—it was a time-consuming process.

One day the chemist called me all excited. "Leigh," he said, "There's an ingredient we took out of a special plant that we thought would test well to relieve pain and discomfort from arthritis and joint pain. We applied the cream we had formulated with this plant extract onto women's hands. Although it didn't alleviate their joint pain symptoms, it did make their hands look much younger!"

I said, "Do *not* give that ingredient to *anyone* else. That is my ingredient, and I'll be right over!"

I dashed over there and checked out the test results and data. Then we made a plan to try it in some of my products. The ingredient is a natural botanical plant extract, and this excited me even more. We made up a formulation and I used it for a while and noticed quite a difference, so I knew we were on to something great. Praise God. Everything came together and we had a line of products to go to market with. For a while, I sold the products on my own and people loved them. One day a licensed esthetician who owned a training school finally returned my sales call and said, "Leigh, I'll give you just a few minutes to demo the products to my estheticians before we break for lunch, but you only have a few minutes. We'll see if you can convince my students.

I prayed, Jesus, "You know I need to sell this product. I don't even have money for dinner tonight—won't even be able to fill my car with gas tomorrow if nothing sells. I'm behind on my rent." Everything depended on my doing well the following day. I prayed while driving in the car to the training center: "Please God—help me demonstrate and sell these products today so I can get Josh the things he needs and to put food on our table."

When I walked into the training center, I didn't even know where to start but I felt impressed upon by the Holy Spirit to choose someone from the audience to help me demo my product. All the while, I could see the estheticians looking skeptical. *Who is Leigh Valentine? What type of training does she have in skincare? What qualifies her to even be here? How can she train us if she's not even a licensed esthetician?* But I plowed through my feeling of insecurity and asked the school owner to select someone.

To my embarrassment she announced that I was looking for someone with really wrinkled and dry skin and I was like, "Help me Jesus!" She pointed to a woman who obviously had some skin challenges. The woman went beet red when she came up front and then she shared that she smoked two packs of cigarettes a day.

I started my story with as much gusto as I could muster. "Now, watch as I mix everything up to activate the ingredients. Now I'll apply the mask to only one side of her face. When you all return from lunch you'll see great change!"

Right before they returned from lunch I removed the mask from our "model" and applied the serum, then the skin renewal booster. Sure enough when they returned an hour or so later the woman's face where I had applied the mask looked amazing—the skin was much fresher, tighter, and smoother looking than the other side. The audience gasped. "WOW! This is unbelievable, amazing. We've never seen anything like this."

I couldn't sell product fast enough; I sold $14,000 in an hour! Within the next few months, credit card orders flew in and I sold thousands more dollars worth of my products.

DON'T GIVE UP IF THINGS LOOK IMPOSSIBLE

For about a month or two, it looked like I was selling products really well. Then, all of a sudden I had problems shipping my products. The boxes were falling apart, the bottles were spilling, I had no help, and I was all alone trying to sell and ship these products. The next thing I knew, products began to spoil in the warehouse, and a deal I thought I had with a network

marketing company fell through the floor when the company went belly up. One minute I thought I was on top of the world, and within months, I was destitute again. Many people whom I trusted began to steal my ideas. Some who promised to pay me for work and promotions, didn't. I realized that the business world was a dog-eat-dog world— I had little to no working capital, and no business partners whom I could trust. Even one man who said he would help me patent an invention I felt the Lord had given me, literally stole the whole idea, patented it himself, and marketed it through another company, and I had no way or means to fight him. At every turn my heart would break. I just couldn't believe how people in the world treated each other. I could write volumes of one business deal after another that just fell through because I trusted everyone, and thought everyone had a pure heart and motive.

I made several trips down to the Home Shopping Network (HSN) outside of Tampa, Florida, and got my products accepted to go live on the air. It wasn't two months later that the person who had accepted my products, was let go. No one there knew anything about my products being accepted to go live on the air. I was totally devastated, worn out, and had lost a tremendous amount of money, energy, and sleep over this whole ordeal.

At this point, my mom and brother said, "Leigh, get a normal job. You've wasted so much time and money on this product." My brother sat me down again and said, in effect, "You have to get a normal job. You're just thinking pie-in-the-sky here. You'll never get ahead doing this. You'll never be able to support your son on your own. Go get a nine-to-five and be done with it!" Even my girlfriends echoed their sentiment. "Leigh, it's just not happening...give it up girl!"

At a loss about what to do and broke again, one night I just lay atop my bed and cried out to the Lord. "What should I do Lord? Am I crazy or is something really going to break loose here?"

The Lord said to me, "Leigh, don't give up. Keep going. You're on to something here."

Not too long afterward, I received an odd phone call from a woman who had found my Website while she was surfing the Internet. Back then my Website was nothing special at all—it just featured my products. I hadn't promoted the site whatsoever. "We'd like to talk to you," she said. "We do infomercials out of Los Angeles, and we promote and distribute products like yours. My bosses would like to talk to you."

She set up a conference call with the company and the next thing I knew I was sending them product to review and then signing a contract. I was so broke at this stage and so geared up to sell product that I quickly signed not wanting to miss the opportunity. A month later I received a phone call asking me to fly out the next day—immediately! I would be cast to promote my own product on the infomercial! *Oh, help me Jesus!* I had so much to do to be ready...one day!

When I arrived, I learned that they had originally wanted a celebrity to promote my product, or at least an L.A. model. But two of the decision makers met accidentally in the lady's room the morning before and talked about how they both were awake the night before thinking about me. They decided that I should be the one to promote the product since I was the one who invented it.

The revelation the two women had must have come from God on my behalf. The moment I landed at the airport, I was whisked to the shopping center for clothes and then I had my makeup done. That first commercial, a shot that lasted only a few minutes, generated $25 million in sales. The company was responsible for taking care of all of the purchasing, commercials, shipping, distribution, telemarketers, and so on, so after everything was paid for and after they received their cut, there wasn't much left for me royalty-wise; but hey, I was on my way, glory to God, and I knew He could make it all up to me someday.

Another time they flew me out at the last minute for some commercials they were about to do using celebrities like Melanie Griffith, Donna Mills, and Deborah Choprh. I was nervous, so I called my friend Byron and said, "What am I going to do? I just landed from Florence, Italy, where I attended Cosmoprof (an international beauty show) and my credit cards are maxed out. My roots are out about an inch, my nails aren't done, and I have nothing new to wear for this important shoot—I can't do this...I just can't do this!" I'm not even certain my nervousness was about my state of disrepair, or just plain fear. I was so stressed out because the flight from Italy had to make an emergency landing at the U.S. military base in Iceland because a young pregnant girl was miscarrying. The stress of the turbulence and landing in a major ice storm was no fun, I can assure you. I love to fly but don't do well in turbulence, I still need deliverance from the fear!

So I resolved that I was not going to California, because I just didn't have time to rest and get ready.

My special friend, a Christian business CEO in Dallas, came to my rescue. "Yes you can, and you will," he said. He picked me up and drove me to my favorite hair salon. "Sorry, we have no openings today," the host said.

"I have to get her on a plane at midnight tonight. You've got to do her hair." At this point, I could hardly hold back my tears. Finally they squeezed me in and did my nails as well as my hair. Afterward, Byron took me shopping—it is so important to have people who champion what God is doing through us.

THE SPIRIT OF EXCELLENCE

Promoter and author Kevin Trudeau called the night I was flying into L.A. and said that he would be interviewing me on my product.

"Great, Kevin," I said, "So, what are you going to ask me so that I can rehearse?"

"Nothing—I want it all to be fresh. Just answer my questions—that's all I need. See you tomorrow!" And that, was that! No coaching, not even a little bit! I didn't even know how to prepare for it.

I arrived in L.A. on the "redeye" and almost immediately was whisked into the AT&T recording studio and advised that there would be no rehearsals, no scripts—all adlibbed, fresh! Now remember, I'm not an actor. But let me tell you what God did. I was so nervous before going on that I just prayed, "Jesus, I'm a wreck, I need your help." I prayed in the Spirit and suddenly a peace washed over me. I could feel God's presence all over, and then it *was* all over. I sailed through the taping beautifully.

"That's a wrap! No retakes!" Later I learned that the taping required no edits either—they used it. That one commercial with no rehearsals, no retakes, just God's stamp of excellence and fingerprints all over it did *$200 million* in sales. Interestingly, the celebrities' commercials didn't do very well at all.

"Jesus, I'm a wreck, I need your help."

The movie stars may have had it all over me with their talent and fame, but I had a higher Power that day to really aid and assist me. I did not say everything I wanted to say, but I know people had to have felt my passion and love for the products. Although Kevin has had some troubles over the years, I have to say, he was a creative genius in front of the camera, and he really cared about people. God helped in the making of my products and I believed in them with fiery passion. This was more than apparent by the success of the infomercial—it broke all the records of its day. The Lord

knew the desperate need in my life to survive with my son, and my prayer made all the difference. The royalty checks were big; and I became what some might term, "an overnight success" in the industry.

My products became a familiar beauty brand around the world at the wholesale and retail levels. For seven years, I've demonstrated my skin care formulas and products on QVC, one of the world's largest televised home shopping broadcasts. I'm a beauty brand there now with this great line of professional anti-aging treatments and mineral-based cosmetics—they continue to do well!

To date, I've sold five million bottles of my Mineral Firm & Lift, and 2.5 million non-surgical facelift kits. It's incredible what God will do when we listen and line ourselves up with His Word and His desire for our lives. It's no secret what God can do!

Because of the prosperity He gave me, I could bless others in the Body of Christ who are in need, thus fulfilling and continuing to fulfill that part of God's call on my life! It wasn't about the money—it was about what God could do through me because of His love for me.

As for the rich in this world, charge them not to be proud and arrogant and contemptuous of others, nor to set their hopes on uncertain riches, but on God, Who richly and ceaselessly provides us with everything for [our] enjoyment (1 Timothy 6:17 AMP).

BE OPEN TO HIS CREATIVITY

It was all about God. He was always there, even through my shame and embarrassment, my sin and the darkness. It gives a girl a whole lot of confidence to know that the Creator of universe is backing up her career or company!

God may indeed give you creative ideas or visions about your career, so be open to seeing His vision and hearing His voice! Don't be close-minded when it comes to the things of the Spirit. We're living in days when God is pouring ideas into His children's hearts and minds to advance His Kingdom here on earth, and we have to take hold of these ideas or someone else will. There's no time to ask, "Why me, Lord?" Let God use you and your ideas because one creative idea from Heaven can set you free. You might be in debt, in poverty, insecure, depressed, but one move of God in your life can transform everything.

Listen, when God spoke the whole world was created and He's never reneged on a single word. Hold fast to His word for your life. Building up my business didn't happen overnight, and there have been challenges that few humans could endure—and others I haven't mentioned. Trust that even when things don't seem to be going along the way you expected, God is working hard on your behalf to make it all right as long as you remain in His will and don't get ahead of Him. God will give you divine appointments and bring to you a strategic team to help it all happen.

The important thing to remember is to invest time with God. Spend a lot of time in worship! Worship is not worrying! Worship is praying to God about everything in your life, telling Him what your needs are, thanking Him for what's He done, and placing Him in the center of everything. It's penciling everything in your day around Him—around your time with Him. He should be the first Person you write into your day—in indelible ink!

Do not fret or have any anxiety about anything, but in every circumstance and in everything, by prayer and petition (definite requests),

with thanksgiving, continue to make your wants known to God (Philippians 4:6 AMP).

Don't worry about things; instead, tell God everything you're going through. If you do this, as you venture forth in God's plan for your life—whether it's in business, at home, or in ministry—you'll experience God's peace and that peace will guard your heart and your mind as you live in Christ Jesus. Worry takes the joy out of things you should delight in. Worry, like bitterness, is self-inflicted torment—the "shoulda-woulda-coulda" game, stuff that we dwell on and scenarios that we stew about. However, worry is a reactive thing and that's dangerous in decision making because it clouds our thinking. Worse, worry can cause emotional and physical problems. Worship, on the other hand, causes God's peace and a sense of wholeness to settle upon us.

Not long ago Firm & Lift wasn't doing well; it seemed as though its success had run its course. I prayed and prayed about it and refused to believe it wouldn't continue selling, and sure enough, God turned it around and it's flying out the window again in sales.

RESTORATION

Over the years, God has restored my name to a good name with national notoriety. I have seen restoration in ministry, too. And many pastors and friends from my past have contacted me. Everywhere I go, at airports, while shopping, people recognize me, and friends I haven't seen in years have reconnected with me through the infomercial and television appearances. Because of my success with all of my products and formulas, I'm now able to afford to travel the world helping people and ministering...just as God promised me I would!

More than anything, He loved me when I felt all alone and helpless. He healed my broken body and my broken spirit. He has started to restore the years I'd wasted doing my own thing and those stolen days too. His unconditional love brought me home again and again; and although I have failed miserably at many things, He has lifted me high and I give Him the glory for that! I can do nothing apart from Him.

God wants to raise your faith level because He's a big God and doesn't want us with less than He wants to give us! Too often, we settle for less than the unlimited He has for us! His purposes for you are far-reaching! We often have such myopic vision because we fail to see the great eternal truths in the Word of God. We have to strive to cast off unbelief because it blinds us to the great truths in the Word of God and shrinks our vision. To stay free from unbelief I had to preserve my relationship with Jesus at all costs if I was to progress in the vision He had planted in me. It took me awhile to become daring and bold but it became easier when I kept focused on the will of God. Beware of the enemy who wants to pervert the desires of your heart and cause you to lust after things for your sole benefit. Trust the Teacher—the Holy Spirit to curb your wrong ambitions and the feeding of your pride. Continue in prayer and worship so that you will remain in obedience to His will, having your living and being in Him and His Word.

The essential in this life is to fulfill life's most exciting adventure of all, God's will in your life; and that takes engaging with God every day—taking Him into every aspect of your life.

Chapter 20

MAINTAINING THE BLESSINGS QUO

"In an amazing spectacle, fire came down from Heaven and consumed not only the sacrifice but also every one of the twelve stones, every piece of wood, every lick of water, every grain of sand."

<hr />

For God's *continual* favor in our lives, we must have a firm foundation and get our foundations right. Once we lay the strong and stable base, God can build upon it. A firm foundation is a sure foundation. If we lay it right, we can stand in assurance, unshaken and unwavering with His seal upon us. The Lord knows who are His by the foundation they build their life on. He knows if you are really His. There's no other foundation than the foundation of Jesus Christ.[84] Jesus, in the Sermon on the Mount, talked figuratively about this foundation saying,

Everyone who hears these words of Mine and acts upon them [obeying them] will be like a sensible (prudent, practical, wise) man who built his house upon the rock. And the rain fell and the floods came and the

winds blew and beat against that house; yet it did not fall, because it had been founded on the rock. And everyone who hears these words of Mine and does not do them will be like a stupid (foolish) man who built his house upon the sand. And the rain fell and the floods came and the winds blew and beat against that house, and it fell—and great and complete was the fall of it (Matthew 7:24-27 AMP).

One of the greatest stories in biblical history about being in God's will and the favor of the Lord is about Elijah the prophet.[85] King Ahab and his people hadn't had any rain for over three years. It was a horrible time of famine, suffering, and death in the dry land. Even the king's horses were about to keel over, and the king and his people sacrificed everything they could to Baal, even their own children, in hopes of getting even a few drops of rain to fall. In their minds, the man responsible for this dry period was Elijah the prophet. There was an all points bulletin out for his hide! Three years previously, Elijah had popped in for a visit to see Ahab and fearlessly said, "Unless you repent of your idolatry you won't see any rain, not even a drop of dew for three years." That said, he was gone as quick as he'd come. The king stubbornly refused to heed the warning and sure enough there was not a spot of rain—not even a measure of dew had fallen since then. (See First Kings 17:1-7.)

While everyone else was keeling over from starvation and thirst, Elijah fared very well in hiding as God supplied him with food supernaturally. Despite being on the king's most wanted list, Elijah came out of hiding and when word came that he was on his way the king went out to meet him. Again, Elijah boldly gave him a message from God. Understand that not only did the king blame him for all the misfortune, but Jezebel and her cohorts were after him too—surfacing could mean certain death. A prophet in those days had to be fearless, bold, and sure, because if what they predicted didn't happen, it was "off with his head!" So convinced was Elijah of the

One True God that he wasn't afraid to get right in the king's face. He said that God had told him to ask of the king, "Why have you caused My children to worship false gods?" (See First Kings 18:1-19.)

Then Elijah set out a challenge. "Tell you what Ahab, you bring your people and I'll bring my people to the mountain and we'll each build an altar. You build an altar to your gods and I will build an altar to my God. Whichever altar either of our gods answers by fire will be the Lord God of Israel—the true God." (See First Kings 18:19-24.)

The contest was on. All of Israel came out for the show. The prophets of Baal built their altar, laid out their sacrifices, and called out to Baal all day long. Not one voice came out of Heaven, not a spark, not one puff of smoke, no sign, no wonder. Elijah mocked, "Cry louder because your god perhaps is meditating or busy, or on a journey, or perhaps he's sleeping and must be awakened." This fueled their determination; they even cut themselves up for sacrifice with knives and lances until blood gushed out of them, but still not a peep or a squeak from the heavens. (See First Kings 18:25-29.)

Evening came along and Elijah prepared the altar and sacrifice to God and then called upon His name. "God, let it be known that You are the Lord God and that You have turned their hearts back to You again" (see 1 Kings 18:37).

In an amazing spectacle, fire came down from Heaven and consumed not only the sacrifice but also every one of the twelve stones, every piece of wood, every lick of water, every grain of sand (see 1 Kings 18:38).

When the people saw this, they fell on their faces and said, "The Lord, He is God! The Lord, He is God!" (1 Kings 18:39). God showed Himself the one true God and made believers out of the king. Every false prophet who had caused the people to turn their backs on the One True God was destroyed.

Divine favor is for you, not just the prophets of old.

Then Elijah told Ahab that it would rain and instructed him to go up to Mount Carmel to eat and drink. Elijah went to the top of the mountain and reminded God of His promise to bring the rain. A servant saw a little cloud the size of a man's fist and Elijah instructed him, "Go tell the king that it's about to rain...hard, and that he better get back before the rains hinder his chariot." (See First Kings 18:41-44.)

The skies darkened with clouds and wind and it rained heavily. Ahab sped away on his chariot to Jezreel but then the hand of the Lord came upon Elijah, and Elijah girded up his loins and ran ahead of Ahab to the entrance of Jezreel. (See First Kings 18:45-46.) It takes superhuman speed to outrun a horse and chariot, don't you think? The favor of the Lord was upon Elijah because he'd done the great things God had told him to do. Trust that you'll run with superhuman speed to outrun anything that stands in your way when you're in His favor!

The rain came after Elijah listened to God, obeyed God, after he built the altar of worship, after he destroyed sin, and after he declared the word of the Lord. If you want to see the rain from the vantage point of a mountain, if you want God to reveal Himself to you, listen to what God is saying in your life. Be someone who stands firm in faithfulness to Him. When you do, signs and wonders in your life will abound. The sound of abundance will come as well as a harvest explosion of restored hopes and dreams and especially peace of mind. The past will let go as you appropriate the joy of the Lord.

Divine favor from Heaven was given to Elijah...the very hand of God was upon him...and available to him even as he supernaturally outran the king's chariot! Divine favor means you can out run and out last anything! Arise and shine for the glory of the Lord is come upon you! Divine favor is for *you*, not just the prophets of old. God promises that He will show favor so great that the whole earth will glorify Him and say, "Surely this must be God!"

The favor of God wasn't only for the prophets. The promise of abundant rain wasn't only for the Israelites. His promises weren't only for the Jewish people. We as Gentiles are joint heirs and heirs to the promise because of the Gospel of Jesus Christ.[86] Paul told the Gentiles that every promise made to the Jewish people in the Last Days is also for those who inherited the gift of God through Christ Jesus—that we will receive the same promises given the Jews.

You can have abundant rain but you have to get some things right first. You have to ask yourself, "What needs to be exposed in my heart and life? What do I need to do to get things right?" When you remove those things that aren't right and tear them down—God will act.

Yes, you already have divine favor—you are given it with eternal life—salvation. But to continually walk with His hand on your life there are things that He requires of you. Do you ever wonder why sometimes it seems as though everything is going right, and at other times, you're in lack and need? As you can see in this book, my life had many ups and downs. When I was in His will, everything went great. Out of His will, my life was a mess. When I was far away from Him, I made horrible choices and suffered tough consequences. When I was close to Him and connecting, there was so much harvest in my life. I was overwhelmed with peace and blessings.

God wants us to live and walk continually in divine favor. He doesn't want us finding ourselves back at square one time and again. It's an upward call that we have—one that moves higher and higher into more and more unbelievable realms of possibility with Him.

Christians don't have anything over anyone else, except the Word of God, His hand and His power—these things help us to continually walk in that upward call. We don't have to be up one day and down the next, triumphant one day and defeated the next. God says that in these last days He will pour out His Spirit on us such that the world will look at us and have no choice but to say that our God is real.[87]

How can you walk in continual blessings? For the next 30 days, why not check yourself out in these areas. I have seen the Lord do unbelievable things if you just give Him 30 days.

1. MAKE UP YOUR MIND.

God can do anything for the person who has made up his or her mind to follow Him and Him alone. "Choose...this day whom you will serve" (Joshua 24:15). Elijah to the people said, "How long will you falter between two opinions? If the Lord is God, follow Him; but if Baal, follow him" (1 Kings 18:21).

God doesn't tolerate fence sitting. Some people make a career out of it, sometimes going with God and sometimes going with the love of something else. But God requires us to make a once-and-for-all decision because He doesn't tolerate polytheism, the serving of more than one god. Not making up your mind to serve and follow the One True God will unmake you. Will you come out on God's side? He will do His utmost for those who do, and for those who don't, frankly you're in danger of being outside of the throne zone of His favor to live in a land of famine and lack rather than within the sound of the abundance of rain.

Former United States President Ronald Reagan learned the benefits of making a firm decision when he was a youngster. He didn't have any shoes so an aunt took him to the shoemaker to have a new pair of shoes custom-made for him. The cobbler asked him, "Do you want shoes with round toes or square toes?" Ronald couldn't make up his mind. "I don't know... how about I let you know what I want tomorrow?" The cobbler told him he'd expect him within a few days to tell him what he wanted. Ronald never showed up as he promised and one day the shoemaker saw him on the street and asked him if he'd made up his mind, did he want round-toed shoes or square-toed shoes. Ronald told him that he still didn't know. So the cobbler told him that was fine and to just come by the shop the next day and he'd have the shoes ready. When the youngster arrived the following morning to pick up his new shoes, one had a round toe and the other a square toe! Of this lesson, Ronald Reagan said, "You know, looking at those shoes everyday taught me that if you don't make your own decisions, somebody else will make them for you."

Former United States President Ronald Reagan learned the benefits of making a firm decision when he was a youngster.

Before my accident I hedged on what I should do—trust God and His desires for me or to go for fame and fortune on my own. Before I knew it, the decision was out of my hands and I was on the road to a personal hell that I couldn't get off. However, in the hospital as I sought the will of God for my life, He met me there and showed Himself strong on my behalf.

We can't be ambivalent, of two minds, hesitant, indecisive, unsure! We have to be sure we want to serve God and then serve Him alone. There's no room in your life for New Age philosophy and God. There's no room for hemming and hawing or for, "Well, I love God and believe in Him for my life but checking out my horoscopes can't hurt." Your career can't take precedence, your relationships can't take precedence, your hobby can't take precedence, your moral values can't take precedence—you cannot believe in God and believe in something that doesn't align with His Word and laws. You believe what His Word says completely or not at all. You align yourself either with His Word, or not at all. No compromise! You can't have a little bit of God's Word and then top it off with a little bit of Karma. God won't tolerate it, and you won't experience the fullness of your calling unless you are totally sold out to Him.

2. KNOW THAT YOU ARE NEVER ALONE.

You may be the last person standing, but it doesn't mean you're alone. You may be the only person in your sphere of influence standing up for what's right, but know that you are not alone. All of Heaven backs you up! All of Heaven rejoices as you stand firm. Stand firm, yes, but not alone!

God emphasizes that He will not forsake those who love Him, no never!

Because he has set his love upon Me, therefore will I deliver him; I will set him on high, because he knows and understands My name [has a personal knowledge of My mercy, love, and kindness—trusts and relies on Me, knowing I will never forsake him, no, never] (Psalm 91:14 AMP).

Charles Spurgeon, a powerful man of God and theologian, knew of God's faithful presence:[88]

When the huge waves of trouble wash over me, and I am completely submerged, not only as to my head, but also my heart. It is hard to pray when the very heart is drowning, yet gracious men plead best at such times. Tribulation brings us to God, and brings God to us. Faith's greatest triumph's are achieved in her heaviest trials. It is all over with me, affliction is all over me; it encompasses me as a cloud, it swallows me up like a sea, it shuts me in with thick darkness, yet God is near, near enough to hear my voice, and I will call him. ...our inmost faith has its quiet heart-whispers to the Lord as to One who is assuredly our very present help.

You can stake your life on the truth that you are never alone and that God never forsakes you. Esther knew it, Moses, Joshua, Abraham, and others all knew it from personal experience. The many such promises throughout the Bible are as true for you today as they were for them. Jesus gave His life for you. How could He forsake you? He is all-powerful God and your very present help.

3. TURN YOUR EYES TO THE KING.

"Turn your eyes upon Jesus, look full in His wonderful face, and the things of earth will grow strangely dim, in the light of His glory and grace!"

Nothing else matters when you focus on Jesus! His face out-lasts and out-shines even the most dazzling earthly and heavenly display! There's a beautiful hymn penned by poet Helen Lemmel: "Turn your eyes upon Jesus, look full in His wonderful face, and the things of earth will grow strangely dim, in the light of His glory and grace!" When you're worried, anxious, or scared about something and you focus on Jesus, those things shrink in significance quicker than a wool sweater in a boiling pot of water.

It might not be "the thing to do," this taking it to Jesus for our needs, but don't give heed to what others think of you for admitting to your Savior that you need help. Blind Bartimaeus, the beggar, called out to Jesus in a loud voice and people in the crowd told him to hush up. He cried all the louder, "Jesus, Son of David, have mercy on me!" (Mark 10:47). He didn't care what others thought. Even if they thought him too unimportant to bother Jesus, that wouldn't stop him. He'd get to Jesus by any means to receive his sight, for as long as it took Jesus to call him over. When Jesus asked him what he wanted, of course Bartimaeus said, "My sight, Lord!" He'd likely been blind for a long time and without any visual contact he just sat there by the road, begging. For sure he must have heard what Jesus did for the other blind men and how they received their sight and how much he must have yearned to be one of those to meet Him. (Read Mark 10:46-52.)

"Out of the abundance of the heart the mouth speaks," (Matt. 12:34). The tone of the voice, its sound and content, reflects the heart—and Jesus heard his heart. Bartimaeus might have had a thousand doubts about calling on Jesus. *What will people say—should I call upon the priests, first to find out what they think about this Man?* The result—he would have remained blind.

Often we're trapped in our thoughts and our reasonings about what other people think, but if we stop seeking Him to stop for us as He stopped for Bartimaeus, we will miss out on life as He meant for us to have it.

People won't always understand or appreciate your passionate pursuit of Jesus. "Don't be one of those Jesus freaks," they might say, or, "Oh no, here comes that religious woman—the one who always says, 'Help me Jesus!'" Don't let them keep you from worship. Only *His* opinion counts. Keep your focus where it needs to be.

Jesus healed him and Bart followed Jesus down the road. He didn't die a blind beggar but a spiritually sighted man who one day would see Heaven because he didn't let people get between him and God.

4. Become obedient to His Word.

Jesus said, "If you love Me, keep My commandments and if you are willing and obedient then you shall eat the good of the land." The good of the land is divine favor. Become obedient to His will, His laws, His commandments, and His voice in every area of your life spiritually, physically, and emotionally. When He speaks, it's time to listen.

What God wants is the most important thing. Defying God for our own way is always wrong and a sin that will lead to painful consequences. King Saul discovered this when he failed to follow God's directions to wipe the Amalekites out completely. Instead, Saul spared the king and the spoils for the people. The prophet Samuel was quite severe with him. *"Behold, to obey is better than sacrifice and to heed than the fat of rams. For rebellion is as the sin of witchcraft, and stubbornness is as iniquity and idolatry..."* (1 Sam. 15:22-23).

God takes disobedience seriously as you can see. Saul's rebellion eventually cost him everything—in fact, his life. God had already sought out David, a man after His own heart, to reign.

When He speaks, it's time to listen.

To be successfully you, obedience is the path to take instead of the "I did it my way highway." Sorry Frank (Sinatra), now I sing, "I did it His way!"

5. Destroy the works of darkness in your life.

We've already covered a lot about deliverance and destroying the work of the enemy in our lives. I want to emphasize again here though, God will not come into an unclean temple. We can't destroy the enemy but we can destroy his works, and it was for this reason that the Son of God was made manifest on this earth. Thus as followers of Christ Jesus we have the power to destroy evil in our lives, to destroy the works of darkness in us. Elijah built the altar and even though the fire came and consumed everything impure, exposing the sin, the rain didn't come until Elijah had destroyed the works of darkness. He destroyed everything that had caused God's people to serve false gods. What hidden sin is in your life that you should destroy? Ask God to expose the sin, so you can repent, get it right, and receive forgiveness.

6. WORSHIP THE LORD.

Come to Him, come to Him! Worship the Lord! Do you actually worship the Lord apart from other people—at home when you're alone, or while driving, or even as you rise in the morning and shake the sleepy cobwebs from your head and plant your feet on the floor.

I've already touched on worship in this book, but it doesn't take rocket science to figure out why it's important to lock it into our lives. First, it glorifies God—that's its most important aspect. Second, worship restores the joy of your salvation. When life happens, it tends to draw all the joy from our lives and can shut us down. There's a link with joy and worship: "...only in [His] presence [through worship], is there fullness of joy" (Ps. 16:11).

Worship, in short, is a divine encounter with God, a coming into His presence, a humble bowing down act of reverence. It's a meeting place where God promises to meet us—it's the meeting place of our heart to God. True worshipers worship the Father in spirit and in truth,[89] which means coming into the Lord's presence adoring and loving Him in the spirit—as He is Spirit.

God doesn't *need* our worship! He seeks worshipers! Why wouldn't we want to minister to God and bless Him? Why wouldn't we want to forget about ourselves in light of Who He is? Why wouldn't we want to meet Him in that place! Awesome God and His awesome presence!

It's a responsibility and a privilege of every believer to worship the Lord. It's critical and key to God's presence in our lives; for worship brings us into intimacy and fellowship with the Father. The atmosphere of worship—His very real and tangible presence in our lives—is what helps us endure. Therefore, worship is vital to withstanding hard times and restoring to us the joy of our salvation when things get difficult.

Your goal? To worship, which means to magnify, exalt, love, cherish, and adore the only true God! He's worthy of our praise! We can join in with the angels: the cherubim, the seraphim, and join the prophets, the apostles, all of those elders around the throne falling down to exalt Him! (Read Revelation 7:11-12.) Worship should always be your response to God.

7. DEVELOP INTIMACY WITH HIM.

Favor will come when you draw near to God. If you want to see continual favor, oh yes, draw near to Him with more than a passing "Hey God, how ya doin' today!"

The closer you are to Him the more of His favor will cover you because it grows out of relationship. Gradually, God will trust you with great and greater things, and you'll trust God to step out of all your comfort zones. Don't mistake favoritism with favor. He loves us all the same—His love is the same yesterday, today, and forever, but to those who come into abiding relationship with Him, He extends the scepter. We all have the same privileges as believers and the same access to God through Jesus, but His favor rests upon those who want to know and are willing to take every step to learn and know Him more.

What are God's desires for you? Do you even know what they are specifically for you? Do you follow His desires—the ones you know about from reading the Bible? Do you seek to draw close to Him just for who He is rather than for what He can do for you? Trust me—you'll know when your focus is on Him alone!

Let the Psalms kick-start you into hungering for that secret place of His presence because God wants to be close to you—personally there for you! He waits up there on high to have compassion on you.

Therefore the Lord will wait, that He may be gracious to you; and therefore He will be exalted, that He may have mercy on you. For the Lord is a God of justice; blessed are all those who wait for Him (Isaiah 30:18).

When you get alone with Him and you experience His presence—oh wow—you'll have such holy hunger and you'll want to get there more and more. He wants you to develop intense hunger but you'll never attain the level of hunger He has to be with you—He wants intimacy with you even more than you could ever want it with Him.

This intimacy—this increasing knowledge of Him—will increase your favor and His benefits toward you but not only for you, for your family as well! His benefits are your godly inheritance and your children and their children and their children's children will benefit too! When we come into alignment with God's will for our lives, we'll have greater influence on others to do the same.

8. Declare His Word in your life every day.

Stop being so negative and speaking words of doubt and unbelief. Believe in God enough that you will declare what He says in His Word about your situation. Elijah spoke God's word back to Him, reminding Him that He'd promised rain.

...The Word (God's message in Christ) is near you, on your lips and in your heart; that is, the Word (the message, the basis and object) of faith which we preach, because if you acknowledge and confess with your lips that Jesus is Lord and in your heart believe (adhere to, trust in, and rely on the truth) that God raised Him from the dead, you will be

saved. For with the heart a person believes (adheres to, trusts in, and relies on Christ) and so is justified (declared righteous, acceptable to God), and with the mouth he confesses (declares openly and speaks out freely his faith) and confirms [his] salvation. The Scripture says, No man who believes in Him [who adheres to, relies on, and trusts in Him] will [ever] be put to shame or be disappointed (Romans 10:8-11 AMP).

When you speak the Word of God—when it rises from your heart to your lips you speak the word of faith and it moves! It moves when you declare it! Declare that God is your Healer—by His stripes you are healed. Declare that He is your Peace, your "I shall not want." Declare Him as "The Lord is my Banner," your Banner of Love going into the world, going into battle, going before you into your circumstances. Declare that blessed be the Lord, who daily loads you with benefits, the God of your salvation![90] Selah!

Watch divine favor come into your life in a big way. Ask for fire from Heaven—the fire of righteousness that comes by faith and by simply asking God for it! We all need the fire of Heaven in our lives.

9. CHECK YOUR MOTIVES AND HEART.

God wants to inspire your dreams, to fuel them with His power, to guide them with His love and faithfulness. He wants you to trust Him as the source of your success, and if you do, how much more you'll enjoy the spoils of divine success!

I didn't handle the pressures of the world well without the wisdom and inspiration of God. He lifted me up with favor, and I let Him down. If God suddenly raised you up with sudden fortune or fame, how would you handle the pressure? Trust that the enemy will be your paparazzi, following your

every move and looking for an opening to destroy you. God means to give you every blessing He has for you, but the enemy wants to steal it all. He'll find inroads through the strongholds of your mind and home in through the idols of your heart. If anything other than God fills those places, satan will use that for his gain and your destruction.

Holy Spirit counsels us, urges us to give attention to His words, tells us to "incline" our ears to His sayings, to not let them depart from our eyes, and to keep them in the midst of our heart because His words are life to those who find them and health to our flesh.[91]

Does the love of money; your 501-K, your stocks, your real estate, your home, drive you or the love of God? Ask God to check the motives of your heart and search your ways for anything that proves an obstacle to your pressing forward toward the mark with endurance. It's not a race to be won but one to be endured so that you can say that you finished it well—and so that God can say, "Well done! You're faithful!"

Motives can do an about turn when we sear God's Word on the altar of our hearts and firmly plant His Word in our minds! This is when the revelation of God's character, nature, and His desires for us happens! We can avert much sin when this happens! The more Scripture in our hearts, the less we'll sin.

FINAL THOUGHTS

As you go about becoming successfully you—know that God loves you. Choose excellent pursuits, the excellence of godly satisfaction, and an Excellent Helper, and watch the blessings flow into your life! Watch as torment, anger, and bitterness leave. Watch as relationships are restored and families are put back together. Watch God heal your emotions and physical conditions!

I've included a few prayers at the end of the book—prayers and Scripture passages that have given me great comfort and peace over the years. I wish the same for you.

Feel free to write me and let me know how God has transformed things in your life—I want to hear your testimony echo across the land! See you at the top!

Successfully Yours,

Leigh Valentine

SALVATION: THE DRAWING POWER OF GOD

S ALVATION is just the beginning of your walk with the Lord!

Heavenly Father, I come in Jesus' name. I feel You drawing me unto You in a new way. I confess that I have sinned and I'm sorry for my sins. Help me to see my sin so I even know what I need forgiveness from. I ask you to work a thorough work of repentance in my heart and continue to show me the areas in which I need forgiveness. I do humbly ask You to forgive me of all of the areas where I have missed the mark, and cleanse me of all my sins with Your blood. I believe in my heart that You raised Jesus from the dead so that I can now have eternal life. I receive the Lord Jesus Christ into my heart as my personal Lord and Savior. I confess Jesus is Lord over my whole life! I will spend time in Your Word because I need daily salvation and help. I look to you for eternal life and I choose this day to put my stake in the ground, to live the rest of my life for You Jesus, as you teach me how to open up my heart to You. Continue to show me daily the condition of my heart and how to cry out to you daily for everything I have need of. I never want to be separated from You again and I desire to spend eternity with You in heaven. Heavenly Father, I thank You for delivering me out of the kingdom of darkness and bringing me in to Your Kingdom. Thank You for making me Your child and for all you are doing in my life. I pray all this in Jesus' name, Amen!

Study: John 1:12; John 3:36; Romans 6:23; Ephesians 2:8-9.

———◆———

BAPTISM OF THE HOLY SPIRIT

Heavenly Father, I come before You right now with an open heart to receive all You have for me. I am not afraid. I have already accepted Jesus Christ as the Lord and Savior of my life, so now I open myself to receive the power of Your Holy Spirit, just as You filled believers in the Upper Room on the Day of Pentecost. You said that if I ask anything in your Name, that You would give it to me. So I ask You to fill me to overflowing with Your precious Holy Spirit. I receive You now, Holy Spirit, by faith and expect to speak in that beautiful heavenly prayer language that you will give me.

In Jesus' name, Amen. Thank You Lord Jesus for baptizing me in the Holy Spirit!

Study: Luke 11:11-13; John 14:16-17; Acts 2:38, 39; 1 Corinthians 14:2,18.

———◆———

PRAYER FOR OVERCOMING FEAR

Heavenly Father, I come in Jesus' name. I confess and believe that You want me to walk with you courageously, with faith in You to protect me and my home and family. I believe as I truly surrender to you that your divine protection will be upon my life and family. I do not have to fear the weather conditions because you bring peace to every storm. No weapon formed against me shall prosper and any tongue that rises up against me shall be shown to be in the wrong. I believe You will never leave me without support or forsake me or let me down. You will not in any degree leave me helpless or relax Your hold on me.

I know that I dwell in the secret place of the Most High and that You are my strength and my refuge; in You alone will I trust. You have given the righteous authority through the name of Jesus, and standing on Your Word, that the name of Jesus is above every fear that would come my way. I can trust you to help me when I am alone, with others, on a crowded subway or airplane. You are with me and no harm will come my way if I walk with you. Help me to walk with you always and be bold for you. In Jesus' name, Amen!

For I have not received the spirit of bondage again to fear; but I have received the Spirit of adoption, whereby I cry, Abba, Father! The Spirit itself bears witness with my spirit, that I am a child of God![92]

I speak to the mountain of fear right now, and command you to move and be cast into the sea, in Jesus' name. I bind every spirit of fear and I command you in the name of Jesus to loose me and let me go.

NOTE: After you have prayed this prayer, thank the Father that the spirit of fear is bound from operating against you. Stand firm, fixed, immovable, and steadfast on your confessions of faith as you walk in that joy and peace that surpasses all understanding.

Study: Isaiah 54:17; Psalm 91:1; Proverbs 29:2; Mark 11:23; Philippians 2:9; Hebrews 4:14; 13:5.

ENDNOTES

1. I've paraphrased excerpts from a lost letter I received from this Good Samaritan, a minister who attended to me and comforted me at the scene of the accident until the ambulance arrived. To the best of my ability, I have recounted what he witnessed. I am forever grateful to him for his kindness and comfort. He had been returning to Denver from St. Louis with his family when it happened.

2. Paraphrase of Proverbs 4:23 New Living Translation.

3. Adam Clark, "Commentary on Psalm 54." "The Adam Clarke Commentary" http://www.studylight.org/com/acc/view.cgi?book=ps& chapter=054, 1832.

4. Doris McMillon, WJLA-TV (ABC Affiliate) and broadcast professional, best known for her 27 years of work at NBC News, WABC-TV in New York, Fox Television, WJLA-TV in Washington, DC, and around the world on the U.S. Information Agency's WORLDNET.

5. Kevin Miller, "Surviving Career Devastation," Profile on Doris McMillon, Media Consultant, Former News Anchor, WJLA-TV (ABC Affiliate) Washington, DC. www.secretsofsuccess.com/people/McMillon.html, accessed March 20, 2008. For more information about Doris McMillon, visit her Website: http://www.mcmilloncommunications.com/.

6. Please refer to and study Psalm 16:6; Ephesians 1:18; Romans 8:17; 1 Peter 1:3.

7. Paraphrased John 14:12.

8. Matthew Slick, "Why Believe in Christianity over Other Religions?" Basic Christian Doctrine, www.carm.org/basicdoc.htm; accessed March 20, 2008. Paraphrased.

9. "Nobody Knows the Trouble I've Seen," Harry Thacker Burleigh, 1917 (1866-1949).

10. Words: Sabine Baring-Gould, 1864. Music: Arthur Sullivan, 1871.

11. Words: Isaac Watts, *Hymns and Spiritual Songs,* 1707, Refrain: Ralph E. Hudson, 1885; Music: Various.

12. *Edward Payson* (1783-1827) pastored the Congregational Church of Portland, Maine during the Second Great Awakening. From a collection of sermons with a memoir by Asa Cummings, originally published 1828, *Memoir, Select Thoughts and Sermons of the late Rev. Edward Payson* (3 vols. Portland, 1846; Philadelphia, 1859).

13. Sermons by Edward Payson, published 1828, Shirley and Hyde, Portland; (public domain).

14. Elizabeth Prentiss, *Stepping Heavenward,* public domain: Project Gutenberg Release #2515 (February 2001), http://onlinebooks.library.upenn.edu/webbin/gutbook/lookup?num=2515.

15. Please read the Book of Hebrews chapter 4.

16. See 2 Kings 20:1; 2 Chronicles 32:24.

17. Isaiah 38:9-20.

18. Annie Johnson Flint. Taken from Streams in the Desert by Mrs. C.E. Cowman, 230.

19. Psalm 118:24.

20. The prayer language commonly referred to as *speaking in tongues.*

21. See Ezekiel 22:30.

22. Years later, I met Mrs. Allen's grown children as they came to hear me speak at a church in Tampa. They shared that she had just gone Home to be with the Lord and how multitudes of young people had attended

her funeral, each testifying how her life and testimony had radically transformed and permanently wrecked them for God. Mrs. Allen introduced me to a God who is total love and had the power to deliver me from all of my fears. Mrs. Allen risked her position at the university by being bold for God so that many would come out of death and destruction. I am determined that I will continue her work to bring thousands, hundreds of thousands, even millions of people into Heaven's gates with me.

23. What is intercession? Study Daniel 9:1-19. For further study on effective intercession, read: Repentance, Romans 10:1-4; Deliverance, 1 Samuel 7:5-9; Blessings, Numbers 6:23-27; Change God's mind, Exodus 32:7-14; Restoration, Ezekiel 22, Job 48:8-10; Judgment, Numbers 14:11-13. Also study the Book of Daniel.

24. See Psalm 25:6-7; 86:5; 86:15; 89:1,4,8.

25. See Psalm 91:1-4; 103:8-15.

26. See Psalm 63:6-8; 77:11-15; 105:4-5; 143:5-6. See if you can relate to any of these heart cries found in the Book of Psalms: 19:14; 51:1-4; 55:1-3; 61:1-4; 64:1-4; 77:1-2, 7-9; 94:1-3; 130:1-4; 141:1-4; 142:1-3a.

27. I don't recommend anyone write a check without the knowledge of adequate funds to cover it. I knew somehow that my dad would cover the expense.

28. See Romans 8:37.

29. Paraphrased from article "Seeker of Souls," reported by Subir Bhaumik and Meenakshi Ganguly/Calcutta; *TIME* magazine: Time Inc., June 24, 2001.

30. See Esther chapter 2.

31. Article: "The Moon is Not Enough" by Charlie Duke, *Secrets of Success;* www.secretsofsuccess.com, accessed March 20, 2008.

32. See John 10:10 and Proverbs 10:22.

33. See Deuteronomy 30:19-20.

34. See Ecclesiastes chapters 2-4.

35. See First Peter 5:7.

36. One of the saddest and most glaring problems in the Church today is there are so many preachers who do not understand the full message of Jesus. Some have denigrated the most basic, precious principles of the Bible. They erroneously teach that after the Bible was written, God went deaf and dumb and no longer speaks to us. On top of that terrible misconception, they teach that the age of miracles is over. They have portrayed our omnipotent God as mortal man, stripped of all power. This misinformation leaves people bereft of hope. I would not allow myself to fall prey to such thoughts. I knew better. God still speaks and He still heals.

37. See Isaiah 53:5b.

38. Annie J. Flint (1866-1932), *What God Hath Promised,* 1919.

39. Isaiah 6:1-8.

40. See Matthew 11:28.

41. See John 1:38-39.

42. Author of this quote (which I've paraphrased) is unknown.

43. See Psalm 119:105.

44. See Psalm 17:5.

45. It is not certain that David penned this psalm, but most theologians are of the mindset that he did.

46. See Matthew 22:37.

47. See Deuteronomy 6:5.

48. See Second Corinthians 5:17.

49. See Matthew 9.

50. For I know the plans I have for you, says the Lord, plans for welfare and not for evil, to give you a future and a hope (Jer. 29:11).

51. Bruce Alberts, Alexander Johnson, Julian Lewis, Martin Raff, Keith Roberts, and Peter Walters (2002). *Molecular Biology of the Cell; Fourth Edition* (New York and London: Garland Science). Information from http://en.wikipedia.org/wiki/DNA; accessed March 6, 2008.

52. See Jeremiah 1:5.

53. See Proverbs 13:12.

54. Religious (usually evangelistic) meeting held in a large tent or outdoors and lasts several days: Definition source: word-net.princeton.edu/perl/webwn.

55. Greek: *word*–derived from the verb "to speak." (See Romans 10:17: "So then faith cometh by hearing, and hearing by the word [rhema] of God.") A *rhema* is a word or an illustration God speaks directly to us, and it addresses our personal, particular situation. It is a timely, Holy Spirit-inspired Word from the *logos* that brings life, power and faith to perform and fulfill it. Its significance is exemplified in the injunction to take the "sword of the Spirit, which is the word [rhema] of God" (Eph. 6:17). It can be received through others such as by a prophetic word, or be an illumination given to one directly during personal meditation time in the Bible or in prayer. The *logos* is the fixed Word of God—the Scriptures—and the *rhema* is a particular portion in line with the logos brought forth by the Spirit to be applied directly to something in our personal experience. Source: *All For His Glory Ministries,* Bible Terms: http://www.allforhisglory.net/ofhoc/terms.html; accessed March 9, 2007.

56. For more information about evangelist Sandy Brown, visit www.sandybrownministry.com.

57. See Matthew 15 and Mark 7.

58. See Acts 13:2-3; 14:23.

59. See examples in Luke 2:37; 5:33.

60. There is much information concerning biblical models of fasting and it would be worthwhile to do extra study, as I do not have space to expound on it here. The late Bill Bright of Campus Crusade for

Christ wrote *Your Personal Guide to Fasting and Prayer,* and it is available free on the Bill Bright Website: http://www.billbright.com/howtofast/.

61. References for study: John 14:26; 15:26; 16:13.

62. References for study: Matthew 17:5; John 12:27-33; Acts 9:1-16; 10:9-16; Revelation chapter 1.

63. As an example, Ezekiel may have heard with the inner audible voice when God spoke to him when he was with the elders. He said, "The Word of the Lord came to me...." Study further in Ezekiel 14:2-4.

64. See First Corinthians 6:16.

65. See Luke 4:16-19.

66. *Rejuvenate.* Dictionary.com. *Dictionary.com Unabridged* (v 1.1). Random House, Inc. http://dictionary.reference.com/browse/rejuvenate; accessed March 2, 2008.

67. See Romans 3:23; Job 1:6-12; Revelations 12:10; 1 John 2:1.

68. See Joel 2:21.

69. See Philippians 3:13-14.

70. Paraphrased 2 Chronicles 7:14.

71. See Daniel 9:5,13

72. See Genesis 37.

73. See Psalm 19:1.

74. See Ephesians 3:16-21.

75. I've paraphrased the story briefly from the Book of Ruth, chapters 1-4. Read the entire Book of Ruth for greater detail.

76. Read the Book of Esther for greater detail.

77. See Malachi 2:16.

78. See Genesis 22:10-12.

79. A few months later we had a ceremony in the U.S. for our family and friends.

80. See Exodus 3:11.

81. See John 9:31.

82. See Isaiah 6:9; Matthew 13:15; Acts 28:27-28.

83. See Ecclesiastes 5:1.

84. See First Corinthians 3:11.

85. Read First King chapters 17-19 for the whole story.

86. See Romans 8:17.

87. Read Acts 2:14-21.

88. Charles Spurgeon, *Treasury of David,* Psalm 61:2.

89. See John 4:23-24.

90. See Psalm 68:19.

91. See Proverbs 4:20-22.

92. See Romans 8:15-16.

**For additional information or to setup
a speaking engagement contact the author at:**

141 Laurel Hill Dr., Suite 2
Rutherfordton, N.C., 28139
1-828-286-4226

Additional copies of this book and other
book titles from DESTINY IMAGE are
available at your local bookstore.

Call toll-free: 1-800-722-6774.

Send a request for a catalog to:

Destiny Image® Publishers, Inc.
P.O. Box 310
Shippensburg, PA 17257-0310

*"Speaking to the Purposes of God for This
Generation and for the Generations to Come."*

For a complete list of our titles,
visit us at www.destinyimage.com.